STUDIES IN
EDUCATIONAL
ETHNOGRAPHY

Volume 1 • 1998

CHILDREN LEARNING
IN CONTEXT

STUDIES IN EDUCATIONAL ETHNOGRAPHY

CHILDREN LEARNING IN CONTEXT

Editors: **GEOFFREY WALFORD**
ALEXANDER MASSEY
Department of Educational Studies
University of Oxford

VOLUME 1 • 1998

 **JAI PRESS INC.**

Stamford, Connecticut   *London, England*

CONTENTS

WITHDRAWN

PREFACE

Ethnography has become one of the major methods of researching educational settings. Its key strength is its emphasis on understanding the perceptions and cultures of the people and organizations studied. Through prolonged involvement with those who are being studied, the ethnographic researcher is able gradually to enter their world and gain an understanding of their lives.

Each volume of *Studies in Educational Ethnography* focuses on a particular theme relating to the ethnographic investigation of education. The volumes are closely linked to an annual two-day residential conference which explores various elements of ethnography and its application to education and schooling. The series of ethnography and education conferences began in the late 1970s, and was originally held at St. Hilda's College, Oxford University. The series later moved to Warwick University and back to the Department of Educational Studies, Oxford University in 1996. Each year a broad theme for the conference is chosen and participants are invited to contribute papers. The conference meeting itself is a period of shared work: papers are pre-circulated to participants and critically yet supportively discussed. In their revisions for possible publication, participants are thus able to take account of the detailed critique offered by their colleagues.

The chapters presented in each volume of *Studies in Educational Ethnography* are of two types. Most are revised versions of papers presented at the annual ethnography and education conference, but each volume also includes some further specially commissioned pieces. They are selected on the basis of their high quality, their coherence as a group, and their contribution to both ethnographic methodology and substantive knowledge.

The series recognizes that the nature of ethnography is contested, and this is taken to be a sign of its strength and vitality. While the idea that the term can be taken to be almost synonymous with qualitative research is rejected, chapters will be included that draw upon a broad range of methodologies that are embedded within a long and detailed engagement with those people and organizations studied.

Further details of the education and ethnography conference or the *Studies in Educational Ethnography* series of volumes are available from the series editor.

Geoffrey Walford
Series Editor

INTRODUCTION

Geoffrey Walford and Alexander Massey

The papers in this collection are bound together by their ethnographic focus on children learning within a range of contexts. They illustrate the rich and intricate patterns which can be revealed through ethnographic exploration of the diversity of forms and settings for children's learning. The title "Children Learning in Context"—rather than "Children's Learning in Context"—reflects the book's emphasis on the dynamic nature of learning and the learner as the primary agent who moves between different learning environments.

In the first chapter we set out our understanding of the utility of ethnography in investigating children learning. We argue that there has been a coalescence of developments in psychology and sociology such that the benefits of an ethnographic approach are increasingly accepted by both disciplines. We then set out seven elements that we see as being the most relevant features of ethnographic research on children learning and suggest that there are many interesting similarities between the ways ethnographers and children learn. We suggest that, in many ways, children act as ethnographers in their learning processes. Finally, we argue that ethnography can give voice to the child—an essential aspect of understanding children learning.

This first analytical, conceptual, and programmatic chapter is followed by a series of chapters that give empirical examples that illustrate the utility of ethnography in studying the ways children learn. The first group focuses on how young children learn in a variety of home, school, and other settings, through interaction with playmates, siblings, and other family members.

In chapter two Eve Gregory and Ann Williams investigate the nature of literacy activities in the lives of five- and six-year-old children from white monolingual English and Bangladeshi British families. They also examine the reading histories of the families, as well as the teacher's own current reading practices and reading histories. Ethnographic and ethnomethodological approaches are used to identify and compare the reading progress of children from different backgrounds during both in- and out-of-school reading activities. They show that there are patterns of continuity and discontinuity between home and school practices as well as a complex pattern of syncretism in older/younger sibling/child interactions.

In the next chapter Susi Long looks at one aspect of a broader study that investigated an American child's adjustment to a new cultural setting. After moving from the United States to Iceland, eight-year-old Kelli (the author's daughter) experienced life in a new neighborhood, school, and community. During the first nine months fieldnotes, audio tape, and video tape were used to record participant observations, planned interviews, and spontaneous conversations at school, at home, in the homes of friends, and during extracurricular and community activities. Long focuses on Kelli's acquisition of Icelandic and the role played by her peers in that process. The research suggests that Kelli's acquisition of Icelandic was most significantly supported by her play-based interactions with friends. At play with friends, Kelli heard the language used in meaningful contexts and was comfortable enough to experiment, receive feedback, and adjust language use. The implications of such a finding are that parents and teachers might best support children in second language settings by providing opportunities for involvement with native-speaking peers in activities that are meaningful, enjoyable and rewarding—from the child's perspective—and by constructing environments in which children feel comfortable and have reason enough to experiment with language in response to feedback.

Next, Dinah Volk describes teaching and learning interactions at home between a five-year-old Puerto Rican boy (Nelson) and his older siblings. Ethnographic and ethnomethodological approaches were used to explore these interactions while the concept of activity setting was used as a mediating context between the levels of culture and individual lives. Activity settings were defined by their components: personnel, cultural values, tasks, immediate motives, and scripts. The chapter describes how interactions between the siblings took place in a poor Puerto Rican family that valued both preparation for school and family togetherness. The siblings taught Nelson school-related knowledge and skills using two types of scripts: sibling lessons and sibling guidance. In both, the older siblings and Nelson co-constructed the activity settings, skillfully creating teaching and learning within their joint activity. The interactions complemented Nelson's interactions with his parents and syncretized cultural styles from diverse aspects of their lives.

Mari Boyle and Peter Woods consider the experiences of a group of bilingual children on starting school. They argue that children are inducted into a pupil role based on an anglicized model which fails to take their own background cultures fully into account. The new identity becomes designated in the ritual of registration, based on English custom, which checks presence, marks pupilhood, reminds, and establishes formality. A different status is attached to play (a child's activity) and work (a pupil's activity), a distinction which inhibits bilingual children in particular. The children quickly learned the rules attached to dress and undressing, but pride in mastering the new pupil skills was mixed with shame emanating from their own cultural experiences. Older children from the same ethnic group were used to acquaint the new recruits with school rules involving movement and behavior. The school did incorporate many of the cultural differences of the children into everyday aspects, but all within a basically anglicized framework. This was particularly the case with regard to language where teachers permitted children to converse in the language of the home in class, but did not actively promote it, nor otherwise use the children's bilingualism to their mutual advantage. Many different cultural strands make up these children's identities. The authors argue that the latter will be the stronger and the richer where the former are given equivalent status and recognition.

This leads to a second smaller group of chapters that focus on the various ways in which older children learn about social conventions (most notably around sexuality) and are tempted to conform to some but resist others.

Shereen Benjamin presents some of the results of a study of an interventionist project about masculinities with a group of 10 to 12-year-old boys in a special school in London. The chapter is written from her own perspective as a teacher/researcher, and describes how a combination of ethnographic and interventionist research methods was used to investigate the boys' constructions of masculinities and to explore ways of making counter-hegemonic understandings available to them. The study suggests that two dominant discourses of masculinity—predatory heterosexuality and sporting (especially football) stardom—were central to the boys' construction of their gender/sexual identities. As working-class boys, already excluded from mainstream schooling and thus categorized as "failing," their investment in these competitive discourses is highly problematic. Their struggle to achieve successful positionings within these discourses was carried out through their enactment of masculine performances based on what can be described as fantasy identifications. In collaborative activities designed to engage with the realms of fantasy as well as cognitive, the boys interrogated these discourses and began to explore alternate meanings as they learned to "do boy" in and beyond the social worlds of the school and classroom.

Mary Jane Kehily's chapter is concerned with the controversial subject of teenage magazines such as *More!* and *Sugar*. Media attention has claimed that such magazines are too sexually explicit for young women and one member of the British Parliament has declared that the magazines "rob girls of their innocence." In contrast, this chapter looks at the ways in which magazines aimed at an adolescent female market can be seen as a cultural resource for learning about issues of gender and sexuality. It explores the ways in which sexual issues are presented to young women through the magazine format, and analyzes the ways in which young women and men read, discuss, and negotiate these media messages. Using ethnographic material drawn from school-based research and textual analysis of teenage magazines, the chapter suggests that there is a complex process of negotiation where young people read the material and the messages within the social context of friendship groups and personal experiences. Acts of readership within the school context produce enactments of femininity and masculinity which can be seen as gender displays, offering a sphere for the construction and public exhibition of sex-gender identities.

Gwen Wallace and her colleagues draw on data from a longitudinal study of 85 secondary school students. Their chapter focuses on student experiences of the annual, within-school tradition of "moving up" from one year grade to the next. Student comments show that in the first two or three years of secondary school, academic learning takes second place to the social excitements of moving up to the "big" school and negotiating social relationships with peers and staff. The chapter shows that toward the end of year nine, as they choose their subject options, students begin to feel more responsibility for their learning. Motivation becomes instrumental as they begin to "learn the ropes" and become aware of the consequences of getting (or not getting) good GCSE grades. Years 10 and 11 are marked by a growing gulf between those who manage to keep up and those who give up. Students' comments reflect the meanings they give to the choices they must make between their immediate personal and social lives and their imagined futures, in the context of schooling and assessment processes which work to institutionalize the differences.

This set of studies is completed by a chapter on the idea of a "learning community" and empirical work on what might be the best environmental conditions in which children can learn. Barry Cocklin argues that within certain schools there is a perception by people both within and outside that the school "works," that it is "successful," and an environment in which effective learning—by staff, students, and community—occurs. There is a strong sense of constructive interaction, and support for the school often derives from the wider community. This is usually accompanied by a feeling of ownership by all stakeholders, demonstrated in a particular allegiance to the school and the learning that occurs within. With qualitative literature on "creative teachers" and "learning communities" as the backdrop, this chapter reports an ethnographic case study of a small rural primary school in New South Wales. The aim of the research was to consider the attitudes, relationships, beliefs, context, and teaching and learning which appear to create an environment wherein learning is relished by all involved. Particular emphasis was placed on eliciting participant perceptions of their own lived realities. The notions of "learning communities" and "creative teachers" are explored as they contribute toward the development of the self and children learning.

Taken together, the chapters in the book illustrate the promise and success of ethnographic research in adding to our knowledge of children learning. The richly descriptive data presented in the chapters are used to ground new theoretical understandings and to challenge existing ones. The chapters show the increased methodological and empirical sophistication of such research.

CHILDREN LEARNING: ETHNOGRAPHERS LEARNING

Alexander Massey and Geoffrey Walford

LEARNING, PSYCHOLOGY, AND ETHNOGRAPHY

The use of ethnography to study the processes by which children learn might be seen as contentious. The study of learning traditionally has been dominated by psychology rather than sociology and, indeed, many psychologists would see learning as the focus of their discipline. For sociologists and ethnographers to enter this territory might be regarded as an invasion.

Yet, it is an invasion which many other psychologists welcome. The defences are down and there is a growing recognition by psychologists and sociologists of the applicability of methodologies drawn from a wide range of disciplines to the study of learning. This new openness is in sharp contrast with the past. Between the 1950s and 1970s, the study of learning was based mainly on laboratory-based studies, where investigations were conducted in "controlled" environments. By changing

Studies in Educational Ethnography, Volume 1, pages 1-18.
Copyright © 1998 by JAI Press Inc.
All rights of reproduction in any form reserved.
ISBN: 0-7623-0436-7

just one variable at a time, it was thought that the independent influences of each of the variables could be evaluated. But, within psychology since the 1980s, there has been a shift away from decontextualized experiments in learning toward more naturalistic enquiries. Learning is now much more likely to be viewed as a situated activity where children are seen as active constructors of their own meanings. There has been an increased appreciation of the importance of the context within which learning takes place, and a greater concern with the need to allow children and other learners to show how they learn through realistic and meaningful tasks.

At a theoretical level, within psychology, Piaget has largely given way to Vygotsky. As Pollard explains (1987), Piaget's ideas had their apogee in Britain during the 1960s and were given prominence in the Central Advisory Council of Education's report *Children and their Primary Schools* (The Plowden Report; Central Advisory Council 1967). The developmental framework put forward by Piaget was not entirely new, for it could be traced back through Froebel and Pestalozzi to Rousseau, but Piaget appeared to offer a coherent model that had applicability to schooling and to the role that adults should adopt in the process of education.

As is well known, Piaget (1969) believed that young children live in a moment-by-moment world and that their intellectual development proceeds by stages and substages which are followed in the same order by every child. The most important consequence of this idea was that infants were seen as qualitatively different in their thinking from young children and adults. The nature of the thinking was said to be determined by the stage of development, which implied that children learn effectively only if their educational experiences are matched to their current stage of development. Put simply, children have to be "ready" to learn.

Children were also seen by Piaget as actively and individually constructing their own development through interactions with the environment. The belief was that infants and young children need direct concrete experiences and should be left to "discover" things for themselves. They were perceived as "little scientists," having an active role in their own development, but having to follow their own predetermined path in this process.

The reasons for the decline in Piaget's influence are many. One reason is that psychologists began to have doubts about his empirical work. The classic work by Donaldson (1978), for example, showed that some of Piaget's experiments and interpretation of results were flawed. In essence, Donaldson showed that children's understanding of the use of language affected their interpretations of the tasks that were set them by psychologists. Her work was largely an attempt to develop new experiments that explored similar issues to those studied by Piaget but did so in ways that were likely to be more easily understood by the children involved. She found that, where the testing situation made "human sense," children were capable of quite subtle and sophisticated reasoning at a much younger age than Piaget had found.

But the laboratory-based experimental method in which Donaldson still showed great faith has at least three serious flaws. First, there are the problems identified by Donaldson of children not understanding the instructions. Second, there is the basic assumption in her work that what a child "knows" can be measured and is not itself context-dependent. The laboratory is itself a very strange context for children. Third, she ignores entirely the possibility that many children may well not wish to demonstrate their knowledge to researchers. The dichotomy of "failing to reason" and "failing to understand" needs to be supplemented by "not prepared to play the researcher's game."

During the 1970s and 1980s, some psychologists began to look to sociology for a new model which would emphasize other aspects of children's learning. They applied their own label of social constructivism rather than accepting the idea of social construction wholesale. Nevertheless, some psychologists clearly looked to the work of G.H. Mead and symbolic interactionism. Others found their inspiration in the social constructivist work of Vygotsky, Bruner, and others.

Like Piagetian thinkers, social constructivists were interested in the complex reality of children's learning and development. But their "bundle of insights" was drawn from such diverse sources as "symbolic interactionism, phenomenology, ethnomethodology, analytic philosophy and some forms of Marxism and structuralism" (Pollard 1987, p. 3). Psychologists had begun to look outside the experimental paradigm and were beginning to see that more naturalistic research might give greater insights.

The strange thing about social constructivism is that, in essence, as developed in the 1980s and 1990s, it offered little that was new. It simply recognized the importance of understanding meaning and interaction from the point of the participants, and viewed meanings as being created and conveyed through the interaction of people. It recognized that children do not discover the world purely through being solitary "little scientists" and emphasized the cultural knowledge and social processes underlying development.

It drew from various acknowledged and unacknowledged developments in sociology and psychology so that, for example, while Vygotsky (e.g., 1966) and Bruner (e.g., 1991 [1972]) were the favored references, many studies might equally well be seen to owe a debt to the sociological work of Berger and Luckmann (1966). What Vygotsky provided was a specialist language in terms of "Zones of Proximal Development" that encouraged psychologists to believe they were saying something new. Such scientific language has the power potentially to mystify and separate the initiated from the uninitiated.

This does not mean that social constructivism is not a useful model for understanding. Indeed, it has many strengths. Bruner's concept of "scaffolding" has been particularly important because it gives a powerful role to teachers, other adults, and more knowledgeable peers in helping children to learn. Children can be given a safe framework for building upon existing knowledge and relating it to new situations. It is worth noting that this model of teaching and learning is in accordance with the more authoritarian 1990s. In the 1990s, teachers try to construct scaffolding of particular shapes and sizes, such that some types of "building" are easily possible while others demand a questioning of the appropriateness of the scaffolding and erection of new supporting structures. If education is to be mainly about utilitarian preparation of a differentiated workforce for particular places in the economy, independent, inquiring "little scientists" are not an appropriate model.

The move toward social constructivism in psychology has been accompanied by a shift to more qualitative and ethnographic methods of research. At the same time, ethnographers have become more interested in the learning process, so that there is now a growing number of studies that begin to take the social context of learning seriously enough to place learning at the center of an extended ethnographic period of observation. Recent edited collections, such as that by Jessor et al. (1996), provide some excellent examples of such studies.

However, there are still relatively few such studies, and even fewer that examine learning beyond the classroom. There is still a great need to provide further accounts of classroom learning and to investigate some of the wide range of learning activities that take place in homes and other organizations as a result of interaction with parents, peers, the wider family, and other possible "teachers." This volume presents some examples of where we believe ethnography has been well used in the study of children learning.

THE NATURE OF ETHNOGRAPHY

We believe that ethnography is a strategy especially well-suited to the study of children learning. To defend such a claim, we need to give some idea of what we understand ethnography to be. Rather than attempt to provide an exhaustive definition, we have confined ourselves to identifying what we see as the minimum requirements for a research project to be called ethnographic, as opposed to, say, just qualitative or naturalistic. Furthermore, we have concentrated on those elements that we see as most relevant to studying children learning.

For a study to be called an ethnography, it needs, at the very least, each of the following seven elements.

1.   A Study of a Culture

Ethnographers stress that we move within social worlds and that to understand the behavior, values, and meanings of any given individual (or group), we must take account of some kind of cultural context. In this respect, ethnography balances attention to the sometimes minute everyday detail of individual lives with wider social structures.

The word "culture" is notoriously difficult to define, but it is hard to avoid it in a discussion of ethnography. A culture is made up of certain values, practices, relationships, and identifications. An ethnographer will try to define a particular culture by asking questions such as, "What does it mean to be a member of this group?" and "What makes someone an insider or an outsider here?" The ethnographer tries to make sense of what people are doing by asking, "What's going on here? How does this work? How do people do this?" and hopes to be told by those people about "the way we do things around here" (Deal 1985).

Answering those questions requires an openness to learning from those who inhabit that culture and a willingness to see everything and suspend premature judgment on what should be selected as data. This quality of openness lies at the heart of ethnography, in its processes, purposes, and ethics.

2. Multiple Methods, Diverse Forms of Data

Cultures are complex and multifaceted. To reach even a rudimentary understanding of them requires an openness to looking in many different ways. Different situations must be sampled many times—including the now widely accepted parameters of people, place, and time—to establish what and who counts as being part of a culture.

Data may consist of written documents, the researchers' own field-notes (including records of discussions, chance conversations, interviews, overheard remarks, observational notes), audiotapes, and videotapes; quantitative data may also be included, such as survey or experimental findings. Gold (1997, p. 393) suggests that the fieldwork phase of an ethnography is complete only when "both the ethnographer and his or her informants have exhausted their ability to identify other kinds of informants and other sorts of questions of relevance to the research objectives."

In order to "develop the story as it is experienced by participants" (Woods 1994, p. 311) and gain a multidimensional appreciation of the setting, the ethnographer must be prepared to consider many different types of data. These can be generated only through the use of multiple methods, which may include interviewing, observing, quantitative work, and assembling cultural artifacts. It makes sense, then, that a study which uses only one field technique (however exhaustively) does not constitute an ethnography, since it can generate only one kind of data.

3. Engagement

The ethnographer believes that "observation of culture in situ" (Denscombe 1995, p. 184) is the best way of getting to know it intimately. Hence, Woods's (1994, p. 310) description of the "most prominent features of an ethnographic approach" as "long-term engagement in the situation as things actually happen and observing things first-hand." Ethnographers work on the premise that there is important knowledge which can be gained in no other way than just "hanging around" and "picking things up."

The principle of engagement by the researcher contains two elements: human connection with participants, and an investment of time. There is an assumption that, as the researcher becomes a more familiar presence, participants are less likely to behave uncharacteristically. Gold (1997, p. 394) explains: "The fieldworker uses face-to-face relationships with informants as the fundamental way of demonstrating to them that he or she is there to learn about their lives without passing judgment on them." The idea is that participants "perform" less and, as trust builds, reveal more details of their lives. So the success of an ethnography depends on the researcher developing and maintaining a positive personal involvement with participants (Denscombe 1995, p. 178), staying as close as possible to what and who is being studied, and returning perhaps many times to the field.

Part of how an ethnographer learns about a culture is through a process of enculturation, which takes time. Participants and settings need time to show what is going on. As the researcher enters the culture more deeply, new questions and avenues open up, requiring further investigation. "Blitzkrieg ethnography" (Rist 1980), where the researcher spends only two or three days in the field, is therefore a contradiction in terms: a prolonged period of investigation is essential for an ethnographer to get to know the ways of a culture.

4.   Researcher as Instrument

Denscombe (1995) points out that much detailed and useful background information on a setting is often subjectively informed, echoing Woods (1994, p. 313), who describes an ethnographer as "his or her own primary source of data." Whether the researcher's subjectivity is a weakness or strength is not the issue. It is seen simply as an inevitable feature of the research act.

The ethnographer must aim to keep an open mind about "what is going on here" and what might be the best ways to talk or write about whatever is being studied. But recognizing the presence of subjectivity is not the same as saying "anything goes." Somehow, a balance must be struck between suspending preconceptions and using one's present understandings and beliefs to enquire intelligently. Dey (1993, pp. 63-64) puts it this way:

> there is a difference between an open mind and empty head. To analyse data, we
> need to use accumulated knowledge, not dispense with it. The issue is not
> whether to use existing knowledge, but how....The danger lies not in having
> assumptions but in not being aware of them.

To achieve such awareness, the ethnographer must constantly review the evolution of his or her ideas, reflecting on why particular decisions were made, why certain questions were asked or not asked, why data were generated a particular way, and so on. Above all, the ethnographer must try to articulate the assumptions and values implicit in the research, and what it means to acknowledge the researcher as part of, rather than outside, the research act. For Hammersley and Atkinson (1995, p. 192), reflexivity, which demands "the provision of.. a 'natural history' of the research" as experienced and influenced by the researcher, is a "crucial component of the complete ethnography."

5.   Participant Accounts Have High Status

Each person's account of the world is unique. What the researcher offers is an account which can be examined critically and systematically, because the means by which it was generated are clearly articulated. It is often in the nature of ethnography that participants' accounts and actions appear to be in the foreground and that the researcher has managed to "get out of the way," acting only as "information broker" (Goodson and Mangan 1996, p. 48). However, whether easily visible or not, it is the researcher who remains the highest authority, who selects from what has been seen and heard and constructs the final account.

The researcher's power in this respect needs to be tempered for this account to be credible, such that we as readers feel that something of the culture has been illuminated rather than further obscured by the idiosyncrasies of a single observer/commentator. This can—and should—be achieved in at least three ways. First, as suggested earlier, the ethnographer must be culturally open-minded from the start, prepared to challenge his or her own theories and understanding, constantly testing them. This also implies that what people other than the researcher have to say has value as well.

Second, all claims about the culture must be based on some kind of empirical experience of that culture. Such evidence must be presented to or be available to the reader so that he or she can evaluate the claims made by the writer. Compared to quantitative work, qualitative writers are much more able to get away with unsupported claims based on non-specific impressions. It is in the nature of ethnography that a wealth of data is generated, recorded, and stored; the writer's job is to share with the readers precisely which data have led to a particular claim.

A researcher may well be able to discover and articulate things about individuals and groups that they cannot see themselves, as well as things that neither the participants or researcher can see at the outset of the study. However, participants hold knowledge about themselves which nobody else has. Thomas (1928, p. 572) argued that "if men define situations as real, they are real in their consequences." If this is true, then what people believe to be the reality of their world must be important information in understanding their activities, values, meanings, and relationships and in working out "what is going on." The most direct means of getting this information is to ask those people.

The third way, then, to temper the researcher's power is to give high status to participants' own accounts of their experiences and allow them to influence the researcher. This has methodological implications.

Rather than relying on a preconceived framework for gathering and analyzing data, ethnographers use their interactions with informants to discover and create analytical frameworks for understanding and portraying that which is under study. The procedures used in this direct and intimate acquaintance with the empirical world provide assurance that the data collected are grounded in informants' actual experiences (Gold 1997, p. 399).

An ethnographic approach is no automatic protection against an overly "researcher-centric" view of a culture, but it does at least allow the possibility of including multiple perspectives.

6.   Cycle of Hypothesis and Theory Building

The openness that has underpinned many of the elements so far is particularly evident in the ethnographer's constant commitment to modify hypotheses and theories in the light of further data. Gold (1997, p. 395) describes it as the "running interaction between formulating and testing (and reformulating and retesting)."

In this type of enquiry, developing a theory is not so much an event as a process. As new data emerge, existing hypotheses may prove inadequate, the ethnographer's sense of what needs to be looked at and reported on may change, and explanations of what is going on may be supplanted by ones which seem to fit better. Such an approach is consonant with emergent design, another distinguishing feature of ethnography.

7.   Intention and Outcome

The ethnographer aims "to discover how people in the study area classify or label each other, how they find meaning in activities they care about in life, and how they engage in processes in which they individually and collectively define (antecedents and consequences of) their situations" (Gold 1997, p. 391). Any attempt to generalize findings beyond the case itself should be regarded as suspect, since statistical random sampling is rarely a feature of ethnographic research. Rather, as with other kinds of qualitative work, the intention is to achieve some kind of understanding of a specific case, whether it be a culture, people, or setting.

In describing the outcome of this kind of research, Denscombe (1995, p. 182) draws attention to the "storytelling" aspect. An ethnography contains descriptions of local places, snapshots of people's lives and relationships, their inner thoughts and feelings, their outward appearances, anecdotes of personal triumphs and disasters, rules, contradictions and meanings. And at the end of all of this, through a judicious blend of empirical experience, systematic activity and appropriate theory, the ethnographer hopes to construct a coherent story that takes the reader into a deeper and richer appreciation of the people who have been studied.

ARE CHILDREN ETHNOGRAPHERS AT HEART?

It is not difficult to find similarities between ethnographers and children in their curiosity, spontaneity, and responsiveness to the fluidity of their learning environment. Knupfer (1996, pp. 139-140) writes:

> Both [the ethnographer and child] are, in essence, learning the social rules of a particular culture. Like children, ethnographers are viewed as hypothesis-makers and testers and builders of their own cultural knowledge. This knowledge is itself a "cultural artifact," and, similar to children's learning experiences, it is built largely upon the interactional nature of ethnography.

Such claims would have to be tested, of course, but they prompt the question of what other similarities there might be. No doubt there are differences as well. If so, what might these differences be? And could children and ethnographers enhance their own ways of learning by picking up a few tips from each other?

While any claims we make in this chapter about how children learn must be speculation at this stage, we thought it would be interesting to consider how our characterization of ethnography mapped onto what, broadly speaking, children's learning might be like. The reader may like to go back over our seven elements and substitute the word "child" for ethnographer/researcher, and "learning" for ethnography.

Our comparisons are based on the seven elements of ethnography already identified.

1. A Study of a Culture

Part of children's motive for learning is to work out "the way we do things around here" (Deal 1985) in order to find a way of fitting into the culture. This requires an openness to that culture, shown in both a willingness and capacity to absorb information from all available sources. The usefulness of the information may not be immediately apparent but is often collected and stored anyway.

An ethnographer's motive for learning about a culture may be very different from a child's, for there is usually no intention of becoming or remaining a member of the culture beyond the life of the study.

2. Multiple Methods, Diverse Forms of Data

Children often adopt a "magpie" attitude to information, picking up anything that looks interesting. They will keep generating data until they feel they have enough to make sense of what is going on, developing a multidimensional understanding. In order to satisfy their curiosity, children may need many different kinds of data, employing a variety of methods to generate it—looking, listening, asking, watching, experimenting, and so on. Many learning tasks simply could not be completed unless more than one method were used.

3. Engagement

As they learn the ways of the world, children do not stand apart but immerse themselves in that world—the principle of engagement. The investment of time is lifelong, and relationships with members of the culture play an essential role.

One of the criticisms sometimes leveled at ethnography is that the researcher gets too close to the people and setting, such that what is being studied either is distorted or cannot be seen sufficiently dispassionately. It is interesting that, far from criticizing a child learner for heavy engagement, we often positively encourage this behavior, regarding it as a necessity and strength in the learning process.

4.   Researcher/Learner as Instrument

To borrow from Woods's (1994, p. 313) description of the ethnographer: "A child/learner is his or her own primary source of data." Experiencing the world subjectively is a way of life, and not one that we can choose. Because of this, we can sometimes be swayed too easily by whim, or be subject to methodological and substantive "blindness." To guard against this, the ethnographer works systematically and reflexively.

Perhaps one of the key differences that distinguishes ethnographers from child learners is that the former learn "in awareness" while the latter may not. A child may not know how he or she learnt something and, therefore, be unable to justify that knowledge, but the reflexivity of the ethnographer should be able to provide the basis for a "reconstructed logic of enquiry" (Hammersley and Atkinson 1995, p. 21). The ethnographer is able to say what he or she has learnt, and how he or she learnt it.

Perhaps those children who are not reflexive could learn more effectively if this capacity were encouraged and developed. Conversely, since children learn so much so successfully without reflexivity, we wonder what an ethnographer could gain by leaving reflexivity and self-awareness to one side?

5.   Participant Accounts Have High Status

However many sources of information they draw upon as learners, ethnographers and children ultimately have to construct their own picture of a culture. The traditional ethnographer affords high status to participant accounts on the basis that group members' knowledge and perspectives are particularly valuable. Children, too, seem to rely at least partially on the help, insights, knowledge, and advice of "native experts" (adults, teachers, friends, siblings, etc.).

Researchers would expect to elicit participant accounts systematically and challenge/problematize them. It is possible that children are more trusting, and liable to accept what they are told at face value; in this respect, they could perhaps adopt the ethnographer's greater scepticism. Of course, some children are much shrewder than adults when it comes to deciding whether they are being told the truth!

6. Cycle of Hypothesis and Theory Building

For the child, theories of "what's going on" and "how to do x" are likely to be challenged repeatedly as new information is assimilated. There can be a continuous cycle of theory formulation, testing, and reformulation. What the child theorizes about will depend on what is most important at the time, and that may be governed above all by the need to succeed and survive in the setting. In this respect, the ethnographer may be more dispassionate.

7. Intention and Outcome

Both ethnographers and children ask (though perhaps not in so many words), "How do things work around here, and what does it mean to be a member of this group?" Both hope to reach some kind of understanding and to construct a coherent picture.

But their purposes are different. First, the ethnographer intends to provide an account for some kind of audience, becoming a storyteller. Unless the child is asked to account for him- or herself, he or she is not looking for an audience: the knowledge acquired is used simply for getting on with life. Perhaps without the ethnographer's need to explain or articulate what has been learnt, there is less external pressure for the child to be reflexive.

Second, for the ethnographer, partial enculturation is the means by which the final story is reached, and the ethnographer then leaves the field in order to tell other people about what has been learnt; the ethnographer rarely needs or intends to stay around afterwards. For the child however, enculturation is an end in itself, and learning becomes crucial for survival in that setting.

What might an ethnographer do differently if he or she expected to become or remain a member of the group under study? And what might be different about what and how children learned if fitting into the culture were not an issue?

STUDYING CHILDREN LEARNING

To talk about "children's learning" seems almost to reify learning (as a product?), suggesting perhaps that it can somehow be separated from the child. To study "children learning" is to place emphasis on the child and what he or she is actually doing (process), and these can be understood only by reference to some kind of social context. If how children learn is to be understood within a social context and the meanings given to these learning contexts explored in detail, then ethnography, as described in this chapter, provides an ideal strategy. Further, ethnography can capture the proactive nature of learning, where children are no longer seen as passive absorbers of knowledge but are recognized as active constructors of their own meanings and understandings. This would still leave the question, of course, of whether an ethnographic approach illuminates certain forms of learning better than others.

Denscombe (1995) suggests that the methods and values implicit in a particular research approach will have a bearing on both access issues and the receptiveness of those who read the final report. Speaking of teachers, he writes:

> To a large extent they [teachers] have power of veto, effectively being able to prevent would-be researchers from entering "their" domain unless they feel comfortable with the aims of the research and trust the people who propose to conduct the research. For this, if no other reason, teachers' attitudes to research need to be treated seriously as a crucial factor affecting the type of research that gets undertaken in educational settings....They have preexisting attitudes and opinions, views and preferences—an "intellectual baggage" which shapes their receptiveness to research.

Ethnographers studying children learning need to get a very wide-ranging kind of access—to child learners, siblings, teachers, parents, and many others. This research strategy has many elements which might appeal to such participants and gatekeepers:

- The assumption that how a child learns is context-dependent and can be understood only by reference to many different factors;

- The suitability of ethnography as a way of studying children learning;
- The openness of the researcher to simply watching and listening;
- The partial suspension of preconceptions about what should be looked at by the researcher;
- The willingness to engage personally with participants, and the high status given to their accounts (implying also the principle of respect);
- Grounding claims in first-hand empirical experience gained through close and prolonged engagement in the field;
- The principle of nonintervention (i.e., minimal disruption); and
- The emphasis on telling the story of the case studied rather than on generalization (thereby heading off the criticism "it's not like that here!").

Such factors can give credibility both to the ethnographer and the research strategy, and could be used to persuade gatekeepers to allow access.

Denscombe (1995, p. 175) also points out that "researchers...need to write with an audience in mind." Many of the arguments used about gaining access could equally apply here. A reader's receptiveness to an ethnography may depend partly on the degree of sympathy both with the values and methods of ethnography and with its appropriateness for studying children learning. Teachers, parents (and children) may be especially in tune with the "storytelling" aspect which focuses on examples from situations to which they can relate directly. Interestingly, policymakers may be less well disposed to this, perhaps seeing it as too discursive; and the lack of easy generalizability to larger populations might make widespread innovation more difficult to justify.

THE LEARNER'S VOICE

If we want to know more about children learning, it makes sense methodologically directly to investigate those who know best what it is like to be a child learning. Might an account of learning as seen through the eyes of learners challenge existing images of them and what they do? Almost certainly. As Fine and Sandstrom (1988, p. 12) write:

> Perhaps the most obvious goal of qualitative research with children is to get to know them better and to see the world through their eyes. On a deeper level, this style of research additionally assumes that minors are knowledgeable about their worlds, that these worlds are special and noteworthy, and that we as adults can benefit by viewing the world through their hearts and minds.

Hargreaves (1991, p. 11) claims that "failure to understand the teacher's voice is failure to understand the teacher's teaching." Perhaps we should also say that failure to understand the learner's voice is failure to understand the learner's learning. Such a gap in our understanding of children would surely hamper any moves toward school improvement.

Enabling a relatively unheard voice to come to the attention of a wider audience is always a political act. This becomes even more significant when those individuals are speaking about matters of which they hold unique knowledge and which directly concern them. One could argue that people even have a right to have a say in matters directly affecting them. There are both methodological and ethical implications of high-lighting child learners' perspectives.

Adopting an ethnographic approach is no guarantee that participants will be fully honored. As Knupfer (1996, p. 135) asks, "how do we write the ethnography to most fully present the children's perspectives?" An adult researcher engaging with a child and eliciting views may be behaving against the child's cultural norms, and the final academic account may lose important aspects of the child's communication, much of which may not be confined to verbal language. Much work has yet to be done on how to study children respectfully and responsibly, and how to present data which have been generated through spending time with children.

CONCLUSION

Our understanding of what and how children learn must be incomplete unless the learners' voices are heard, and heard within their social contexts. Ethnography is ideal for reaching an understanding of children learning in context. Furthermore, children, teachers, and caregivers may be well disposed toward permitting ethnographic enquiry because of the kind of information which is valued and how it is generated. For the same reasons, they may be more receptive to the findings of such research. Whatever insights can be gained through psychological approaches, the picture of children learning would be dangerously incomplete without the unique contributions of ethnography.

ACKNOWLEDGMENT

The authors would like to thank Thomas Spielhofer for his comments on earlier drafts of this chapter.

REFERENCES

Berger, P., and T. Luckmann. 1966. *The Social Construction of Reality.* Harmondsworth, UK: Penguin.

Bruner, J. 1991. "Nature and Uses of Immaturity." In *Becoming a Person*, edited by M. Woodhead, R. Carr, and P. Light. London: Routledge (originally published 1972).

Central Advisory Council for Education. 1967. *Children and Their Primary Schools* (The Plowden Report). London: Her Majesty's Stationary Office.

Deal, T.E. 1985. "The Symbolism of Effective Schools." In *Culture and Power in Educational Organisations*, edited by A. Westoby. Buckingham, UK: Open University Press.

Denscombe, M. 1995. "Teachers as an Audience for Research: The Acceptability of Ethnographic Approaches to Classroom Research." *Teachers and Teaching: Theory and Practice* 1(1): 173-191.

Dey, I. 1993. *Qualitative Data Analysis: A User-Friendly Guide for Social Scientists.* London: Routledge.

Donaldson, M. 1987. *Children's Minds.* London: Fontana (originally published 1978).

Fine, G., and K. Sandstrom. 1988. *Knowing Children: Participant Observation with Minors.* London: Sage.

Gold, R. 1997. "The Ethnographic Method in Sociology." *Qualitative Enquiry* 3(4): 387-402.

Goodson, I., and J.M. Mangan. 1996. "Exploring Alternative Perspectives in Educational Research." *Interchange* 27(1): 41-59.

Hammersley, M., and P. Atkinson. 1995. *Ethnography: Principles in Practice.* London: Routledge (first published 1983).

Hargreaves, A. 1991. "Restructuring Restructuring: Postmodernity and the Prospects for Educational Change." Unpublished paper, Ontario Institute for Studies in Education.

Jessor, R., A. Colby, and R.A. Shweder, eds. 1996. *Ethnography and Human Development: Context and Meaning in Social Enquiry.* Chicago, IL: University of Chicago Press.

Knupfer, A.M. 1996. "Ethnographic Studies of Children: The Difficulties of Entry, Rapport, and Presentations of their Worlds. *Qualitative Studies in Education* 9(2): 135-149.

Piaget, J. 1969. "Advances in Child and Adolescent Psychology." In *Learning to Think*, edited by P. Light, S. Sheldon, and M. Woodhead. London: Routledge.

Pollard, A. 1987. "Introduction: New Perspectives on Children." In *Children and Their Primary Schools: A New Perspective*, edited by A. Pollard. Lewes, Sussex, UK: Falmer.

Rist, R.C. 1980. "Blitzkrieg Ethnography: On the Transformation of a Method into a Movement." *Educational Researcher* 9(2): 8-10.

Thomas, W.I. 1928. *The Child in America*. New York: Knopf.

Woods, P. 1994. "Collaborating in Historical Ethnography: Researching Critical Events in Education." *International Journal of Qualitative Studies in Education* 7(4): 309-321.

Vygotsky, L.S. 1991 [1966]. "Genesis of the Higher Mental Functions." In *Learning to Think*, edited by P. Light, S. Sheldon, and M. Woodhead. London: Routledge.

FAMILY LITERACY HISTORY AND CHILDREN'S LEARNING STRATEGIES AT HOME AND AT SCHOOL:
PERSPECTIVES FROM ETHNOGRAPHY AND ETHNOMETHODOLOGY

Eve Gregory and Ann Williams

INTRODUCTION

The teacher goes over to where Shuma sits and says "Choose one of these books. Quietly read through the book. If you don't know a word, write it down." She points to the book as she repeats, "Write the words down, OK?" The child nods...

Shuma has not understood the task—she has written down the words she DOES understand. "No, honey, I don't want you to write down the words you know, but the ones you don't understand," she says with emphasis, "OK, so that I can help you." Another child comes along to show the cut-up words and stands a couple

Studies in Educational Ethnography, Volume 1, pages 19-46.
ISBN: 0-7623-0436-7

of minutes to show her. Soon after, Shuma approaches and requests permission
to "play" on the computer. "Well, I'd like to see what you've done first," states
the teacher. However, some confusion arises and Shuma does go off to the computer.

What takes place in the excerpt above is just one incident in a school day
for five-year-old Shuma and her friends learning in their East London
Primary class, where all the children speak English as an additional language. When Shuma leaves school, she enters a very different world...

It is a blustery June evening when I walk toward the community building that
houses the Arabic class of the Flower and Dean estate, notorious for being the site
of one of Jack the Ripper's killings in East London just one hundred years ago.
In this particular class, there are two male teachers, one of whom is working with
the more advanced children, who are tackling the complicated word structures of
the Qur'an. The other group consists of younger children who are in a different
part of the room with the other teacher, grappling with sounds and letters and oral
verse. Everyone sits on the mat swaying to the sound of his or her own voice.
Although on initial appraisal the noise level seems high, little of this is idle chat-
ter. It is the expressed wish of the teachers that children read aloud, partly to assist
their learning, but more importantly so that Allah can hear. Children are encouraged to develop an harmonious recitation in unison with the gentle rocking to and
fro which accompanies the reading, as they are told that Allah listens to his ser-
vants and is pleased if they take time to make their reading meaningful...."Now,
repeat after me," the teacher solemnly requests, "Kalimah Tayyabh, la ilaha ilal-
laho, mohammadan rasolallahe." He tells them to look at him as they repeat....I
leave the room on the third recitation of the prayer and notice that the children
have not wavered at all; they remain seated on the floor as they have done for the
last hour and a half (Rashid 1996).

Although many linguistic minority children will experience such contrasts, little recognition has been given in Britain to cultural differences
in learning practices. A number of factors might be responsible for the
lack of research in this area. Since the debate on linguistic and cognitive
"deficit" or "difference" (Bernstein 1971; Labov 1972), researchers and
teachers have been anxious to emphasize similarities rather than differences in language use in the homes of different social classes (Wells
1981; Tizard and Hughes 1984). A second reason may stem from the
strong British tradition of child-centredness in early years education,
grounded in Piagetian child development theory which is focused on the
child as individual rather than as a member of a cultural or ethnic group.
Finally, recent government policy in Britain stresses the need to promote a "common culture" (Tate 1995) which will iron out cultural dif-

ferences between groups. This aim is practically reinforced by the English National Curriculum (National Curriculum Council 1995), which fails to acknowledge the learning practices of different minority groups. "Equality of opportunity," a promise made in the Education Act of 1988, is currently interpreted as "the same" provision. In practice, this means that both school and home-school literacy programs are generally designed for the "common" (English) culture.

As a consequence, teachers in Britain are unable to call upon a bank of research studies into the literacy and learning practices of different cultural groups in the British context to inform their classroom practice. This contrasts with their colleagues in the United States, where there is a long tradition of research investigating continuities and discontinuities of home and school learning practices (Scollon and Scollon 1981; Heath 1983; Rogoff 1990; Volk 1994; Duranti and Ochs 1996; Reese and Gallimore 1995) as well as the learning styles of different cultural groups and the effect of awareness of them on teaching styles (Au 1980; Michaels 1986). Nevertheless, some recent studies in Britain are beginning to reveal the rich variety of literacy practices of minority groups, which may remain unknown to their children's teachers (Barton and Hamilton 1992; Gregory 1994, 1996; Saxena 1994). The ethnographic study outlined below aims to contribute to this growing fund of knowledge, to compare the literacy and learning practices of indigenous English and Bangladeshi British families with those of their children's teachers and, further, to investigate the transfer of learning strategies by young children from home to school and vice versa. Ultimately, the research aims to provide data showing whether and how a child's home learning strategies and home/school interaction might be theorized as part of the school learning process.

BACKGROUND

The poor literacy and numeracy achievement of young children from economically disadvantaged families in British schools has been well documented over the past 20 years (Chazan and Williams 1978; Ofsted 1996) and public debate has been renewed since the introduction of the national standard attainment tasks in 1992 (Ofsted 1996). The performance of children of Bangladeshi British origin has recently been highlighted as particularly low (Select Committee to the House of Commons 1986/1987; Ofsted 1996). Government response to poor achievement has resulted in considerable investment in basic skills programs through the Adult Literacy and Basic Skills Unit (ALBSU) (1993). Programs currently in use in Britain rest on a firm belief in the intergenerational effect of literacy and numeracy failure. Their evidence is based on data from the National Child Development Study, whose sample was drawn from people born in the United Kingdom between March 3 and March 9, 1958. However, this cohort excludes most families from ethnic minority groups, who only entered Britain in larger numbers during the 1960s. Therefore, although the intergenerational factor is presented as a general conclusion (ALBSU 1993), it has so far not been substantiated through empirical studies across cultural groups.

"Family literacy" programs, which provide the "double bonus" of helping parents and children, have been promoted as a model which is "truly generational" (Brooks et al. 1996, p. 6) for developing literacy skills in Britain. However, such programs have been criticized for suggesting "literary impoverishment" and ignoring the considerable scope and variety in the existing literacy practices of both indigenous and minority communities (Barton and Hamilton 1992; Williams 1997). Other cross-cultural studies on cognitive development highlight differences by caregivers in the "scaffolding" of children's learning (Rogoff 1990). Both groups of researchers suggest that important questions need to be explored as to the literacy practices of different cultural groups and the relationship between these home learning practices and children's cognitive strategies at school. Our project started, then, with the following set of research questions.

Research Questions

- What place do literacy activities have in the out-of-school life of five-year-old inner-city children and their parents?
- To what extent do family practices and literacy histories shape the child's strategies in early literacy lessons? In mainstream school?
- In what ways do children restructure their home learning patterns during the initial period in school, and what role does the teacher play in this?
- What influence do "schooled" learning practices have on the learning patterns of the family over time?
- What knowledge do teachers bring of families' literacy practices and how do they use this in their teaching?

METHODOLOGY

Ethnography

In the course of the research we used a combination of ethnographic methods including participant observation, interviews, and field notes, and ethnomethodological techniques such as of conversation analysis. Ethnography was important in its aim to produce a "cultural grammar" or a set of rules which need to be known in order to become a competent member of the group. The researchers themselves were teachers and shared in many of the experiences of the participants, spending considerable time in homes and classrooms and accompanying the families on shopping or other visits. At the same time, their task was to remain "strange" to the situation in order to make explicit what was already known to the group. The ethnographic fieldwork went through the following stages:

1. Carrying out prolonged and repetitive data collection during contextualized observations which disturbed the interactions of the participants as little as possible.
2. Formulating questions and multiple hypotheses until a pattern was formed from the data to provide an analytic framework.
3. Narrowing the focus to generate a limited number of hypotheses, or "typologies," which were then subjected to further investigation.
4. Producing "trustworthy" evidence through a full and explicit description of the social world in which the events studied took place.

Ethnographic methods enabled us to give a detailed account of the literacy practices taking place in homes, communities, and classrooms as well to examine patterns of difference and similarity between groups. However, it did not provide insight into the moment-by-moment construction of meaning between child and partner during reading sessions.

Ethnomethodology

The vital aspect of an ethnomethodological approach was to show how child and adult (or older sibling) created "cultural knowledge" in the home or classroom together, rather than viewing knowledge as pre-constituted by cultural or social class background. The aim was to show how adult (or older sibling) and child "situate" themselves in the reading "lesson" and how they both participated in teaching and learning through interaction and negotiation.

DESIGN OF THE STUDY

Selecting the Sample

Two groups of children: seven Bangladeshi British children and six white monolingual English children, were recruited from two primary schools situated 500 yards apart in the East End of London. The Bangladeshi British children came from a Year 1 class, but changing demographic patterns in this part of the capital meant that we were unable to find sufficient white monolingual Londoners in the Year 1 classes and had to work instead with Year 2 children. After discussions with the class teacher and the head teacher, the parents of the white monolingual children were contacted by letter, and follow-up phone calls were made after parental consent had been obtained. In the case of the Bangladeshi British group, however, different procedures were followed, and after discussions with the head teacher, the parents were visited in their homes by a Bangladeshi British researcher, who then explained the project. Letters in both Bengali and English with details of the project were sent out, and parental consent for the children to take part in the project was obtained. All the families approached agreed to take part. We refer below to the teacher working with the monolingual English children as Teacher 1 and her colleague working with the Bangladeshi British children as Teacher 2.

Collecting the Data

A member of each family, in most cases the mother, was interviewed once a term. In the Bangladeshi British families, the father was sometimes present. In the case of one monolingual English family, the father was present at all interviews and the grandparents were also present on one occasion. Each interview lasted between one and two hours. Interviews with the monolingual English mothers were carried out in the home, in the parents' room in the school, in the school refectory, or in a local cafe, and all were recorded on a portable tape recorder and transcribed by the research officer. The Bangladeshi British mothers were interviewed in their homes but did not wish to be recorded. The bilingual research officer, therefore, interviewed the families in Sylheti and made detailed fieldnotes in English immediately after each interview. One morning per week throughout the school year was spent in classroom observation. During this time, fieldnotes were taken which were written up as soon as possible after the session. The data for each child consisted of:

1. One or two recorded reading sessions with the class or group teacher (in the case of the children in Reading Recovery, one session with the specialist teacher) together with fieldnotes on each child participating in a variety of classroom reading activities;
2. One recording of the child reading at home with a parent or older sibling;
3. One recorded interview between the child and a researcher;
4. Three interviews with a parent of each child; and
5. Fieldnotes from each Bangladeshi British child's Bengali and Qur'anic class.

We also interviewed the two mainstream teachers involved in the project and the school caretakers, both of whom had worked for more than 20 years in their respective schools. Data on the general history of the area and changing migration patterns were collected through secondary sources.

Analyzing the Data

The data analysis was conducted using the method of multi-layering (Bloome and Theodorou 1987). This approach enabled us to combine three layers of analysis, the focus moving from the outer layer, or social context, in which the individual functioning is embedded, through a middle layer in which we examined and quantified the teaching strategies used by teachers, parents, and children, to the inner layer in which ethnomothodological techniques were used to analyze in detail the roles of teacher and child in individual reading interactions. A useful example of the value of combining qualitative and quantitative approaches was found in Rogoff and Gauvain's (1986) pattern analysis used to examine instructional discourse in mother/child dyads.

Layer 1: The Ethnographic Analysis

Patterns of similarity and difference were sought between:

1. The demographic characteristics of each group;
2. The literacy histories and current reading practices of the two groups of children and adults;
3. Parents' and teachers' views of the role of the school and the family in children's reading development; and
4. The children's reading in different domains.

Layer 2: The Coding of Teaching Strategies

Teacher/child and parent/child reading sessions were examined and a list of strategies used by the "teachers" to facilitate the reader's progress through the text was drawn up (Campbell 1981; Hannon, Jackson, and Weinberger 1986). Twelve broad categories of strategies were identified which could be grouped under two headings:

1. *Modeling strategies* whose aim was to initiate the learner into being a "good reader." They included imparting knowledge about books, relating the text to real-life experiences, using the text to extend the reader's language development, and so forth.
2. *Scaffolding strategies* which concentrated on the text itself and were used to support the reader in decoding the text (see below).}

Examples of the strategies used by Teacher 1 and Teacher 2 in their teaching of reading include:

a. *Modeling Strategies*—that is, strategies used to promote reader-like behavior in their pupils:

1. Opening and closing moves:

T1: We can start reading clockwise or anti-clockwise

2. Imparting knowledge about books:

T1: We've just reached the middle. How do I know this is half way? I could tell roughly by the story or perhaps I could tell by the number of pages but I'm just going to do this....That's the middle

How do I know? Look!

Child: Oh, because there are staplers there.

3. Positive feedback:

T2: Well done, and so forth.

4. Negative feedback—no examples in teachers' transcripts.
5. Text-to-life interactions:

T2: Do you like Jelly beans? No? Have you had them before? Well, I like them.

6. Language development:

T1: ... wearing her of the rabbit holes?

Child: ... off the rabbit holes

T1: Does that make sense?

Child: wear ... he

T1: So if her dad is speaking to her and is telling her about rabbit holes, tree roots and ... what's he doing he's ... warn ...

Child: He's warning her....

b. *Scaffolding Strategies*—that is, strategies used by teachers to help readers decode the text.

1. Providing text:

T2: Then?

Child: A... M...

T2: Came

2. Phonic strategies:

T1: ....Do you remember? If you see a letter E and the letter A together ... can you remember the sound? Child: edie ... eddie..

T1: beady.... beady... beady eye...

3. Breaking down words—no examples of this in the teachers' transcripts.
4. Establishing meaning:

T1: Heads.... How do you know head?

Child: Because look ... (points to picture)

T1: You noticed that in the picture already. Well done

5. Pausing and prompting:

T1: Give Sarah a chance to think. Sarah, what is it?

Child: daughter

T1: daughter

6. Insisting on accuracy:

Child: it had blue leaf and yellow branches...

T2: It had blue what?

Child: Blue branches.

T2: Blue branches?

Child: Yellow branches

Reading sessions conducted by parents, school teachers and siblings were analyzed. Moves made by these "teachers" were allocated to one of the 12 categories of strategies and the number of moves in each category was expressed as a percentage of total moves in the reading session. It was then possible to compare the relative frequency of use of all the strategies across three sets of "teachers": parents, school teachers, and siblings. In addition, reading sessions in which two project children read with younger readers were analyzed, thus providing insights into the types of strategies the young readers had learned from their "teachers."

Layer 3: The Ethnomethodological Analysis

Conversation analysis or "talk-in-interaction" (Sacks, Schleghoff, and Jefferson 1974) was then used to show how joint cognitive activity in the form of "scaffolding" (Mercer 1994) or "guided participation" took place, whereby the child was active in managing the pace and nature of the interaction (Rogoff 1990). A comparison was made between reading sessions with Bangladeshi British older siblings reading with a younger brother or sister and monolingual English "book-oriented" caregivers and their infants.

RESULTS

Our layers of analysis reflect the broad aims of our project: to compare the literacy histories and current practices of the two communities with practices taking place in school and to trace ways in which these are reflected in individual reading interactions.

Layer 1: The Ethnographic Analysis

Demographic Data

The data we collected included information on the educational background of the parents, the child's position in the family, the parents' employment and, accommodation (see Tables 1 and 2).

Four factors contributed to differences in the children's home literacy practices. First, the different pattern of employment between the two groups highlights the relative isolation of the Bangladeshi British families living in this area in comparison to the monolingual English families. No mother of the Bangladeshi British group was in employment outside the home, in contrast with all but one of the monolingual mothers, whose work or studies demanded literacy skills. Three out of seven Bangladeshi British fathers were unemployed and the remaining four fathers were employed in the immediate area with colleagues from the same country of origin. Second, the educational level of the Bangladeshi

Table 1.   Family Background: Bangladeshi British families

	Position in Family	Father's Occupation	Mother's Education	Accommodation
Uzma	4/5	Restaurant-owmer	Grade 5	Flat
Maruf	5/5	Shop worker	Grade 5	Double flat
Shima	5/5	Unemployed	Grade 5	House
Shuma	2/4	Waiter	to age 15	Flat
Akhlak	9/11	Unemployed	Grade 7	Flat
Henna	3/4	Unemployed	Grade 4	Flat
Shanaz	2/3	Factory owner	Grade 5	Flat

Table 2.   Family Background: Monolingual English Families

	Position in Family	Father's Occupation	Mother's Education	Mother's Occupation	Accommodation
Susie	1/1	Policeman	Age 16	Childminder	Flat
Sally	3/3	Publican	Age 16	Works in family pub	Week—flat Weekend—house
Anne Marie	1/1	Builder	Age 16	Insurance clerk	House
Naomi	2/2		Age 16	Unemployed	Flat
Richard	3/3	Unemployed	Age 16	Access course	Flat
Stewart	2/2	Plumber	Age 16	Playleader in chilren's playground	Flat

British mothers meant that, although literate in Bengali, only one was able to read or write English. This contrasted with the monolingual mothers, three of whom had GCE passes. Third, unemployment and cramped accommodation meant that the array of educational toys found in some of the monolingual English family homes was not available to many of the Bangladeshi British children. Finally, in contrast to the monolingual children, the Bangladeshi British children had a number of older siblings living at home who played a significant role in the children's reading development.

Literacy Histories and Current Reading Practices of Parents and Teachers

Each group looked back on very different memories of learning to read and now associated reading with very different purposes and materials. The two teachers remember learning to read at home and in school as pleasurable. Both still read for enjoyment, although Teacher 2 distinguished between challenging or "good" reading and other kinds. Reading was largely an individual affair between the reader and the book.

In contrast, the white monolingual English mothers all made a clear distinction between school reading and home reading. Their overriding school memory was of truanting, bullying by other pupils, a lack of encouragement by their teachers, and their consequent feeling of having "missed out" in some way on education. Two mothers spoke of having been being dyslexic. However, all had happy memories of early reading outside school, mainly because their parents "provided lovely books, comics or literacy materials." One spoke of attending Hebrew classes, which she really enjoyed "because you could relate to people." Five out of six mothers still loved reading and spent considerably more time than the teachers engaged in a variety of literacy activities such as informal book discussions or pub quiz groups, acting as chairperson for the local Residents' Association, as well as being crossword or autobiography addicts. In contrast with Teacher 2, no mothers mentioned "educational" or "good" books. Reading was seen purely as a pleasurable activity and was often a joint or social affair.

For all the Bangladeshi British mothers, learning to read had a serious purpose, often associated with religion. As children in Bangladesh, most had attended Mosque and Bengali school for equal amounts of time. Reading any kind of fiction had been strongly discouraged by parents. Five of the seven mothers had left school by the end of class 5 (aged 11), which was a normal age for girls to leave school. In contrast to the monolingual English group, limited schooling was accepted by these women as a necessity of life. The religious purpose of reading remained with them throughout adult life. Although one woman borrowed Bengali novels from the library, reading generally meant "reading the Qur'an'." The Arabic word for "reading" (*qara'a'*) also carries the meaning "learning by heart" (Wagner 1993; Baynham 1995).

Pleasure was reserved for news-telling—that is, meeting with friends and neighbors to exchange news, ideas, and views, a regular occurrence in the women's lives. Both reading and news-telling were group activities.

Our findings, therefore, indicate very different interpretations of both reading and schooling by each of the three groups. These findings reflect those of recent studies in the United States into different cultural models of education held by different groups (Reese and Gallimore 1995).

Adults' Perceptions of the Role of School and the Family on Children's Reading

Both teachers indicated that the parents' role was listening to children's reading using the PACT materials (Parents and Children Together—a home reading scheme) and felt that some parents were not strict enough in using these. The teachers' perceptions of their own role on the other hand were very different. Teacher 1 felt that the teaching of reading was very much her responsibility. She was very experienced and had developed her teaching methods "by observing and working with children, rather than adhering to any one particular orthodoxy." Observations and recordings of Teacher 1 throughout the year demonstrated a close link between her aims and practice. In contrast, Teacher 2 thought her parents should become more involved in their children's reading. It seems fair to say that the views of Teacher 2, who worked with the Bangladeshi British group, contrasted sharply with those held by the parents of her pupils; they reflected her own childhood experiences of reading as a pleasurable activity and she consequently wanted parents to enjoy reading with their children. Neither teacher seemed to be fully aware of the scope of reading practices their pupils were engaged in outside school.

All the parents, without exception, were keen for their children to benefit from the educational opportunities they themselves seemed to have missed, and they provided all they could to foster their young children's reading development. Nevertheless, the teacher was held to be the expert, and parents viewed their own role as complementing hers. Neither group had a very clear idea of how reading was taught in school; nor were they very sure what the teachers expected of them at home. The Bangladeshi British parents believed that the English teacher would use the same teaching methods as were used in the Bengali and Qur'anic class and judged their children's progress accordingly. Although the monolingual English parents felt equally unclear about teaching methods, they appeared less concerned, possibly because all were extremely pleased with their children's progress, which they attributed to Teacher 1's "brilliance." Both groups of parents wanted more work to be sent home; the PACT reading books taken regularly by children were not generally regarded as serious homework.

The Children's Reading Practices in Different Domains

Common to all children except the two monolingual English speaking boys was that less time was spent on school reading taken home than on other reading and literacy activities. Apart from this, out-of-school literacy activities of the two groups differed in terms of context, participants, purpose, scope, and materials (see Tables 3 and 4).

The monolingual English children read mostly in informal contexts and for enjoyment, using a variety of books, comics, and other materials. Reading could be an individual or a social activity, as during "playing schools," where the girls modeled themselves on the teacher. A distinction must be made between the girls in this group and the boys, who rarely read at all outside school. In contrast, the Bangladeshi British boys and girls learned in both formal contexts, such as learning standard Bengali using primers and learning to read the Qur'an in Arabic, and in informal contexts, learning to read English with siblings using books from school. Both contexts had a serious purpose for the Bangladeshi British children, whose older siblings viewed themselves as teaching reading and English.

There were both similarities and differences in the organization of reading in the two school teachers' classrooms. Both schools had a policy of quiet reading. Both used a combination of different reading schemes and other materials, color-coded for difficulty, and both had purchased sets of books which the children could read in groups, according to ability. However, Teacher 1 (with the monolingual children) worked almost entirely through group reading or shared reading with the whole class, while Teacher 2 (with the bilingual children) listened to the children individually. Consequently, the groups with Teacher 1 read for considerably longer than did the individuals with Teacher 2. Teacher 1 also spent longer explaining tasks and discussing expectations with the whole group. An immediate explanation for the unequal amounts of time spent on reading might be that the white monolingual children who read in groups were in Year 2, while the Bengali British children who read individually were in Year 1. Nevertheless, we noted that all these young children were able to concentrate for longer

Table 3. Children's Out of School Literacy Activities: Bangladeshi British Children

Type of Practice	Context	Participants	Purpose	Scope	Materials	Role of Child
Qur'anic class	Formal: in class-rooms or in some-one's living room	Group of 0 - 30 mixed age-range	Religious: to read and learn the Qur'an	Approximately 7 hours per week	Raiel (wooden book stand); preparatory primers or Qur'an	Child listens and repeats (individully or as group); practices and is tested
Bengali class	Formal: in class-rooms or in some-one's living room	Group of mixed age range. Can be children of one family up to group of 30	Cultural: to learn to read, understand-ing, and write Stan-dard Bengali	Approximately 6 hours per week	Primers, exercise books, pens	Child listens and repeats (individully or as group); practices and is tested
Reading with older siblings	Informal: at home	Dyad: child + older sibling	"Homework": to learn to speak and read English	Approximately 3 hours per week	English school books	Child repeats, eches, predicts, and finally answers comprehension questions
Videos/Television	Informal: at home	Family group	Pleasure/entertain-ment		TV in English Videos (often in Hindi)	Child watches and listens. Often listens to and joins in dis-cussions. Sings songs from films

34

Table 4. Children's Out of School Literacy Activities: English Monolingual Children

Type of Practice	Context	Participants	Purpose	Scope	Materials	Role of Child
Playing School	Informal: at home	Group or individual	Play		Blackboard, books, writing materials	Child imitates teacher and/or pupils
PACT (Parents And Children Together: Home reading scheme)	Informal: at home	Dyad: Parent/child	Homework: to improve child's reading		School reading book	Child reads and is corrected by parent using "scaffolding" or "modeling" strategies
Comics, fiction, non-fiction	Informal: at home	Individual or dyad (parent or grandparent/child)	Pleasure		Variety of comics, fiction, nonfiction books	Child as "expert" with comics or books; as interested learner reading adult nonfiction, magazines, etc.
Drama class	Formal	Group	Pleasure and to learn skill	2 hours per week	Books: poetry and plays	Child performs in group; recites as individual
Computers	Informal	Individual or in dyad with friend or sibling	Pleasure			
Video/Television	Informal	Family group or individual	Pleasure/entertainment		TV/videos	

periods during their community classes than was expected of them in mainstream school.

Layer 2: Teaching Strategies

Transcripts of recorded reading sessions in different contexts revealed very different patterns of interaction between the participants. We began to examine these by coding the teaching strategies used by:

1. Teacher 1/children in class group reading sessions (Teacher 1 always worked with groups of children);
2. Teacher 2/individual child dyad;
3. Older Bangladeshi British sibling/child dyad at home;
4. Monolingual English mother/child dyad at home; and
5. Child/younger child dyad in class.

Community classes were not included because taping was not permitted. Nevertheless, the pattern of Listen, Repeat, Practice, Test ran through all sessions observed in the Bengali and Arabic classes and has been noted in Qur'anic classes in many countries (Wagner 1993). In view of our aim to analyze patterns of joint activity appearing in the interactional context of multiple cases, we used variables tied functionally to the purpose of the interaction, which allowed us to: (1) consider the actions of the participants as interrelated rather than separate, and (2) incorporate changes over the course of tuition rather than impose a static conception of the participants' actions (see also Layer 3).

Prompted by observations of Qur'anic classes where teachers all used a single strategy (providing text), in contrast with the English teachers who used a whole variety, our coding focused on what we refer to as "modeling" and "scaffolding" strategies (Mercer 1994)). Our initial hypotheses were: (1) that the English reading sessions would be characterized by a pattern of "modeling" strategies, in contrast with the Qur'anic and Bengali classes where "scaffolding" would dominate; and (2) that the monolingual English children would not be as strongly accustomed to "scaffolding" strategies as their Bangladeshi-origin peers and would be more disposed to adopt the strategies of their English teacher.

However, our findings found a similar pattern emerging from all interactions except those of Teacher 2/child. The strategy of providing text which, indeed, dominated the Qur'anic class, was also the main strategy used by all other "teachers" (see Figures 1, 2, 3, and 4).

We had expected strategies used by the Bangladeshi British siblings to reflect those of their community classes and, indeed, these did consist largely (though not entirely) of providing text. However, this strategy also figured large in the teaching by mothers and by the two monolingual English girls who "taught" younger children, and was the most common strategy during the group reading sessions of Teacher 1. In contrast, it seldom appeared in the interactions between children and Teacher 2. Figures 2 and 4 also highlight a symmetry between the teaching of Teacher 1 and that of Naomi, a monolingual English child whose mother did not read to her but provided literacy materials with which she loved to "play schools."

Teacher 1's work is, however, very different from both the Qur'anic teacher and the siblings. Although both teachers used a whole variety of both "scaffolding" and "modeling" ,strategies Teacher 1's lessons revealed a balance of approaches, whereas those of Teacher 2 (with the bilingual Bangladeshi British group) were based almost entirely on "modeling" strategies, which were unfamiliar to the children and not used in their community class lessons.

Layer 3: "Teacher"/Child Interaction in Different Domains

In Layer 3, ethnomethodological analysis of transcripts of children and siblings reading together demonstrated that the extent to which guided participation takes place, depends on the way in which "modeling" and/or "scaffolding" strategies are used. As a final step, patterns of interaction between the home reading of the Bangladeshi-origin siblings and the young children were compared with transcripts of Western "mainstream" caregivers and their two-year-old infants.

Analysis of reading sessions between the Bangladeshi British children and their older siblings reveal an intricate and finely tuned "scaffolding," which is gradually removed as the child's proficiency develops. A syncretism results whereby the sibling gradually grafts school "modeling" strategies onto the familiar pattern of providing text from the Qur'anic class. Consequently, the way in which text is provided by the sibling is closely linked to the child's development as a reader. To summarize, the younger children's strategies are characterized by: repeating word-by-word or phrase-by-phrase, sometimes antic-

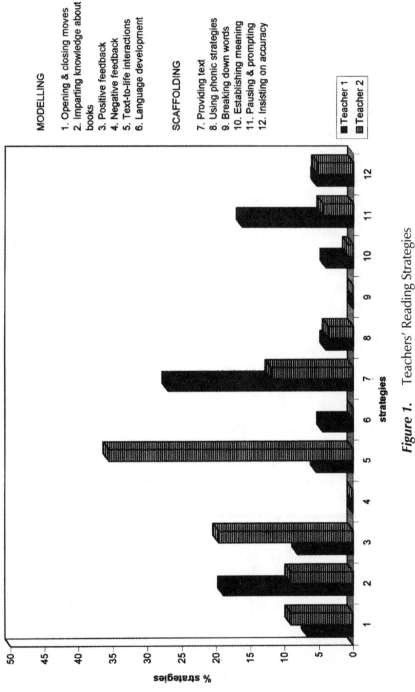

MODELLING

1. Opening & closing moves
2. Imparting knowledge about books
3. Positive feedback
4. Negative feedback
5. Text-to-life interactions
6. Language development

SCAFFOLDING

7. Providing text
8. Using phonic strategies
9. Breaking down words
10. Establishing meaning
11. Pausing & prompting
12. Insisting on accuracy

■ Teacher 1
▦ Teacher 2

Figure 1. Teachers' Reading Strategies

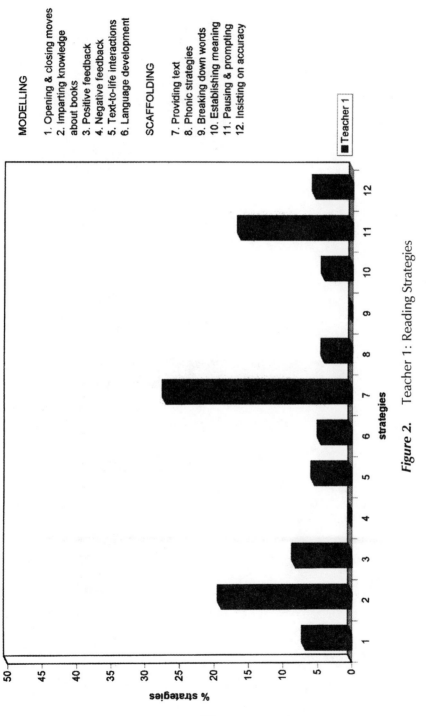

MODELLING

1. Opening & closing moves
2. Imparting knowledge about books
3. Positive feedback
4. Negative feedback
5. Text-to-life interactions
6. Language development

SCAFFOLDING

7. Providing text
8. Phonic strategies
9. Breaking down words
10. Establishing meaning
11. Pausing & prompting
12. Insisting on accuracy

Figure 2. Teacher 1: Reading Strategies

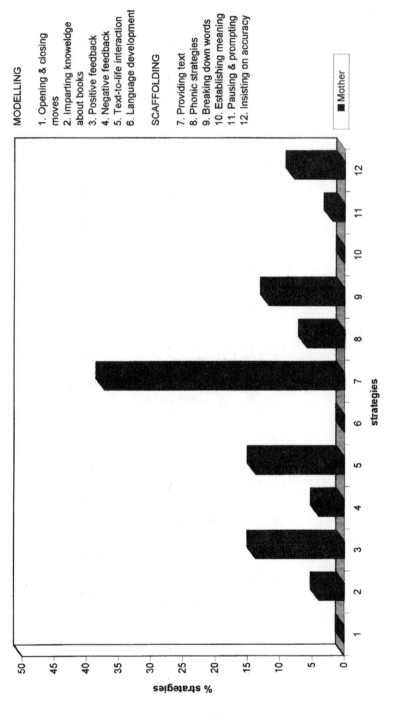

MODELLING

1. Opening & closing moves
2. Imparting knoweldge about books
3. Positive feedback
4. Negative feedback
5. Text-to-life interaction
6. Language development

SCAFFOLDING

7. Providing text
8. Phonic strategies
9. Breaking down words
10. Establishing meaning
11. Pausing & prompting
12. insisting on accuracy

■ Mother

Figure 3. Mother Reading with Susie

40

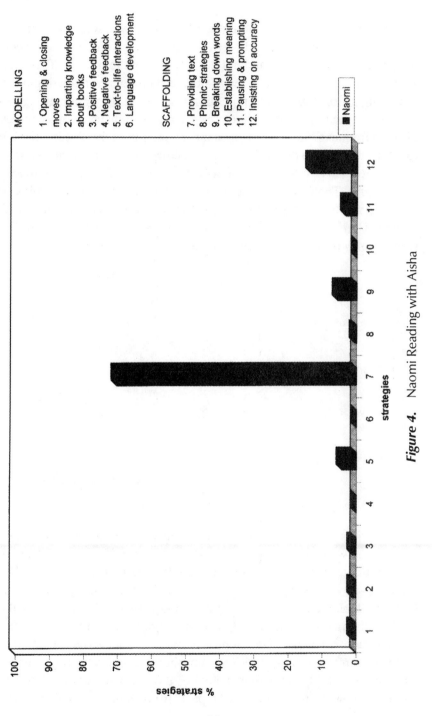

MODELLING

1. Opening & closing moves
2. Imparting knowledge about books
3. Positive feedback
4. Negative feedback
5. Text-to-life interactions
6. Language development

SCAFFOLDING

7. Providing text
8. Phonic strategies
9. Breaking down words
10. Establishing meaning
11. Pausing & prompting
12. Insisting on accuracy

Figure 4. Naomi Reading with Aisha

41

ipating the next word(s); echoing words and phrases, which sometimes results in "telegraphic" speech; always repeating a word after being corrected before continuing; and not hesitating about joining in. The older sibling's strategies are characterized by: sustaining a fast-flowing pace; providing a firm "scaffold" (repetition or echoing only gradually gives way to prediction by the child); expecting a high level of accuracy through frequent (though not constant) correction of the child; allowing (perhaps expecting) the child to repeat a correction before continuing; a lack of evaluative comment; and a lack of text-to-life comment during the readings. The whole interaction is characterized by a high number of exchanges between participants with no breakdown in communication.

Here, Uzma and her eight-year-old sister are reading together. The strategy of repeating and extending the utterance is evident:

Uzma	Sister
	1 with lots
2 lots of windows	
	3 or a
4 or a carpet	
	5 What else could it be?
6 What else could it be?...triangle	
	7 little
8 little triangles	
	9 How many big triangles?
10 How many big triangles are there?	

Transcripts of reading sessions recorded in both mainstream school classrooms were then examined to see whether evidence of the home pattern of interaction between the Bangaldeshi British siblings could be found in school reading sessions. Transcripts of the reading interactions between Teacher 2 and the Bangladeshi British children, showed the teacher giving a very different type of support, in some respects reversing the home pattern. Her approach was characterized by making text-to-life references, questioning on phonics, and repeating the last word of the child rather than allowing the child to repeat after her. Excerpts show the reversal of the "repeat" move, a procedure that results in truncated interactions very different from the fast flow of reading at home.

Child	Teacher
	19 O.K. Point to the words like you did last time
20 (There) string	
	21 *string*
22 *string*. (0) on the (.) upstairs	
	23 upstairs

Note: (0) = longer pause; (.) = short pause

In contrast, group reading sessions in Classroom 1 reveal the use of many strategies which characterize the Bangladeshi British sibling/child interaction. Thus we trace the fast flow of reading, repeating text, echoing, chained reading, insisting on accuracy, and so forth that is familiar from interaction between siblings. Interestingly, however, it is mostly the other children in the group who provide this support, and the teacher who orchestrates the whole.

Here, we see the same Listen and Repeat plus extension strategy which characterized the reading of Uzma and her sister:

(Teacher 1 is reading with a group of monolingual and bilingual children. It is Child 1's turn to read).

1. *Child 3:* daughters! daughters!

2. *Child 1:* help

3. *Child 2:*because

4. *Child 1:* because it gave him a

5. *Child 2:* change

6. *Child 3:* chance

7. *Child 1:* chance to have a quick smoke. They were very

8. *Child 4*: close

9. *Child 1:* close. One...

Finally, a comparison of reading interaction between our siblings and transcripts of English-speaking mothers who regularly read stories to their toddlers revealed unexpected similarities in the use of "scaffolding" though patterns of repetition, echoing, and prediction (Gregory 1998). Such interaction has been referred to as "a reciprocal dialogue," which is precisely how we would characterize the siblings' reading sessions.

Thus, far from discovering considerable differences between "school-oriented" and "non-school-oriented" groups as documented in previous studies (Scollon and Scollon 1979; Heath 1983), we found remarkable similarities in both the strategies and in the finely tuned "scaffolding"of the Bangladeshi British siblings which was only slowly and carefully removed in order to give the child maximum confidence in completing the task.

CONCLUSION

Findings from this study reveal clearly the strengths of combining ethnography and ethnomethodology to provide a dynamic framework within which child/adult (or older sibling) interaction may be viewed. The ethnographic approach presented in Layer 1 allows us to see the different interpretations of reading brought by children from home and community literacy experiences as they enter school but is not able to detail whether and in what ways dyads exchange meanings during reading sessions. Layers 2 and 3 highlight the effects of different interpretations on "teachers" (teacher/adult/older sibling) strategies during the child's first years in school. The ethnomethodological approach, using a finely tuned analysis of repetitions, echoing, and so forth, is able to trace both successful and truncated exchanges. It is also able to highlight the syncretism taking place as older siblings combine school and community class teaching strategies in their work with their younger brothers and sisters. The small scale of the study, however, means that the results should be seen as preliminary and interpreted as providing an overview of the strategies used by "teachers" rather than as a controlled comparison of methodologies. Nevertheless, the combination of ethnography and ethnomethodology must be seen as a powerful tool in analyzing discourse in educational contexts in the homes and classrooms of the many cultural groups that make up our society.

ACKNOWLEDGMENT

This research was supported by the Economic and Social Research Council (R 000 22 1186) from 1994 to 1995. The authors whould like to acknowledge the assistance of Jane Mace, co-director in this project, and Nasima Rashid, research officer, the families, the schools, and particularly the two teachers in whose classrooms the research took place.

REFERENCES

Adult Literacy and Basic Skills Unit (ALBSU). 1993. *Parents and their Children: The Intergenerational Effect of Poor Basic Skills.* London: ALBSU.

Au, K. 1980. "Participation Structures in a Reading Lesson with Hawaiian Children: Analysis of a Culturally Appropriate Instructional Event. *Anthropology and Education Quarterly* 17: 115-152

Barton, D., and S. Hamilton. 1992. *Literacy in the Community.* Final Report of ESRC Project R 000 23 3149.

Baynham, M. 1995. *Literacy Practices:Investigating Literacy in Social Contexts.* London: Longman.

Bernstein, B. 1971. "A Sociolinguistic Approach to Socialization with Some Reference to Educability. In *Directions in Sociolinguistics*, edited by D. Hymes and J. Gumperz. New York: Rinehart and Winston

Bloome, D., and E. Theodorou. 1987. "Analysing Teacher-Student and Student-Student Discourse." In *Multiple Analysis of Classroom Discourse Processes*, edited by J. Green, J. Harker, and C. Wallat. Norwood, NJ: Ablex.

Brooks, G., T. Gorman, J. Harman, D. Hutchinson, T. Kinder, H. Moor, and A. Wilkin. 1996. *Family Literacy Works: The NFER Evaluation of the Basic Skills Agency's Demonstration Programmes.* London: The Basic Skills Agency.

Campbell, R. 1981. "An Approach to Analysing Verbal Moves in Hearing Children Read." *Journal of Research in Reading* 4(1): 43-56.

Chazan, M. and Williams, P. 1978. *Deprivation and the Infant School.* Oxford, UK: Basil Blackwell.

Duranti, A., and E. Ochs. 1996. "Syncretic Literacy: Multiculturalism in Samoan American Families." San Francisco, CA: National Center for Research on Cultural Diversity and Second Language Learning.

Gregory, E. 1994. "Cultural Assumptions and Early Years' Pedagogy: The Effect of the Home Culture on Minority Children's Interpretation of Reading in School." *Language, Culture and Curriculum* 7(2): 114-125.

Gregory, E. 1996. *Making Sense of a New World: Learning to Read in a Second Language.* London: Paul Chapman.

Gregory, E. Forthcoming. "Siblings as Mediators of Literacy in Linguistic Minority Communities." *Language and Education: An International Journal.*

Hannon, P., P. Jackson, and J. Weinberger. 1986. "Parents' and Teachers' Strategies in Hearing Young Children Read." *Research Papers in Education* 1(1): 6-25.

Heath, S.B. 1983. *Ways with Words: Language, Life and Work in Communities and Classrooms.* Cambridge, UK: Cambridge University Press.

Labov, W. 1972. *Sociolinguistic Patterns.* Philadelphia, PA: University of Philadelphia Press.

Mercer, N. 1994. "Neo-Vygotskyian Theory and Classroom Education." In *Language, Literacy and Learning in Educational Practice,* edited by B. Stierer and J. Maybin. Clevedon: Multilingual Matters.

Michaels, S. 1986. "Narrative Presentations: An Oral Preparation for Literacy with First Graders. in In *The Social Construction of Literacy,* edited by J. Cook-Gumperz. Cambridge, UK: Cambridge University Press.

National Curriculum Council. 1995. *The National Curriculum for English.* York: National Curriculum Council.

Ofsted. 1996. *The Teaching of Reading in 45 Inner London Primary Schools.* (Ref. 27/96/D5) London: Ofsted.

Rashid, N. 1996. Fieldnotes from a visit to a Qur'anic class in the London Borough of Tower Hamlets.

Reese, L., and R. Gallimore. 1995. "Ethnotheories and Practices of Literacy Development among Immigrant Latino Parents." Paper presesented at the American Association for Educational Research Conference, New York, April 8-12.

Rogoff, B. 1990. *Apprenticeship in Thinking: Cognitive Development in Social Contexts.* Oxford, UK: Oxford University Press.

Rogoff, B., and M. Gauvain. 1986. "A Method for the Analysis of Patterns, Illustrated with Data on Mother-Child Instructional Interaction." In *The Individual Subject and Scientific Psychology,* edited by J. Valsiner. New York: Plenum Press.

Sacks, H., E.A. Schleghoff, and G. Jefferson. 1974. "A Simplest Systematics for the Organisation of Turn-Taking for Conversation. *Language* 50(4): 696-735.

Saxena, M. 1994. "Literacies among Panjabis in Southall." In *Worlds of Literacy,* edited by M. Hamilton, D. Barton, and R. Ivanic. Clevedon: Multilingual Matters

Scollon, R., and S. Scollon. 1979. Linguistic Convergence: An Ethnography of Speaking at Fort Chipewya. New York: Academic Press.

Scollon, R., and B.K. Scollon. 1981. *Narrative, Literacy and Face in Interethnic Communication.* Norwood, NJ: Ablex Publishing.

Select Committee to the House of Commons. 1986/1987. *The Achievement of Bangladeshi Children in School.* London: Her Majesty's Stationary Office.

Tate, N. 1995. "Final Speech." Presented at the International Conference Supporting Additional Language Learners, London, April.

Tizard, B., and M. Hughes. 1984. *Young Children Learning.* London: Fontana.

Volk, D. 1994. "A Case-Study of Parent Involvement in the Homes of Three Puerto Rican Kindergartners." *The Journal of Educational Issues of Language Minority Students* 14(Fall): 1-25.

Wagner, D.A. 1993. *Literacy, Culture and Development. Becoming Literate in Morocco.* Cambridge, UK: Cambridge University Press.

Wells, G. 1981 *Learning Through Interaction.* Cambridge, UK: Cambridge University Press.

Williams, A. 1997. "Investigating Literacy in London: Three Generations of Readers in an East End Family." In *One Child, Many Worlds: Early Learning in Multicultual Communities,* edited by E. Gregory. London: Fulton.

THE SIGNIFICANCE OF PLAYMATES IN THE ACQUISITION OF A SECOND LANGUAGE:

IMPLICATIONS FROM A STUDY OF CROSS-CULTURAL ADJUSTMENT

Susi Long

INTRODUCTION

Daily, in my role as mother, I observe my daughter, Kelli, learning to get along in many cultures or "interrelated contexts" (Almy and Genishi 1979) that make up her world. Such observations became scientifically based just before Kelli's eighth birthday, when we moved from the United States to Iceland. Interested in how children learn to get along in new cultures and the potential implications for parents and teachers, I designed a study to look closely and systematically at Kelli's day-to-day

Studies in Educational Ethnography, Volume 1, pages 47-67.
Copyright © 1998 by JAI Press Inc.
All rights of reproduction in any form reserved.
ISBN: 0-7623-0436-7

experiences during her first nine months in Iceland. The purpose of the study was to gain "a deeper understanding of [one child's] every day experiences" (Van Manen 1990). I asked, "What does it mean to be an eight-year-old girl learning to get along in a new cultural setting?" Committed to the collection and analysis of data in as contextualized a manner as possible, the question was intentionally broad. I did not want to focus so narrowly that I would neglect the spectrum of interwoven factors that I assumed would make up Kelli's experience. Because of the contextualized and culture-based nature of the question—attempting to understand how a child views and learns to operate within a new cultural environment—ethnography provided an appropriate paradigm on which to base the research design. The resulting story is one of cultural adjustment which includes discussions of friendship development, peer group entry, classroom adjustment, second language acquisition, and literacy development. This paper focuses on one aspect of that story: the significance of playmates in the process of Kelli's acquisition of Icelandic.

THEORETICAL PERSPECTIVE

The theoretical perspective guiding the study was drawn from a constructivist paradigm which views children as constructors of knowledge through supported involvement in their worlds. Roots of this perspective are found in the work of Piaget, who believed that "children develop through activity by acting upon their environment" (Genishi 1985) and in Vygotsky's discussion of a zone of proximal development in which learning is extended through interaction with more knowledgeable partners (Vygotsky 1978). Particularly helpful in the clarification of this perspective are the basic tenets of an interactionist approach to language acquisition. From this point of view, the learner is seen as biologically predisposed to acquiring language as well as a creative constructor who, with the support of a communicative partner, formulates, tests, and reformulates hypotheses, thereby building an understanding of language structure and use (Bruner 1983; Genishi and Dyson 1984; Wells 1986).

Although other bodies of research were reviewed with respect to the entire study, those discussed as relevant to this paper are: acculturation in middle childhood, bilingualism, and second language acquisition. Key understandings from those studies include the notion that children learn about activities, routines, behaviors, and values through interaction within peer groups (Corsaro 1988; MacKay 1991) and that social knowledge becomes more complex as children face new cultural norms in bilingual and bicultural situations (Tammivaara and Enright 1986). The process of learning to operate within systems that guide behavior in a culture other than one's own is termed, acculturation (Ellis 1985). It is viewed as a reciprocal process resulting in changes to attitudes and behaviors of members of the host culture as well as to the newcomer (Spradley and McCurdy 1990). In terms of bilingualism and second language acquisition, studies illustrate a process of language learning that occurs at different rates determined to a large extent by the learner's participation in the second language world (Genishi 1989; Hester 1984; Wong-Fillmore 1986). Also suggested as factors affecting second language acquisition are age, personality, cognitive development, attitude, and parental influence. Critical to the success of the developing bilingual is the role played by native speakers, who provide authentic contexts for language practice as well as important language data and feedback (Dulay, Burth, and Krashen 1982; Ervin-Tripp 1974; Hakuta 1986; Levine 1990; Wong-Fillmore 1986). As they interact with native speakers, learners have opportunities to experiment with meaning, function, and pronunciation before freeing themselves from dependence on native speakers' support (Ellis 1985; Hakuta 1986; Wong-Fillmore 1976).

THE STUDY

The Research Site and Collection of Data

On August 22 1991 Kelli and I moved from the United States to Iceland, joining my husband who had lived there for a year. Our new home was in Njarðvík, a town of 2,800 residents located at the southwestern tip of the country. Two weeks after our arrival, at the start of the academic year, Kelli entered *þriði bekk* (third class/year) at the local Icelandic school. For the next nine months, I observed her in as many contexts as possible as she interacted with the children and adults in her new worlds. Using field notes, videotape, and audiotape, I collected data at home, in the homes of friends, at school, and during her participation in extra-curricular and community activities. I listened and questioned as Kelli talked about the joys and struggles of her new life. Formally (in prepared interviews) and informally (in spontaneous conversations), I talked to Kelli's teachers, friends, and parents of friends about her experiences. Documental data were also collected and included Kelli's school work and progress reports, artifacts from informal play, letters and stories written by Kelli, and still photographs.

Participants

With the exception of Kelli, her father, and me, all participants in the study were native-speakers of Icelandic. It is a language that has changed little from that brought to the country by Norse settlers in the tenth century and possesses a complex grammatical structure that includes four cases, three genders, and 48 potential forms of nouns and adjectives (Magnusson 1990). Many adult Icelanders with whom Kelli came in contact spoke English as a second language, having studied it as a compulsory school course from the age of ten. Adult Icelandic participants included Kelli's classroom teacher (who welcomed me as a participant observer in her classroom), parents of Kelli's friends, the school's reading specialist, the school's librarian, Kelli's piano teacher, and her choir director. These teachers and parents of friends played particularly important roles in Kelli's Icelandic experience and contributed invaluably to the study. Regularly and frequently, they talked with me about their observations and interpretations of Kelli's experiences. Two parents helped with the translation of data from Icelandic to English.

The Icelandic children who played key roles in the study were Kelli's closest friends—Birna, Elva, and Guðbjörg. As eight-year-olds, the girls had not yet begun to study English at school but exhibited knowledge of approximately 20 English words, learned primarily from watching British and American television programs. The girls lived within walking distance of our home and were in Kelli's class at the local school. Throughout the study, one or more of the girls played with Kelli almost every day, usually at our house but also in their homes and around the neighborhood.

Intimately involved in Kelli's life, her father and I were also key participants in the study. In planned interviews and spontaneous conversations with each other and with Kelli, we worked through issues related to our daughter's experiences and developed our own understandings of language and culture.

The primary participant was, of course, Kelli. She was almost eight years old when we moved to Iceland, having lived in Germany, The

Netherlands, and the United States. Kelli's experiences living in The Netherlands (from the time she was 10 months old until just before her sixth birthday) appeared to have a significant impact on her attitude about life in Iceland. Remembering that she had learned a new language and played exclusively with Dutch children during those years, Kelli expected that the same would be possible in Iceland: she would make friends, learn the language, and play.

Mother as Researcher

As mother/researcher, I was involved in aspects of my daughter's life that provided excellent arenas for the collection of naturalistic data. At the same time, important ethical issues (faced by all researchers but magnified in parent-child studies) emerged: (1) how to avoid taking advantage of access to intimate situations, comments, and behaviors and (2) how to ensure the autonomy necessary for Kelli to work through understandings about life and language—particularly at school—without the excessive intrusion of mother as data collector. These issues were addressed by: consistently and frequently sharing data and interpretations with Kelli, learning to listen to and respect her solicited and unsolicited concerns about the study, developing a sensitivity to the point at which she perceived interviews to be uncomfortable and intrusive, eliminating aspects of the study that violated her privacy or embarrassed her, and, after the first six weeks, reducing my presence in Kelli's classroom from daily observations to one day per week. In spite of these measures, it must be acknowledged that Kelli may not have voiced (or could not articulate) every discomfort she felt.

The Story: The Role of Playmates in One Child's Acquisition of a New Language

Focusing on one part of a broad study that looks at many aspects of a child's cross-cultural adjustment, the data and interpretations presented in the following pages describe the role of playmates in my daughter's acquisition of Icelandic. Although it appeared to be the most significant factor, play-based interaction with peers was not the only factor that affected Kelli's language learning. The broader study describes other elements, which include: family involvement, the support of teachers, contributions of parents of playmates, and Kelli's attitude about the move, the country, the people, and the feasibility of learning a new language. This paper focuses on the role of playmates by looking at: (1) strategies used by Kelli and her playmates to facilitate communication, (2) a brief chronology of Kelli's acquisition of Icelandic, (3) contexts that supported language learning, and (4) contrasts between Kelli's language use at play and at school. Concluding paragraphs consider findings and potential implications for parents and teachers.

Strategies Used by Kelli and her Playmates to Facilitate Communication

From our first days in Iceland, Kelli wanted to meet children who would play with her. She made herself available to potential playmates by wandering up and down the street in front of our house. She was not yet comfortable enough to knock on doors but was eager to accept an invitation to play. On the evening of our second day in Iceland, the doorbell rang. We opened the door to find two Icelandic children—Elva and Birna—standing on the front porch wearing roller skates. In a carefully rehearsed sentence, Elva asked, "Do you want to play?" Excited that she had been invited to join them, Kelli quickly put on her skates and followed the girls outside. They skated up and down the hill in front of our house and then stood in our driveway looking at each other. They uttered no words but smiled and giggled. As the first strategies used by Kelli and her Icelandic playmates, smiles, giggles, and involvement in a mutually comprehensible activity (skating) made interaction possible. During Kelli's first months in Iceland, the children developed a variety of communicative strategies that supported interaction and facilitated communication. Using those strategies, they built relationships, established a common play history, and constructed a comfortable environment, all factors that affected Kelli's eventual acquisition of Icelandic. Following is a discussion of those strategies as they evolved in the play worlds of Kelli and her Icelandic peers.

Laughing

During their first evening of play, after skating outside, Kelli brought Elva and Birna into our kitchen, where she gave them juice and cookies. As she opened the rubbish bin to throw away juice cartons, Kelli wrinkled her nose at the foul-smelling rubbish. The Icelandic girls laughed.

Kelli gestured toward the rubbish, wrinkled her nose again and, once more, the girls laughed in response. Kelli then looked around the kitchen, picked up a cooking timer and set the dial. As the timer rang, the girls giggled. Over and over again, Kelli set the dial, the timer rang, and the girls laughed. In this way, laughter (and, as discussed later, the use of physical objects) became a strategy that, prior to the establishment of a mutually comprehensible language, allowed Kelli not only to participate communicatively but to initiate interaction with Icelandic peers.

As they played together during the first weeks, the girls' laughter often seemed to have a nervous tone and was used somewhat self-consciously to fill silences. Kelli's laugh took on an exaggerated quality—more forced than a natural giggle and more assertive than a giddy reaction to something silly or funny. She seemed to use it to announce and emphasize her role as an active participant among peers. For the first three weeks, laughter was an important communicative tool. Its significance diminished as other strategies evolved.

Intonating Sounds

The girls' repertoire of communicative techniques broadened immediately to include intonated sound. Used to communicate intent, emotion, reaction, and instruction, sounds acquired meaning when supported by intonation (shortening or lengthening the sound, deepening or raising the voice), facial expression (raising eyebrows, frowning, furrowing the brow) and gesture. This is illustrated in an excerpt from their first attempt at indoor play. Kelli, Birna, and Elva were sitting on Kelli's bedroom floor putting together a puzzle. Their utterances occurred as they picked up puzzle pieces and considered options for placement:

Birna:	Hmmm.	Picking up a puzzle piece and examining it, furrowed brow.
Kelli:	Mmmm. Mmm?	Picking up a puzzle piece and testing possibilities for placement, voice rising in tone, raising eyebrows.
	Hmmm.	Trying to place the piece—voice deepening in tone.
	Mm mmm.	Shaking her head as the piece does not fit, short, staccato voice.

(Videotape, August 28, 1991)

Sounds continued to be used as important communicative tools even after Kelli began to speak Icelandic. As she experimented with the new language, she frequently used sound to fill gaps. For instance, one evening, as she was playing with friends, I told her to play quietly (to stop screaming). Attempting to communicate that message to her playmates, Kelli constructed a sentence by using the Icelandic she knew combined with sound. She said, "Ekki ahhhhhh (screaming sound)" meaning, "Don't scream" (Field Notes, September 20, 1991). As Kelli gained competence with Icelandic, reliance on sound decreased but its use never disappeared.

Using Action and Facial Expression

Supporting all other communicative strategies, action and facial expression were essential to the success of communication between Kelli and her Icelandic friends. By pointing, miming, demonstrating, raising an eyebrow, and/or nodding a head, the children gave meaning to their use of sounds and words. For example, during the second week, action and facial expression supported Birna's limited use of English to describe a newly invented game. Pointing and miming, Birna explained that one child should run downstairs and outside into the front garden to catch toys dropped by another child from an upstairs window. Using similar strategies, Kelli confirmed the plan and communicated her father's rejection of it:

Birna:	Come you this	Pointing to the stairs.
	and come you this	Pointing outside the house.
	and whooooo	Pretending to blow a whistle.
Kelli:	So I this	Pointing down the stairs.
	And you this?	Pointing to the window.
(Father intervenes, telling Kelli that this game is not a good idea.)		
Kelli:	We	Pointing to herself and Birna
	are not allowed	Shaking head and finger
	to do this.	Rotating finger in a circle, raising eyebrows.

(Field Notes and Audiotape, September 3, 1991).

Action and facial expression also supported communication outside of play. For example, in early September, Kelli used gesture and mime to tell Guðbjörg that she would call her on the telephone, saying, "I (pointing to herself) ding-a-ling (pretending to dial a telephone) you (pointing to Guðbjörg)" (Field Notes, September 7, 1991). When Kelli gained enough proficiency with Icelandic to use it as a primary means of communication, action and facial expression were no longer essential to successful interaction but were still used to support and extend the meaning of many utterances.

Performing

From her earliest interactions with Icelandic children, Kelli and her friends used performance as a basis for communication. During the first week, for example, Kelli was sitting at the top of a little hill that sloped down from our yard to Elva's yard next door. From her vantage point, Kelli could see Elva sitting inside her kitchen watching from the window. As Elva watched, Kelli hugged her knees, leaned back in the grass, kicked her feet in the air, turned on her side, and rolled down the hill. Then she somersaulted, climbed up and down the clothesline pole, and rolled down the hill again. Occasionally, Kelli glanced at Elva, who had begun a performance of her own by crawling along the inside window ledge (Field Notes, August 27, 1991). A form of communication, performance attracted attention and seemed to propose the potential for future interaction. Other performances that facilitated communication included ballet lessons in Kelli's bedroom (Kelli directing Elva and Birna by demonstrating and physically positioning their bodies), producing puppet shows for one another, and playing, singing, and dancing at the piano.

Using Physical Objects

Particularly during Kelli's first weeks in Iceland, the children used physical objects as foundations for interaction. Skates, balls, jump ropes, and playground equipment provided bases for activities that allowed them to play together with little need for verbalization. They also sought and spontaneously employed the use of everyday objects such as books, photographs, placemats on the lunch table, and even shoes. Other objects that provided foundations for communication and sparked ideas for interaction included board games, puzzles, dolls, and musical instruments.

When Kelli began using Icelandic consistently, physical objects supported opportunities for language practice and for receiving important feedback about the effectiveness of her attempts to communicate. In January, for instance, a deck of cards provided a basis for language exposure, practice, and feedback as Kelli and Guðbjörg invented a card game. As the girls asked one another for cards, Kelli rehearsed and extended her own language use:

Kelli:	Sjáðu, okay?	Look, okay?
	Átt þú svona?	Do you have like this?
		Holding up a card.
Guðbörj:	Nei.	No.
Kelli:	Áttu ekkert?	Do you have nothing?
	Ekki svona?	Not like this?
		Holding up the card again.
Guðbjörg:	Nei.	No.
Kelli:	Áttu svona?	Do you have like this?
		Holding up a two of hearts.
Guðbjörg:	Tvö. Já.	Two. Yes.

(Videotape, January 11, 1992)

Using Charts, Books, and Dictionaries

Shortly after our arrival in Iceland, I posted vocabulary, pronunciation, and conjugation charts on the refrigerator door and kitchen walls (primarily for the purpose of supporting my own acquisition of Icelandic). Sometimes Kelli referred to the charts to support attempts to use Icelandic with friends. On her birthday, for example, she used a pronunciation chart to make it possible to call out letters and numbers in a Bingo game, and on November 14, Kelli picked up a vocabulary chart and said, "Hey, you found out what 'think' is! I was trying to tell the girls that they 'think' something" (Field Notes, September 26, 1991). Word charts sometimes stimulated the exploration of grammatical details. On December 4, for instance, Kelli looked at the conjugation of *vera* ("to be") and asked, "Mom, how come 'vera' is 'to be' and then it's 'er, eru, erum,' nothing like 'vera?'" (Audiotape, December 4, 1991).

Also useful as a support for Kelli's language use with playmates was the Icelandic/English dictionary. In one of many instances, Kelli looked in the dictionary to find the Icelandic word for "already." When I asked about her interest in the word, she said, "It's just a word I want to use all the time" (Audiotape, October 17, 1991). In the same way, alphabet books, songbooks, and labeled puzzles provided sources of support. They were used as references as well as props and foundations for play.

Using English

During their first evening of play, Kelli and her Icelandic playmates used a few simple Icelandic words as well as their limited English vocabulary ("this," "here," "yes," "no," "me," and "you"). Within the next few days, Elva and Birna stopped using Icelandic when communicating with Kelli and relied instead on the English vocabulary that they had in common with her. Kelli reciprocated by simplifying the use of her native tongue to the same few English words. Thus, conversations became exchanges of simple English words and phrases used to convey complex messages. Typical of their abbreviated use of English were phrases such as, "Me this" (meaning, "I want to play with this toy") and "You no this" (which meant, "You may not play with this toy"). Throughout the first three months, abbreviated English phrases supported by other communicative techniques became a standard means of communication between Kelli and her Icelandic playmates. Representative of that strategy use is the following example, in which Kelli uses simple English supported by gesture to direct an episode of block-building:

Kelli:	Okay. Now we make house. There.	Pointing to a spot on the floor.
	Okay. That. There.	Pointing to blocks.
	We have little house. There.	Pointing to a space.
	Too little. What we need.	Shaking her head, pointing.
	This. This. This. There. There.	Pointing to blocks and spaces on the floor.
		(Videotape, September 3, 1991)

Particularly interesting was the continued use of simple English by Elva and Birna even after Kelli began to use Icelandic. For almost six weeks, the girls continued to speak to Kelli using their limited English vocabulary. Typical of their conversations at that time is the following exchange in which Elva (the native speaker of Icelandic) used English and Kelli (the native English speaker) used Icelandic. As she speaks, Kelli gives apples to Elva and Birna:

Kelli:	Þetta fyrir þú.	This for you (Elva).
	Þetta fyrir þú.	This for you (Birna).
Elva:	Kelli, this you.	Kelli, this is for you.
	This you.	This is for you.

| Kelli: | Epli krakkar! | Apples, kids! |
| | Epli krakkar! | Apples, kids! |

(Videotape, October 20 1991)

Altering English Pronunciation and Inventing Words

During the first weeks, Kelli not only abbreviated the use of her own language but she altered its pronunciation. In what seemed to be an attempt to foreignize her use of English, Kelli made alterations such as "mo-uh" for "more"and "wahm" for "warm." In some cases, Kelli's altered English was an obvious mimicry of Elva and Birna's pronunciation—an attempt to sound as much like her peers as possible. For example, when I asked how she invited the girls to play, Kelli said, "I don't know it in Icelandic. I just say, "Dooo youuuu want tooo puh-layyy?" clearly an attempt to approximate the Icelandic girls' careful and deliberate English use.

During the first weeks of play, Kelli also invented words. Instead of saying, "this," "that," and "there" when playing with Elva, Birna and Guðbjörg, Kelli used "dis," "dat," and "dere." Again, her inventions appeared to be attempts to move away from English toward something "foreignized"—something she perceived to be more comprehensible to the Icelandic girls and that would allow her to be more like them.

By the end of the first month, Kelli's alterations and inventions became less "English-like" and began to reflect her growing familiarity with the sounds of Icelandic. Instead of "better" and "here," for example, she said "bay-tar" and "heh-tah," both closer to the Icelandic "betra" and "hérna" (pronounced "beh-truh" and "hee-airt-nuh") than to their English equivalents. As Kelli and her peers began to use Icelandic with one another, altered and invented words gradually disappeared from their interactions. By the end of December (the fourth month), they were no longer in use.

A Chronological Look at Kelli's Acquisition of Icelandic

Facilitating interaction between Kelli and her Icelandic playmates, the communicative strategies described in the preceding pages also contributed to her acquisition of Icelandic. As the children used laughter, mime, sounds, simple English, and so on, they constructed an environment in which risk-taking was comfortable and experimentation was the norm, conditions that proved to be essential to Kelli's language development. Also, in that environment, Kelli observed her friends using Icelandic with one another thereby receiving repeated demonstrations of meaningful language use.

Kelli used Icelandic conversationally for the first time in just such a setting. During our fourth week in Iceland, Kelli turned to Guðbjörg while playing with dolls and said, "Þú kom" ("You come") (Videotape, September 14, 1991). Used in this way—functionally in the context of play with friends—much of Kelli's early Icelandic was directly traceable to phrases frequently uttered by playmates. When I asked how she had learned, "sjáðu" ("look"), for example, Kelli said, "Everybody says it . . . I just heard 'sjáðu,' something like that" (Audiotape, October 10, 1991) and when asked how she knew the exclamation, "Hættu þessu!" ("Stop it!"), she said, "Everybody says it when they don't want people to do things" (Videotape, October 10, 1991).

As Kelli's use of Icelandic evolved, she often combined both English and Icelandic in the same sentence, substituting an English word when she did not know the Icelandic equivalent. Through October (the second month), although Kelli was sometimes able to construct completely Icelandic phrases, simple English continued to be useful for clarifying and completing most messages. An illustration of utterances typical of that time is Kelli's response to Birna's suggestion that they play outside. Using both Icelandic and English, Kelli said, "Ekki núna. Á eftir this" ("Not now. After this") (Videotape, October 18, 1991).

Data collected in mid-October illustrate Kelli's use of Icelandic in informal play settings to initiate and direct play as well as to participate in it. With friends, she ventured to try the language whether or not she was certain that she would use it correctly. By the next month, Kelli's Icelandic had progressed significantly to include a more extensive vocabulary and new word combinations. Her growing fluency is illustrated in this November utterance in which Kelli used Icelandic to teach Elva how to play a board game:

Svona og svona og svona.	Like this and like this and like this.
Eða koma hér ef þú veit. Okay?	Or come here if you know. Okay?
Sjö. þú má ekki sjá. þú má	Seven. You may not see. You may
einn, tveir, þrír, fjorir, fimm, sex	one, two, three, four, five, six,
sjö, átta. Oh, Elva, þú fara heim!	seven, eight. Oh, Elva, you go home (meaning back to "home" on the game board)!

(Video Tape, November 21 1991)

By early January (the fifth month), Kelli and her playmates used Icelandic exclusively in their interactions with one another. In much the same way that Kelli simplified her use of English for them, the Icelandic girls reduced the complexity of their own language to accommodate their perception of Kelli's comprehension. As Guðbjörg explained:

Ég þurfti að tala svo Kelli	I had to talk so Kelli
skildi mig. Ég talaði alveg	understood me. I talked always
... svo hún skidi mig ...	... just so she understood me ...
Við vorum alveg eins og	We were always just like
smábörn.	small children.

(Audiotape, May 24 1992)

In February, conversations with friends required much less support from strategies constructed during the first months. Frequently, Kelli translated for her father and me, corrected our Icelandic, explained the meaning of words, and taught us vocabulary and pronunciation.

During March and April (the seventh and eighth months), Kelli continued to refine her pronunciation of Icelandic as she adopted speech mannerisms typical of the children with whom she played. She mastered the breathy quality of the "hn" and "ekk" sounds and emphasized certain syllables (pronouncing, "America," as "Ah-mer-i-kuh" instead of the Americanized "Uh-mer-i-kuh," for instance). Kelli was also able to use Icelandic humorously, recognize puns and plays-on-words, stop to correct her own misuse of verb tenses, and, as illustrated in the following example, express her understanding of the expanded forms of contractions:

Kelli:	Ég dró'nn.	I drew't.
Mother:	What did you say?	
Kelli:	Ég dró'nn.	I drew't.
Mother:	Ég drone?	
Kelli:	Ég *dró hann.*	I *drew it.*

(Audiotape, April 11, 1992)

Confident in her ability to use Icelandic in the company of friends, in May Kelli organized a neighborhood production of "Öskubuska" ("Cinderella"). Working with Guðbjörg, she invited 13 classmates to meet at our house for a rehearsal. Samples of Kelli's utterances during that afternoon illustrate her easy use of Icelandic to plan, direct, maintain order, settle disputes, and solve problems:

Situm þá níður. Ég ætla að sitja hér.	Then sit down. I am going to sit here.
Bíddu, ég ætla fyrst að skrifa sem allir segja sko.	Wait, I am first going to write what everyone says.
Þið megið ekki fara í kistuna.	You may not go to the box.
Þið megum ekki fara ná í búning.	You may not go get the costumes.
Þá verður þú að skifta við henni út af því að hún er Lovisa núna.	Then you must switch with her because she is Louisa now.
Við erum til búin núna. Byrja lesa.	We are ready now. Begin reading.
	(Videotape, May 6 1992)

At the end of the study, Kelli's friends used Icelandic with her in much the same way that they used it with native-speaking peers. Explaining that they no longer simplified their Icelandic for Kelli, a friend explained, "We talk to her now just like she is Icelandic" (Translated Interview, May 25, 1992).

Supportive Contexts for Language Learning

Throughout the study, it was obvious that Kelli's rapidly growing proficiency with the new language was directly linked to her association with friends in comfortable, meaningful contexts. In new situations with people outside her close circle of friends, Kelli's confidence and willingness to experiment with language diminished. Familiarity, comfort, and a strong desire to develop and maintain play-based relationships supported her attempts to use Icelandic with playmates. In those contexts, her language use and comprehension far exceeded those in other situations. At play with friends, Kelli enjoyed an environment in which she was comfortable enough to try words and forms of words until, through feedback from peers and repeated exposure to correct usage, she began using correct forms consistently.

Feeling comfortable enough to experiment with the language was a critical factor in Kelli's acquisition of Icelandic. This is particularly evident in data that trace the development of grammatical knowledge. Although lessons in singular and plural verb and noun complements, possessives, and feminine and masculine forms were not a part of her school experience, by the end of the study Kelli had mastered the correct use of many grammatical forms. Data collected during November and December illustrate extensive experimentation with word forms in play-based settings. In mid-December, for example, Kelli alternated between correctly and incorrectly matched verb and pronoun forms. She said to Elva, "Við má vera búin með þetta" ("We is allowed to be finished with this") (Videotape, December 12, 1991), mismatching the singular verb, má, with the plural pronoun, við. A week later, she reversed the mismatch using the singular pronoun, þú, with the plural verb, megum: "Elva, þú megum taka eina heim hjá þér" ("Elva, you [singular form] are allowed to take one home") (Videotape, December 19, 1991). Although she did not correctly match singular and plural forms in either instance, she was aware that different forms existed. In the same way, Kelli experimented for several months with gendered forms. By the end of the study, data indicated less experimentation and more consistently correct usage. The atmosphere of comfortable experimentation also provided opportunities for the rehearsal and reinforcement of pronunciation: Kelli heard and practiced the sounds of the language as the children chanted and repeated words and phrases, sang songs, and created "Icelandic-sounding" nonsense words.

In addition to providing opportunities to experiment, playmates supported language development in other ways. For example, through play-based conversations, they provided demonstrations of correct usage. In March, as I was making lunch for the girls, Kelli asked for bread with "smor" thinking she was using the correct form of the word for "butter." When Guðbjörg asked for butter on her bread, she used the word, "smöri." In Kelli's next utterance, she incorporated the correct form, saying, "Ég vil brauð með smjöri" ("I want bread with butter"). Peers also supported the acquisition of Icelandic by rephrasing utterances when Kelli did not understand them. In February, Kelli was confused about the word, "jeppanum" ("the jeep") and Guðbjörg clarified it by defining the word in terms that Kelli could understand: "jeppanum ... svo mamma þín á" ("jeep ... like your mother has"). Playmates also provided language lessons by directly correcting Kelli's language use. In the following example, Elva corrects Kelli's utterance:

Kelli:	Ég fara til klósette.	I go to toilet.
Elva:	Ekki til klósette—	Not to toilet—
	Á klósettið.	On the toilet.

(Fieldnotes, October 29, 1991)

In an April example, Guðbjörg taught Kelli the word for "egg yolk" while they were cooking:

Guðbjörg:	Veistu hvað þetta er?	Do you know what that is?
Kelli:	Hvað?	What?
Guðbjörg:	Eggjarauða	Egg red (egg yolk).
Kelli:	Ekki eggjagula?	Not egg yellow?
Guðbjörg:	Nei.	No.

(Videotape, April 19, 1992)

Data collected as Kelli and her Icelandic peers played together illustrate over and over again the language learning that occurred in those contexts. Comfortable, interested, and motivated, Kelli heard Icelandic in use, experimented, received feedback, adjusted, and tried again in the supportive context of play with friends.

Contrasts between Language Use at Play and at School

The contrast between Kelli's language use with friends at play and her comprehension and use of Icelandic at school further emphasizes the important role of playmates and a comfortable environment in the process of language learning. Whereas when playing with friends, Kelli began trying Icelandic at the end of the first month and, by the second month, was using the language freely and comfortably, her use of Icelandic at school happened gradually, with more hesitation and much less experimentation. At school, except when interacting informally with friends, Kelli waited until she was sure she would be correct before attempting to use Icelandic and did not use it voluntarily until the fifth month. With friends, Kelli's comprehension of Icelandic was supported by (1) a common knowledge of activities in which the children were engaged and (2) the construction and liberal use of communicative strategies. At school, unsupported verbalizations sounded to Kelli "like la de da de da" (Audiotape, September 10, 1991). Kelli attended to "school talk" only when teachers and classmates used strategies similar to those employed by her friends at play: reference to familiar objects and activities, illustrating, miming, gesturing, demonstrating, varying tone of voice, and altering facial expression.

DISCUSSION

Methodologically, this study provides an example of prolonged, contextualized, naturalistic research as an effective means of looking comprehensively at the process of acquiring a new language. By collecting data in as many contexts of a child's life as possible, important contrasts and connections were made about the significance of many aspects of new cultural experience as they related to second language acquisition.

The findings of the study are clearly supportive of the constructivist and interactionist perspectives in which it was grounded. Kelli learned language by constructing knowledge through long-term involvement in a variety of activities and experiences with native-speaking peers. The most significant of those experiences were her informal, play-based activities (a) with peers with whom she wanted to play and who wanted to play with her, (b) in what were considered by Kelli to be comfortable, safe surroundings in which she felt at ease risking interaction, and (c) that were enjoyable, meaningful, and rewarding to all participants. As they played, Kelli and her friends were comfortable enough and had reason enough to manufacture and utilize a wide range of strategies and resources to facilitate communication. In the same contexts, Kelli's peers used Icelandic with one another, allowing her to observe the language in use. At play with friends, Kelli first ventured to try the language and then to experiment with it while receiving important feedback from playmates. Thus, in environments in which the children were at ease and engaged in activities that they considered to be purposeful and enjoyable, Kelli evaluated and adjusted language use in terms of its effectiveness in the native-speaking world in which she wanted to belong. In classroom settings, Kelli did not take risks to experiment with language and participated verbally only when she was certain she would be correct.

The contrasts between Kelli's willing experimentation with (and, thus, eventual acquisition of) language as she played with friends and her limited language use in most school contexts suggest that educators consider the conditions which support language learning in informal play settings as they construct classroom environments. According to the findings of this study, those conditions include:

- Regular, frequent, and prolonged opportunities for second language learners to interact (and, thus, develop relationships) with native-speaking peers:
- In the contexts of activities that are perceived by the students to be meaningful, rewarding, and enjoyable,

- In environments in which the students feel comfortable and confident enough to attempt participation and to use language, and
- With the support of materials and resources that will encourage and support interaction.

As students develop meaningful peer relationships, teachers may further encourage language use and acquisition by providing motivation for verbal interaction, capitalizing on learning that occurs within those interactions, and extending that learning through teaching which is directly linked to knowledge constructed in those settings.

Viewed in conjunction with research that shows students attaining social language proficiency long before they are proficient in language used in academic content areas (Cummins 1980), the findings of this study further suggest that students may acquire proficiency with school-related language earlier if their educational programs are designed to focus on the development of social relationships and to provide opportunities for students to explore subject matter through socially based means. While it is important to acknowledge differences between academic and social language and to recognize the learner's need for prolonged periods of silent observation, it seems likely that academic as well as social language may be more easily acquired if encountered in supported, meaningful, interactive contexts. In Cummins' terms, this would mean transforming language use at school from what is typically "context-reduced" to that which is meaningfully "context-embedded" (1980).

CONCLUSION

What does it mean to be an eight-year-old girl learning a new language in a new cultural setting? This study links one child's language acquisition directly to her informal, play-based interactions with children in her new community. Supporting other studies that point out the significance of purposeful interaction between language learners and native-speakers, this work suggests that classroom teachers and second language specialists evaluate current classroom practices in terms of the extent to which developing bilinguals have opportunities and motivation to interact meaningfully with their native-speaking classmates.

REFERENCES

Almy, M., and C. Genishi. 1979. *Ways of Studying Children*. New York: Columbia Teachers College Press.

Bruner, J. 1983. *Child's Talk: Learning to Use Language*. New York: W.W. Norton.

Corsaro, W.A. 1981. "Friendship in the Nursery School: Social Organization in a Peer Environment." In *The Development of Children's Friendships*, edited by S.R. Asher and J.M. Gottman. Cambridge, UK: Cambridge University Press.

Corsaro, W.A. 1988. "Routines in the Peer Culture of American and Italian Nursery School Children." *Sociology of Education* 61: 1-14.

Cummins, J. 1980. "The Construct of Language Proficiency in Bilingual Education." In *Current Issues in Bilingual Education*, edited by J.E. Alatis. Washington, DC: Georgetown University Press.

Dulay, H., M. Burt, and S. Krashen. 1982. *Language Two*. Oxford, UK: Oxford University Press.

Ellis, R. 1985 *Understanding Second Language Acquisition*. Oxford, UK: Oxford University Press.

Ervin-Tripp, S. 1974. "Is Second Language Acquisition like the First?" *TESOL Quarterly* 8(2): 111.

Genishi, C. 1985 "Observing Communication Performance in Young Children." In *Observing the Language Learner*, edited by A. Jaggar and M.T. Smith-Burke. Newark, NJ: IRA.

Genishi, C. 1989 "Observing the Second Language Learning: An Example of Teachers' Learning." *Language Arts* 66(5): 509-515.

Genishi, C., and A.H. Dyson. 1984. *Language Assessment in the Early Years*. Norwood, NJ: Ablex Publishing.

Hakuta, K. 1986. *Mirror of Language: The Debate on Bilingualism*. New York: Basic Books.

Hester, H. 1984. "Peer Interaction in Learning English as a Second Language." *Theory into Practice* 23(3): 208-217.

MacKay, R.W. 1991. "Conceptions of Children and Models of Socialization." In *Studying the Social Worlds of Children: Sociological Readings*, edited by F.C. Waksler. London: Falmer Press.

Magnússon, S.A. 1990. *The Icelanders*. Reykjavík: Forskot Publishing Company.

Spradley, J.P., and D.W. McCurdy. 1990. *Conformity and Conflict: Readings in Cultural Anthropology*. New York: Harper Collins.

Tammivaara, J., and D.S. Enright. 1986. "On Eliciting Information: Dialogues with Child Informants." *Anthropology and Education Quarterly* 17(4): 218-138.

Van Manen. 1990. *Researching Lived Experience: Human Science for Action Sensitive Pedagogy*. New York: State University of New York Press.

Vygotsky, L.S. 1978 Mind in Society: *The Development of Higher Psychological Processes*. Cambridge, MA: Harvard University Press.

Wells, G. 1986. *The Meaning Makers: Children Learning Language and Using Language to Learn*. Portsmouth, NH: Heinemann.

Wong-Fillmore, L. 1986a. "The Second Time Around: Cognitive and Social Strategies in Second Language Acquisition." Unpublished doctoral dissertation, Stanford University.

Wong-Fillmore, L. 1986b. "Research Currents: Equity or Excellence?" *Language Arts* 63(5): 474-481.

SIBLINGS AS TEACHERS:
CO-CONSTRUCTING ACTIVITY SETTINGS
IN A PUERTO RICAN HOME

Dinah Volk

Yo encuentro que lo más importante es el que la familia esté unida y se muestre amor. Y allí es donde entonces el niño, pues, puede aprender más. Porque aveces ¿de qué le vale a uno enseñarle a uno una...una matemática o eseñarle a escribir si en la familia no está unida ni hay amor? Ahora cuando toda la familia trabaja junto con todos los hijos, yo encuentro que eso ayuda más a los niños.

[I find that the most important thing is that the family is together and shows each other love. And there is where then the child, well, can learn most. Because sometimes what good does it do to teach someone a...math or teach them to write if the family is not together and there isn't love? Now when the whole family works together with all the children, I find that that helps the children most.]

Señora Maldonado, Nelson's mother

Studies in Educational Ethnography, Volume 1, pages 69-91.
Copyright © 1998 by JAI Press Inc.
All rights of reproduction in any form reserved.
ISBN: 0-7623-0436-7

INTRODUCTION

The purpose of this paper is to explore the teaching and learning of school-related knowledge and skills in the home of a Spanish dominant Puerto Rican five year old, Nelson Maldonado.[1] The teachers, in this case, are Nelson's older siblings and they do their teaching within the context articulated by Nelson's mother. From her perspective, teaching and learning find their meaning in the closeness of family relationships.

This work is part of a broader study (Volk 1997) I conducted that explored continuities and discontinuities in language use during lessons in the homes of Nelson and Mónica, another five year old, and in their bilingual kindergarten[2] classroom. In that study I found that the teacher, a bilingual Puerto Rican, created continuity with the homes by maintaining the children's culture and first language as she introduced them to mainstream American culture and to English. She provided active experiences so children could learn through their play. She believed it was her job not only to teach the children required kindergarten knowledge and skills involving numbers and letters but also to teach them to be more independent and to help them expand their thinking and language abilities.

Despite this range of goals, the teacher did most of the talking during lessons, asking 99 percent of the questions and frequently using the *recitation script*, a typical and restrictive style of teacher talk. This script is characterized by known information questions used to assess children's knowledge (e.g., What number comes after seven?) and by the initiation-response-evaluation (IRE) sequence in which the teacher asks a question, the child responds, and the teacher makes an evaluative comment ("What day is today?" "Tuesday." "Good.").

Nelson and Mónica's parents believed they played a role in preparing their children for school by teaching them to respect their teachers and instructing them in school-related knowledge and skills. They identified the direct instruction of academic content by an adult as "teaching" which they distinguished from "play," an activity children did on their own or with other children, not adults.

Like the teacher, the parents used the recitation script during lessons. However, in contrast to classroom lessons, lessons at home were infrequent and both parents and children played active roles. It appeared that the parents drew on both their knowledge of schooling and their cultural heritage to create some elements of continuity for their children between home and school.

As I observed these parent-child interactions in Nelson and Mónica's homes, I realized that the older siblings also assumed a role in preparing them for school. The older siblings played with the kindergartners frequently and school content was often introduced into the interactions by both the older and younger siblings. Sometimes the interactions involved the required kindergarten content such as numbers and letters. Sometimes they involved more complex skills such as classifying and strategic thinking which were also taught in school. These sibling interactions supported and complemented the formal lessons of both parents and teacher.

After Mónica's family moved back to Puerto Rico I planned a case study of the interactions between Nelson and his older siblings that involved both required and more complex school-related content. My focus was on *activity settings* for teaching and learning within the Maldonado home.

THEORETICAL FRAMEWORK

Neo-Vygotskians (Moll 1990; Rogoff 1990; Tharp and Gallimore 1988) argue that children's development and learning are embedded in a sociocultural process. Children—novices at many culturally appropriate tasks—experience patterns of thinking and communicating in interactions with experts who are more competent members of their culture. These experts may be adults, siblings, or peers (Rogoff 1990). As children participate in the interactions, they appropriate these patterns through their own activity, acquiring the means to be competent members of their cultures themselves.

The concept of *activity setting* provides one way of studying the relationship of culture to children's lives. Activity settings are mediating contexts between culture and individuals; they are goal-directed and collaborative interactions in which teaching and learning occur. Composed of the elements of the environment as well as the social and cognitive aspects of interactions, activity settings are defined by their components: personnel, cultural values, tasks, immediate motives, and scripts (Gallimore and Goldenberg 1993; Tharp and Gallimore 1988).

Within activity settings, people create what Vygotsky called a *zone of proximal development* (zpd), a range of emerging behaviors that are bounded at one end by "*independent performance*, what the child knows and can do alone" and at the other by "*assisted performance*, the maximum [level] the child can reach with help" (Bodrova and Leong 1996, p. 35). Within the zone are levels of assisted performance in which the child will need some help. Since children are always changing and learning, emerging behaviors change along with the kind of assistance needed (Berk and Winsler 1995; Bodrova and Leong 1996).

Within the zpd the expert scaffolds the learning of the novice, providing support that is sensitive to the learner's needs while the novice actively responds and initiates more learning (Bodrova and Leong 1996). For the novice, what occurs is not merely an internal replication of the external process of interaction but an appropriation or active transformation of that process, in which the child makes it his or her own to use in the future (Rogoff 1990). In order for the novice to move to a higher level of functioning, the expert transfers responsibility for the task to the novice and the novice takes on the responsibility (Azmitia and Hesser 1993; Ellis and Rogoff 1986). Thus, assisted performance is the result of mutual negotiation or co-construction by the expert and the novice within their joint activity.

In the study described here, I investigated activity settings in Nelson's home by describing personnel, cultural values, tasks, and immediate motives in relation to the scripts used. Scripts were understood as "stable patterns of behavior" that are of cultural and situational significance to the personnel involved (Tharp and Gallimore 1988, p. 7).

REVIEW OF RELATED RESEARCH

Most of the research on children's socialization has been concerned with the mother-child dyad (Watson-Gegeo and Gegeo 1989). Nonetheless, much cross-cultural research has shown that older siblings often play an important role in the care and education of young children (Cicirelli 1995; Weisner 1989). Weisner and Gallimore, in their landmark investigation of sibling caretaking across cultures (1977), assert that "nonparental caretaking is either the norm or a significant form of caretaking in most societies" (p. 169). Older siblings are described as "cultural and linguistic brokers" (Watson-Gegeo and Gegeo 1989, p. 70), functioning as caretakers along with parents, not instead of them. Parents and older siblings play complementary roles in dynamic relation to each other (Bryant and Litman 1987). These more expert members of a society co-construct social knowledge along with the novice members.

Older siblings accomplish a variety of tasks vis-à-vis younger ones within and across societies. In many they assist parents in caregiving (Weisner and Gallimore 1977). In others they participate in the affective, social, or cognitive development of their younger siblings, even though they may not have direct responsibility for care (Cicirelli 1995; Dunn 1985). As younger children reach middle childhood, homework is often the subject of their joint activity (Bryant and Litman 1987).

Overall, the literature argues against generalizations, describing variablity in sibling interactions between cultures and within them. For example, in Native Hawaiian culture, despite widely held beliefs supporting the autonomy of children's peer and sibling groups, variations in activity settings occur depending on who is involved, what they are doing, and what they want to accomplish (Weisner, Gallimore, and Jordan 1993). These factors constitute "the instantiation of culture at the individual level" (Gallimore and Goldenberg 1993, p. 331). To avoid stereotyping, research must *unpack* the culture in this way, investigating how the culture informs everyday lives and how families adapt to their particular situations (Weisner, Gallimore, and Jordan 1993).

METHODOLOGY

For the data collection and analysis, an ethnographic approach used for the study of cultural goals and practices was combined with an ethnomethodological approach used for the study of discourse patterns in individual interactions (Gregory 1993; Rogoff, Mistry, Goncu, and Mosier 1993). By describing values and motives in relation to the participants and what they did, the analysis kept three overlapping levels in focus: the individual child's development, the interpersonal context, and the cultural process (Rogoff, Mistry, Goncu, and Mosier 1993). The use of the mediating concept of activity setting facilitated movement between the levels of analysis and emphasized the child's embeddedness in the sociocultural context (Weisner, Gallimore, and Jordan 1993).

The data collection for the broader study of home-school continuities and discontinuities was conducted primarily during one school year. I observed in the school and in both homes throughout the fall and, between January and April, conducted audio tapings in both settings of the target children and their speech partners. There were six tapings of between one and three hours in each home for a total of about 21 hours. I also conducted a semi-structured interview with the parents and held many conversations with family members.

Two years later I returned to Nelson's home to learn more about sibling interactions. I interviewed Señora (Sra.) Maldonado along with the children and conducted additional observations. Total observation time in the two homes during both phases of data collection was almost 50 hours.

In the analysis I first described key components of the context—personnel, cultural values, tasks, and immediate motives—in relation to the scripts used. I then identified two types of overlapping activity settings: *sibling lessons* that involved the direct instruction of required school content such as the naming or writing of numbers and letters; and *sibling guidance* that involved indirect instruction in more complex skills such as creating patterns or using strategies to complete a puzzle. The sibling lessons were identified by family members when asked how they supported Nelson's learning in school and by their use of the recitation script. Instances of sibling guidance were called *play* by the family but were identified as relevant to the kindergarten curriculum by the teacher.

Within the activity settings, language use and interaction patterns were identified and compared with those in the adults' lessons analyzed in the broader study and with others described in the literature. Older and younger siblings were viewed as active participants; the co-construction of scripts within zpds and the transfer of responsibility for the activity from the older siblings to Nelson were of special interest (Azmitia and Hesser 1993; Ellis and Rogoff 1986; Rogoff et al. 1993).

ACTIVITY SETTINGS

This section begins with a brief description of the community and then presents the components of the activity settings with a focus on the scripts.

The Community

The study took place in a large midwestern city in the United States that has had a thriving Puerto Rican community since the 1940s. In 1990 there were 22,330 Latinos living in the city, representing about 4.4 percent of the population. About 79 percent were Puerto Rican. Of all the

Latinos living in the city who were 18 years and older, only 20.6 percent had more than a high school education. That same year there were 4,300 Latino children in the city's schools, representing about 6 percent of all the students. Seventy-three percent lived in families below the poverty level (de Acosta 1993).

Personnel

Nelson was 5.9 years old in September, the year the study was conducted. He attended a bilingual kindergarten and, like all the children in the class, he was eligible for the free lunch program provided for low-income families. In January, when the taping began, Nelson was Spanish dominant, an emergent bilingual who used Spanish more competently than English. At home Nelson spoke Spanish with his mother and father. The older siblings spoke English fluently and Nelson frequently used English words and phrases with them.

Nelson's family had come to the city less than a year before the study after living in New York City and Puerto Rico. Nelson's father worked in a small local factory; his mother was a housewife. The parents had attended school in Puerto Rico until the age of 15, dropping out two years before completing high school.

In addition to Nelson and his parents, the family living at home included Robert, Yvette, and Luis; 7, 14, and 17 years old respectively. All three attended school. Nelson's 19-year-old brother, Manuel, and his wife, Nati, lived nearby as did his uncle, Joey, and his wife, Zulma, both in their early 20s. Manuel, Nati, Joey, and Zulma as well as Luis, Yvette, and Robert were all considered "older siblings," members of Nelson's extended family.

Cultural Values

Like other poor and minority parents described in the literature (Vasquez, Pease-Alvarez, and Shannon 1994; Soto 1997), Nelson's parents said that they understood the importance of education in their children's lives. They asserted that parents were responsible for teaching their children the basics and proudly described how they had taught Nelson to write his name and identify colors, numbers, and letters. They said they expected their children to do well because they had provided this academic preparation and because they had taught their children to respect their teachers. In fact, Nelson did do well in the years after kindergarten. In first grade he received an award as the best student in his class.

During one of the interviews I asked Nelson's mother to describe the most important ways parents could prepare their children for school. Her answer, quoted at the beginning of this chapter, highlighted the family's approach to learning. The older siblings also spoke about the closeness of their family. Yvette said that it had always been that way; the older brothers helped her and now she was helping Nelson and Robert. Luis described "the teaching and the enjoyment and being together."

The family's perspective reflects the common Latino understanding of "bien educado," a highly valued personal characteristic. While the term literally means "well educated," it has both academic and moral aspects. Schooling by itself is not enough; people who are "bien educado" are well brought up and know how to act respectfully and correctly with others (Reese, Balzano, Gallimore, and Goldenberg 1995; Valdes 1996).

When I asked Sra. Maldonado to explain why the family was so close, she pointed to their religion. As Jehovah's Witnesses she believed that they had learned to teach and care for each other. They all played a role in keeping the family close and in preparing each other to do well in school and life.

Tasks

The tapings were conducted on weekday afternoons and on Saturdays. Nelson and Robert played with action figures and studied their baseball cards, threw a ball, worked on a jigsaw puzzle with Luis, and argued as they played board games. Sometimes Nelson played alone or read to himself. Nelson and Yvette and then Robert played Connect Four, a draughts-type game. Everyone watched television and all the children worked on homework, occasionally doing each other's work. Nati, Zulma, Manuel, and Sra. Maldonado came into the boys' room to talk or bring snacks. The extended family often congregated around the kitchen table talking and eating.

Immediate Motives

When asked about their motives when teaching, Sr. Maldonado described parents' responsibility to prepare their children for school.

Sra. Maldonado explained that the older siblings helped the younger ones when she was too busy. Robert explained that he often asked his older siblings for help instead of his mother because of her limited knowledge of math and limited command of English. Nelson added that when he did not understand his homeowork, his siblings helped him. "Me explican las cosas. Después yo las escribo"/"They explain things to me. Then I write them down."

Other motives were also apparent. When Luis worked on a puzzle with Nelson and when Yvette played Connect Four with him, they worked hard to teach him needed skills and information while also trying to finish the puzzle or win the game. Nelson was just learning how to do a puzzle and was eager to be taught and to put together pieces faster than his brothers. He knew how to play Connect Four and was eager to beat Yvette and invent his own variations.

SCRIPTS IN ACTIVITY SETTINGS

Sra. Maldonado's perspective on learning in the family context provided two clues to the analysis of the scripts used by Nelson and his older siblings. First, sibling interactions were not discrete events but were embedded in the ongoing flow of family talk and activity. Personnel and tasks continually shifted, as people moved in and out of rooms, playing, arguing, directing, helping out, and just sitting around and talking. Immediate motives might change or conflict with cultural values or with the motives of another. This multilayered, multi-person quality was also apparent in the scripts which mixed different languages and styles of speaking and interacting.

Second, the two interrelated values implicit in the concept of educación—preparation for school and family relationships—undergirded the two types of activity settings, sibling lessons and sibling guidance. Though both values were operative at all times, preparation for school seemed primary in the lessons and family relationships seemed primary in the settings characterized by guidance. The scripts used reflected these values.

Table 1 displays the activity settings identified in the transcripts, noting tasks, personnel, school content, and duration. Following the table are descriptions of the scripts in sibling lessons and sibling guidance that were embedded in the activity settings. Many of the activity settings contain aspects of both types of script.

Table 1.   Activity Settings for Sibling Teaching

Task	Personnel	School content	Duration
(1) play Connect 4	Nelson, Yvette, Robert	colors, numbers, strategic thinking, patterns	23 min.
(2) complete puzzle	Nelson, Luis, Robert	puzzle strategies	60 min.
(3) play Connect 4	Nelson, Yvette, Robert	colors, numbers, strategic thinking	30 min.
(4) play w/stickers	Nelson, Yvette, Robert	same/different, writing name, ordinal numbers	12 min.
(5) coloring	family	colors, days	15 min.
(6) play Connect 4	Nelson, Nati, Sra M. Yvette, Robert	colors, numbers, strategic thinking	8 min.
(7) play w/baseball cards	Nelson, Nati, Robert	reading, classifying	4 min.
(8) talking	Nelson, Nati	animal care, birthdays, ages, numbers	3 min.
(9) talking	Nelson, Zulma, Yvette, Sr & Sra M	addresses, writing, addition/counting, reading animals, drawing, families	100 min.
(10) play Connect 4	Nelson, Luis, Robert	colors, strategic thinking	19 min.
(11) play w/baseball	Nelson, Yvette, Robert	colors, strategic thinking	7 min.
(12) play Chinese checkers	Nelson, Yvette, Robert	colors, strategic thinking	13 min.
(13) play dot-to-dot	Nelson, Yvette, Robert, Sra M	numbers, strategic thinking	20 min.
(14) talking	Nelson, Yvette, Robert, Sra M	family relationships	2 min.
(15) play tictactoe	Nelson, Yvette, Robert Sra M	"strategic thinking	2 min.

Scripts in Sibling Lessons

Example 1, part of activity setting #3, begins when Nelson and Yvette have been playing Connect Four for awhile. Nelson invents a game in which he distributes the red and black pieces equally to each of them, talking to himself as he does so. Yvette interrupts and starts to quiz him about how many black pieces he has. A little later Yvette asks the question again, telling him to take another red piece and this time count the total number of red pieces. She repeats this strategy, adding pieces and asking him to count. (The double slashes indicate overlapping speech).

Several patterns are evident here. The first involves Yvette's use of known-information questions, a key aspect of the recitation script. She uses them to assess Nelson's knowledge and as indirect requests for action that tell Nelson to count. When Yvette asks "¿Cuántas negras tú

Example 1.

Nelson:	(to self) Una para ti. Para mi. [One for you. For me.]
Yvette:	¿Cuántas negras tú tienes? [How many blacks do you have?]
Nelson:	Tres. ¿Y tú? [Three. And you?]
Yvette:	Tres. [Three.]
Nelson:	(to self) Para ti. //Para mi.// [For you. For me.]
Yvette:	//Para mi.// [For me.]
Nelson:	(to self) Para ti. Para mi. Para ti. (to Yvette) ¿Cuántas tú cogiste? [For you. For me. For you. For. How many did you take?]
Yvette:	Mm. ¿Cuántas negras tú tienes? [Mm. How many blacks do you have?]
Nelson:	Uno dos tres cuatro. [One two three four.]
Yvette:	Yo tengo cuatro también. Coge una roja. ¿Cuántas rojas tú tienes? [I have four too. Take a red one. How many reds do you have?]
Nelson:	Uno dos tres cuatro. [One two three four.]
Yvette:	Uno dos tres cuatro. Coge una roja. Uno dos tres //cuatro// cinco. [One two three four. Take a red one. One two three four five.]
Nelson:	(to self) //Cuatro.// [Four.]
Yvette:	Cinco. [Five.]
Nelson:	(to self) Cinco. [Five.]
Yvette:	Una para ti. Para mi. //Una para ti. Ahora tu vas repartiendo.// [One for you. For me. One for you. Now you give them out.]
Nelson:	//No yo las reparto. Yo las reparto.// ¿Cuántas negras tú tienes? [No I give them out. I give them out. How many blacks do you have>]
Yvette:	Una //dos tres cuatro cinco seis.// [One two three four five six.]
Nelson:	//Yo tengo una dos// tres cuatro cinco seis. [I have one two three four five six.]
Yvette:	Yo tengo seis también. [I have six too.] (they continue to give out pieces and count them)
Nelson:	(to self) Para ti. Para mi. Para ti. Para mi. ¿Y estas dos? [For you. For me. For you. For me. And these two?]
Yvette:	¿Cuántas negras tú tienes? Ponlas aquí. ¿Cuántas negras tú tienes? [How many black do you have? Put them here. How many blacks do you have?]
Nelson:	Uno dos tres. Tengo tres allí. Cuatro cinco. Cinco seis siete ocho nueve diez. [One two three. I have three there. Four five. Five six serven eight nine ten.]
Yvette:	Dos tres cuatro cinco seis siete ocho nueve diez. ¿Cuántas rojas tú //tienes?// [Two three four five six seven eight nine ten. How many reds do you have?]
Nelson:	//Diez.// [Ten.]
Yvette:	O pues //coge una.// [Oh then take one.]
Nelson:	//Diez.// [Ten.]
Yvette:	¿Cuántas rojas tú tienes? [How many reds do you have?]
Nelson:	Uno dos tres cuatro cinco seis siete ocho nueve. [One two three four five six seven eight nine.]
Yvette:	Diez. Yo cojo //diez.// [Ten. I take ten.]
Nelson:	//Nueve// y diez. [Nine and ten.]
Yvette:	¿Pues? [Then?]

Example 1. (Continued)

Nelson:	(to self) Nueve y diez. [Nine and ten.]
Yvette:	Una para ti y una para mi. [One for you and one for me.]
Nelson:	Ok. Nueve diez once. [Ok. Nine ten eleven.]
Yvette:	Y yo ten-tú tienes //once rojas y yo once negras." [And I ha-you have eleven reds and I have eleven blacks.]
Nelson:	//Ok vamos a hacer un juego.// Yo empiezo. [Ok let's play a game. I start.]

tienes?"/"How many blacks do you have?," she seems to establish her role as a teacher and this interaction as a lesson. Her series of questions about how many pieces he has after one more is added is similar to the questioning used by Nelson's teacher and his parents when they taught lessons about numbers and letters.

In contrast to the adults' language use, Yvette's use of the IRE sequence is inconsistent. At times she uses repetition for the evaluation turn to confirm the accuracy of Nelson's counting just as the adults do; at other times she does not use that third part of the sequence and she and Nelson alternate turns like peers.

Second, Yvette appears sensitive to Nelson's level of independent performance and the kind of scaffolding he needs within the zpd. She knows he is learning to count and provides support by counting with him in their overlapping turns, modeling counting, and repeating his turns. With her final "¿Pues?"/"Then?," Yvette urges Nelson to add one more to 10 by himself. She provides assistance by giving them each one more piece. This concrete action provides the scaffolding most young children find useful in order to extend their counting and that Nelson needs to perform at a level beyond that of his independent functioning. These techniques illustrate assisted performance and the transfer of responsibility for the task.

Third, Nelson is also an active participant here. He takes control of distributing the pieces just as Yvette offers them back to him, asks Yvette how many pieces *she* has, and completes the final step of adding one to 10 with no verbal assistance. As Yvette counts, Nelson repeats the numbers and works with her at counting and adding. At times he does this aloud and at other times he appears to be using private speech as a way of guiding his thinking and completing the task as it becomes progressively harder. The repetition, private speech, and the many overlapping turns seem to be evidence of Nelson's active appropriation of an understanding of how to add and count. In his final turn Nelson asserts that they will play a game he is inventing, providing evidence of their competing motives.

Example 2, part of activity setting #9, is also a sibling lesson, though it is characterized by a mix of personnel, tasks, motives, and scripts. It begins as several family members sit around the kitchen table. Nelson works with a pencil and paper. Zulma and Yvette tease him to try to get him to say Zulma's address. The adults and older siblings often used teasing with Nelson. Here it seems to function like the assessment questions, requiring Nelson to share some known information. When this does not work, Zulma tries a more direct known-information question, "¿Cuál es el número?"/"What's the number?" Nelson, ignoring the question, indicates that he needs help with spelling, initiating a sequence of assistance by both Zulma and Yvette.

After the others have talked for awhile, Nelson responds to Zulma's earlier question by asking for help with his address. Zulma asks him to read what he has written. Nelson continues to ask Yvette for help writing the numbers as Sra. Maldonado and Zulma talk. His father helps too.

This lesson is similar in some ways to Example 1, different in others. First, Zulma and Yvette share the teaching role though only Zulma uses the recitation script, asking a series of known-information questions beginning with "¿Cuál es el número?"/"What's the number?" She uses the evaluation turn in the IRE sequence, though only once to confirm Nelson's answer with "Mjum"/"Mhum." In contrast, Yvette asks a question to which she does not know the answer to find out what Nelson is writing and then uses a series of directives ("Aquí no. Aquí."/"Not here. Here.") telling Nelson what to do.

Second, the use of scaffolding is minimal. As Nelson tries to write "papá," both Yvette and Zulma provide questions and information ("¿Después?"/"Next?" and "Pero la chiquita."/"But the small one.") that make it possible for him to spell the word, performing slightly beyond his level of independent performance with their assistance. Simultaneously, Yvette supplies him with the letters, providing no scaffolding and doing herself what he cannot do on his own. There is little assisted performance or transfer of responsibility from Yvette and Zulma to Nelson. The zpd is extended only slightly.

Finally, Nelson continues to play an active role. He practices what *he* knows and wants to practice, asking many questions requesting help. The fact that he is working primarily at his level of independent performance means he has no need for private speech or repetition to direct his

Example 2.

Zulma:	El no sabe cual es mi dirección. ...Nelson no sabe cual es la dirección de él, ¿verdad Nelson? [He doesn't know my address....Nelson doesn't know his address, right Nelson?]
Nelson:	Yo la sé. [I know it.] (mother, father, Yvette, and Zulma talk about Nelson and to him about address, he is silent)
Zulma:	¿Cuál es el número? ¿Cuál es el número de aquí? [What's the number? What's the number here?]
Nelson:	(writes P) Después de ᴜsta ¿cuál viene? ¿La A? [After this one which one comes? The A?]
Yvette:	¿Qué tú vas a escribir allí? [What are you going to write there?]
Nelson:	Papá. [Father.]
Yvette:	A.
Nelson:	(writes)
Zulma:	Mjum. //¿Después?// [Mhum. Next?]
Yvette:	//P.// Pero la chiquita. A. [P. But the little one. A.]
Nelson:	(writes)
Yvette:	Y más nada. [And nothing else.]
Zulma:	¿Qué dice allí? [What does it say there?]
Nelson:	Papá. [Father.] (mother, father to talk to each other; Zulma talks to father and Yvette about house Nelson is drawing)
Nelson:	Después de esta ¿cuál viene? West? [After this one which one comes next? West?]
Yvette:	West sesentisiete. [West sixty-seven.] (mother and father talk; Zulma, Yvette, and Nelson talk; Nelson writes)
Zulma:	(to Nelson) ¿Qué es eso? ¿Qué es eso? [What's that? What's that?]
Sr M:	Dirección de acá. [Address here.]
Yvette:	(to Nelson) Na-a. [Na-ah.]
Nelson:	¿Mm? [Mm?]
Yvette:	Seis y un siete. [Six and a seven.]
Nelson:	¿Así es? [Like this?]
Sra M:	¿Tú vas a predicar viernes Zulma? [Are you going to preach Friday Zulma?]
Nelson:	¿Aa? [Huh?]
Yvette:	//Así.// [Like this.]
Zulma:	//Tengo que predicar.// [I have to preach.]
Nelson:	//No. ¿Así?// [No. Like this?]
Sra M:	//¿Desde qué hora?// [At what time?]
Yvette:	//No al revés. Así.// [No the other way. Like this.]
Zulma:	//Voy a tratar de empezar// temprano. [I'm going to try to start early.]
Sra M:	¿Con //quién vas?// [Who are you going with?]
Zulma:	//No tengo (unclear).// [I have no ( ).]
Sr M:	(to Nelson) //Aquí no. Aquí.// [Not here. Here.]
Sra M:	//Pero con// que este. ¿Tú vas en tu carro o no? ¿No? [But with that this. Are you going in your car or not? No?]
Zulma:	No creo. [I don't think so.]

Example 2. *(Continued)*

Yvette:	Pero hazlo acá. [But do it here.]
Nelson:	///(unclear)///
Zulma:	///(unclear)///
Yvette:	Déjalo. Está bien. [Leave it. It's fine.] (Zulma and mother talk; Nelson writes)
Yvette:	No. Escríbelo otrra vez acá. [No. Write it again here.]

own efforts. The overlapping talk seems related to the many simultaneous conversations.

Scripts for Sibling Guidance

In Example 3, exerpts of activity setting #2, Nelson and Robert work with Luis on a jigsaw puzzle. Robert has some experience with puzzles and Nelson very little. As a consequence, Luis plays the role of guide, sometimes telling them what to do but, more often, providing strategies for them to use. Their collaborative work reflects the family's value of close relationships and mutual assistance.

These four exerpts illustrate the most salient patterns in this hour-long interaction. First, it is notable that Luis does not use the recitation script in this setting. Putting a puzzle together was not identified by the family as a school-related skill that requires direct teaching and teacher language. But this skill was a part of the developmental assessment given to all kindergartners. Months later Nelson completed this part of the assessment with ease, noting that his brother had taught him how to do it.

Second, though Luis's assistance occasionally takes the form of directives, most often he shares strategies for finding and matching puzzle pieces that provide scaffolding for Nelson that allows him to participate with his brothers and learn new skills. At first Luis suggests they look for blue pieces and corners; Nelson readily adopts these strategies. At the same time Nelson suggests Luis's first strategy himself. He mentions the sky pieces but asks for confirmation: "¿Verdad del cielo?"/ "Right part of the sky?" Several turns later, Nelson repeats Luis's words about looking for corner pieces and then suggests a strategy himself: look for pieces with the tree. Near the end he tells everyone to look for white pieces. Luis seems sensitive to Nelson's growing ability, providing less assistance and asking Nelson for information, transferring more responsibility for the activity to him.

Example 3.

Luis:	Todas las azules busca el cielo el cielo el cielo el cielo el cielo primero los azules. [All the blue ones look for the sky the sky the sky the sky the sky first the blue ones.]
Nelson:	This one.
Luis:	Las azules. [The blue ones.]
Nelson:	This one.
Luis:	Pues sácalas aquí. [Then get them out of here.]
Nelson:	(to self) Azules... Mira azul. Azul. [Blue ones... Look blue. Blue.]
Luis:	Mjum. [Mhum.]
Nelson:	(to self) Azul. [Blue.]
Luis:	Pues búscalas y pónlas allí. [Then look for them and put them there.] (boys work and talk)
Luis:	Así mira. Así. [Like this, look. Like this.]
Nelson:	Aa del cielo. Del cielo. //¿Verdad del cielo?// [Ah it's part of the sky. Of the sky. Right, part of the sku?]
Luis:	//Ahora necesito la que va aquí ¿ves?// La que va aquí. [Now I need the one that goes here, see? The one that goes here.]
Nelson:	La que va allí. Esta. [The one that goes there. This one.]
Luis:	Tiene que tener esquina. Esquina así. [It has to have a corner. A corner like this.]
Nelson:	(to self) Ah. Una que tenga esquina. (aloud) Ahora una que tiene el palo. [Ah. One that has a corner. Now one that has the tree.]
Luis:	Sí tiene palo. Mírala aquí. [Yes it has a tree. Look at it here.] (boys work and talk)
Luis:	Búscalas. Que están. Mira. [Look for them. They're there. Look.]
Robert:	Look it one here.
Luis:	Mira. Mira. [Look. Look.]]
Robert:	I know I know. Look one here.
Nelson:	Oh yeah. This go here.
Robert:	Hey what about this one? (unclear)
Luis:	Oye Nelson. Chequéate si esto es de allí/ [Listen Nelson. Check if this is from there.]
Robert:	Look. Let me see it. //I'll check.//
Nelson:	//I'll check.''
Luis:	Deja a Nelson que chequese.// [Let Nelson check it.]
Nelson:	I'll check it.
Luis:	Busa tú otras partes que tú sabes más. [You look for other parts that you know better.]
Nelson:	Ok. This go here....I'll check it.
Luis:	Well check it then. (boys work and play)
Robert:	(unclear) Luis ponlo para atrás. [( ) Luis put it back.]
Nelson:	Ponlo. Ponlo. [Put it. Put it.]
Luis:	Nelson watch out.
Nelson:	Esta es de aquí. Yo creo que esta es de aquí. Mm. Esto es blanco esto es blanco. Y blanco blanco. Blanco. [This is one from here. I think this one is from here. Mm. This is white this is white. And white white. White.]
Luis:	Chequéate por allí //también.// [Check around here too.]

Example 3. (Continued)	
Nelson:	Ajá. Ya. Ya puse esta aquí. [Aha. Already. I put this here already.]
Luis:	¿Pusiste esa? [Did you put that one?]
Nelson:	Mjum. [Mhum.]

Third, Nelson's active participation is evident throughout. His abundant use of repetition and private speech support his growing ability to work on the puzzle. As he appropriates strategies for putting a puzzle together, he becomes more confident and uses these two aspects of the script less. In the last exerpt he confidently declares he knows where pieces go, functioning at a higher level than the one at which he began but still within the zpd that he has co-constructed with Luis.

Nelson also plays an active role in the use of English which seems associated with his play with his brothers, particularly Robert. He repeats Robert's phrases and also seems to be using phrases that he has heard elsewhere and repeats here in whole chunks. Like the repetition of puzzle strategies, the repetition of English appears to be evidence of Nelson's active appropriation, in this case of a second language.

DISCUSSION

In a study of families and literacy, Leichter (1984), describes the task of "locating literacy in the stream of family activities" (p. 42). This sense of a stream of multiple and competing activities, most of which did not serve instructional purposes, was also found in Nelson's home. Teaching and learning of school-related content in sibling interactions were frequently embedded in the flow of the family's life. Aspects of the interactions at the three levels of the analysis—individual, interpersonal, and cultural—are discussed below.

First, at the level of individual development Nelson's active role in jointly constructing zpds was amply demonstrated. In contrast to his quiet behavior in the classroom, Nelson was active during lessons with his parents and even more so with his siblings. He asked questions and answered them, initiated topics, and ignored others' questions and directives. In some instances responsibility for parts of a task were given to Nelson and, in others, he took responsibility away from the older sibling.

Previous research suggests that these are common patterns: learners working with child teachers are more active than those working with adults; children working with siblings are especially active (Azmitia and Hesser 1993; Ellis and Rogoff 1986); assisted performance is more likely to occur in families from a variety of cultures than in classrooms where teachers often restrict themselves to the assessment of children's knowledge (Rogoff 1990; Tharp and Gallimore 1988).

Nelson's use of private speech is an important aspect of his active role. Private or self-directed speech has been described by Vygotsky (Berk and Winsler 1995) as a means of self-regulation used for directing one's own behavior and scaffolding one's own thought. It is an intermediate stage between social speech and language used for thinking as a tool of the mind. When children are engaged in difficult tasks, they are more likely to use private speech. As a consequence, private speech is evidence of their active appropriation of new knowledge and skills. The child collaborates first with others, then with himself or herself.

Second, at the interpersonal level this work suggests that the activities of the older siblings together with those of the parents formed a coordinated system of caretaking and teaching as described in the cross-cultural literature (Bryant and Litman 1987; Watson-Gegeo and Gegeo 1989; Weisner 1989). The parents engaged in more formal teaching and provided many informal learning experiences. They did not play with Nelson. Complementing these activities, the older siblings provided a range of informal opportunities for learning that were embedded in play and other meaningful interactions. While the parents used the recitation script, the older siblings occasionally used parts of the script. Most often they eliminated the evaluation turn of the IRE sequence, providing assistance without the element of assessment identified with the adult teaching role.

Within these activity settings the older siblings provided scaffolding for Nelson to engage in tasks that extended his knowledge and skills. Luis and Yvette's sensitive assistance helped Nelson function in ways he could not on his own. There were also instances when the older siblings used directives to tell Nelson what to do. This was another style of teaching that gave Nelson practice with school-related skills.

Previous research provides insight into the role of older siblings. Several studies conducted with American children (Azmitia and Hesser 1993; Ellis and Rogoff 1986) suggest that children are much less able than adults to work within a learner's zpd because they focus on finishing the task and not on communicating concepts or on the learner's ability. In contrast, a study by Farver (1993) comparing sibling pairs and mother-child pairs from Mexico and the United States, found that the Mexican siblings were more skillful at scaffolding pretend play than those from the United States and that their interactions with younger siblings resembled the interactions of the mothers from the United States with their children. The author argues that these findings are related to cultural patterns: the Mexican mothers did not play with their children; the Mexican siblings were very involved in caretaking.

Similarly, Gregory (forthcoming), studying Bangladeshi origin families in London, describes the skillful scaffolding by older siblings of young children learning to read. Older siblings de-emphasized evaluation as they mediated between approaches to reading used in school and those used in the children's community.

In this study Yvette and Luis's teaching skills may have drawn on their learning experiences in school and at home as well as on patterns of caretaking in Latino families and their own family's values. At the same time, their inconsistent use of the recitation script indicates that immediate motives may have conflicted sometimes with cultural values. Though Latino, they are still not adults who play the teaching role with more consistency. Though they had been raised to help each other, there were times when they just wanted to win the game or complete the puzzle.

These findings illustrate the usefulness of the concept of activity setting when unpacking the culture at the level of individual families. Variations in personnel, tasks, and scripts as they relate to underlying motives and values can be teased out of these complex, multilayered settings. Further research of this kind is needed to explore other factors that appeared to have an impact on the process of sibling teaching. For example, there seemed to be differences in teaching scripts when Nelson worked on known tasks with siblings and when he worked on novel ones with them. Activity settings in which Luis participated differed in some ways from those with Yvette, confirming suggestions in the literature (Bryant and Litman 1987; Cicirelli 1995) that the gender of the older sibling may be relevant. Differences in the use of Spanish and English were also apparent. In order to move beyond cultural stereotypes, more research is needed to investigate such complexities inherent in natural settings.

Third, at the cultural level, several different scripts seemed to be used in the activity settings. In the sibling lessons the recitation script identified with many English-speaking teachers on the mainland of the United States was used in conjunction with a more directive and conversational script that has been described in research in a Puerto Rican classroom (McCollum 1989). According to other research (Rogoff, Mistry, Goncu, and Mosier 1993), the recitation script is associated with a cultural pattern of adult-child collaboration common in middle-class homes in Western urban cultures in which adults see themselves as responsible for teaching and, thus, teach their children directly through verbal interactions and play. Children are not integrated into adults' activities. In this home, siblings as well as parents collaborated with Nelson using this script to directly teach lessons with school-related content.

This cultural pattern is contrasted with one common in poorer families and those from rural, non-Western cultures in which children learn by observing and participating in family activities. Children take responsibility for their own learning. Parents provide assistance to children, but they rarely teach them directly or play with them. This pattern is similar to the activity settings in Nelson's home in which sibling guidance occurred. Though the parents did not play with the children, the siblings did, providing indirect instruction as they participated together in activities.

This syncretism of cultural styles is discussed by Duranti and Ochs (in press) in their study of literacy in the homes of Samoan families living in California. Defining syncretic literacy as "an intermingling or merging of culturally diverse traditions [that] informs and organizes literacy activities" (p. 2), they extend the term beyond its usual reference to language to "include hybrid cultural constructions of speech acts and speech activities" (p. 2). Thus, rather than embodying a single, "traditional" style, the activity settings constructed by Nelson and his older siblings represent a comingling of resources from Puerto Rican culture, from the culture of the United States, from schools in both contexts, and from the family's religion. A perspective that recognizes the syncretism of cultures within one home contrasts with the deficit perspective that highlights what families lack as well as the more recent diversity perspective that emphasizes the cultural discontinuities between homes and schools. While discontinuities do exist, it is important to recognize that homes such as Nelson's are a rich and complex source of learning for children. Nelson learned through his collaboration with his parents, with his siblings, and even with himself.

ACKNOWLEDGMENTS

This research was supported in part by Research Development Support Funds from the College of Education and by Faculty Associate Program Funds from the Urban Child Research Center, College of Urban Affairs, both of Cleveland State University, Cleveland, Ohio.

NOTES

1. Pseudonyms are used for all participants and for the school.
2. Kindergarten is the entry-level year of formal schooling for five-year-old children in the United States. In the bilingual kindergarten studied, the teacher used Spanish to teach the children, slowly introducing English through songs and stories.

REFERENCES

Azmitia, M., and J. Hesser. 1993. "Why Siblings are Important Agents of Cognitive Development: A Comparison of Siblings and Peers." *Child Development* 64: 430-444.

Berk, L.E., and A. Winsler. 1995. *Scaffolding Children's Learning: Vygotsky and Early Childhood Education*. Washington, DC: National Association for the Education of Young Children.

Bodrova, E., and D.J. Leong. 1996. *Tools of the Mind: The Vygotskian Approach to Early Childhood Education*. Columbus, OH: Merrill.

Bryant, B.K., and C. Litman. 1987. "Siblings as Teachers and Therapists." *Journal of Children in Contemporary Society* 19: 185-205.

Cicirelli, V. 1995. *Sibling Relationships across the Lifespan*. New York: Plenum.

de Acosta, M. 1993. *The Cleveland Hispanic Community and Education*. Cleveland, OH: Urban Child Research Center, Cleveland State University.

Dunn, J. 1985 *Sisters and Brothers*. Cambridge, MA: Harvard University Press.

Duranti, A., and E. Ochs. In Press. "Syncretic Literacy in a Samoan American Family." In *Discourse, Tools, and Reasoning*, edited by L. Resnick, R. Saljo, and C. Pontecorvo. Berlin: Springer-Verlag.

Ellis, S., and B. Rogoff. 1986. "Problem Solving in Children's Management of Instruction." Pp. 301-325 in *Process and Outcome in Peer Relationships*, edited by E.C. Mueller and C.R. Cooper. Orlando, FL: Academic Press.

Farver, J.A.M. 1993. "Cultural Differences in Scaffolding Pretend Play: A Comparison of American and Mexican-American Mother-Child and Sibling-Child Pairs." Pp.

349-366 in *Parent-Child Play: Descriptions and Implications*, edited by K. Mac-Donald. Albany, NY: SUNY Press.

Gallimore, R., and C. Goldenberg. 1993. "Activity Settings of Early Literacy: Home and School Factors in Children's Emergent Literacy." Pp. 315-335 in *Contexts for Learning: Sociocultural Dynamics in Children's Development*, edited by E.A. Forman, N. Minick, and C.A. Stone. New York: Oxford University Press.

Gregory, E. 1993. "What Counts as Reading in the Early Years' Classroom?" *British Journal of Education Psychology* 63: 214-230.

Gregory, E. Forthcoming. "Siblings as Mediators of Literacy in Lingusitic Minority Communities." *Language and Education* 11.

Leichter, H.J. 1984. "Families as Environments for Literacy." Pp. 38-50 in *Awakening to Literacy*, edited by H. Goelman, A. Oberg, and F. Smith. Portsmouth, NH: Heinemann.

McCollum, P. 1989. "Turn-Allocation in Lessons with North American and Puerto Rican Students." *Anthropolgy & Education Quarterly* 20: 133-155.

Moll, L.C. 1990. "Introduction." Pp. 1-27 in *Vygotsky and Education: Instructional Implications and Applications of Sociohistorical Psychology*, edited by L.C. Moll. Cambridge, UK: Cambridge University Press.

Reese, L., S. Balzano, R. Gallimore, and C. Goldenberg. 1995. "The Concept of *Educación*: Latino Family Values and American Schooling." *International Journal of Educational Research* 23: 57-81.

Rogoff, B. 1990. *Apprenticeship in Thinking: Cognitive Development in a Social Context*. New York: Oxford University Press.

Rogoff, B., J. Mistry, A. Goncu, and C. Mosier. 1993. "Guided Participation in Cultural Activity by Toddlers and Caregivers." *Monographs of the Society for Research in Child Development* 58(8): (Serial No. 236).

Soto, L.D. 1997. *Language, Culture, and Power: Bilingual Families and the Struggle for Quality Education*. Albany, NY: SUNY Press.

Tharp, R., and R. Gallimore. 1988. *Rousing Minds to Life: Teaching, Learning, and Schooling in Social Context*. Cambridge, UK: Cambridge University Press.

Valdes, G. 1996. *Con Respeto: Bridging the Distance between Culturally Diverse Families and Schools*. New York: Teachers College Press.

Vasquez, O.A., L. Pease-Alvarez, and S.M. Shannon. 1994.*Pushing Boundaries: Language and Culture in a Mexicano Community*. Cambridge, UK: Cambridge University Press.

Volk, D. 1997. "Questions in Lessons: Activity Settings in the Homes and School of Two Puerto Rican Kindergartners." *Anthropology and Education Quarterly* 28(1): 22-49.

Watson-Gegeo, K.A., and D.W. Gegeo. 1989. "The Role of Sibling Caretaking in Socialization." Pp. 54-76 in *Sibling Interaction across Cultures: Theoretical and Methodological Issues*, edited by P.G. Zukow. New York: Springer-Verlag.

Weisner, T.S. 1989. "Comparing Sibling Relationships across Cultures." Pp. 11-25 in *Sibling Interaction across Cultures: Theoretical and Methodological Issues*, edited by P.G. Zukow. New York: Springer-Verlag.

Weisner, T.S., and R.G. Gallimore. 1977. "My Brother's Keeper: Child and Sibling Caretaking." *Current Anthropology* 18: 169-190.

Weisner, T.S., R.G. Gallimore, and C. Jordan. 1993. "Unpackaging Cultural Effects of Classroom Learning: Hawaiian Peer Assistance and Child-Generated Activity." Pp. 59-87 in *Coming Home to Preschool: The Sociocultural Context of Education*, edited by R.N. Roberts. Norwood, NJ: Ablex.

BECOMING A PROPER PUPIL:
BILINGUAL CHILDREN'S EXPERIENCE OF
STARTING SCHOOL

Mari Boyle and Peter Woods

INTRODUCTION

Starting school is one of the great status passages in life, having profound repercussions for identity. Before starting school children already
have multiple identities. They are a son or daughter; brother, sister, only
child or particular-placed sibling; Pakistani, Indian, Bengali, African
Caribbean, or English; friend of someone; and a young child. On starting school children acquire another identity, that of "pupil" (Edwards
and Knight 1994). For many children it is their first step toward secondary socialization (Berger and Luckmann 1967), their first major break in
the day-to-day regularity of family life where the primary caregivers are
the focus of the child's world and "what is mediated through the family
is the only reality that is known" (Woods 1990, p. 145). Secondary

Studies in Educational Ethnography, Volume 1, pages 93-113.
Copyright © 1998 by JAI Press Inc.
All rights of reproduction in any form reserved.
ISBN: 0-7623-0436-7

socialization involves children's first regular experience of institutional life and the internalization of specific roles. The first of these is that of pupil. The shaping of this new role is not a negotiated one, but very much dependent on the teacher image of the "good pupil" (Waterhouse 1991). Burns (1992, p. 155) argues: "All organisations seek to impose an identity on their members, allocating to each of them a character and a conception of self which is consonant with the organisation's values, requirements, and expectations." This involves "a thoroughly embracing conception of the member—and not merely a conception of him (sic) qua member, but behind this a conception of him qua human being" (Goffman 1961, p. 179). In school the notion of the "good" or "ideal" pupil is a "construction which is drawn primarily from the lifestyle and culture of the teacher concerned" (Wright 1993, p. 28).

"Culture" is a crucial concept here. Tyler (1871) defines it as "that complete whole which includes knowledge, beliefs, art, morals, law, customs and any other capabilities acquired by man as a member of society." Yet any one society might be made up of several different cultural bases. For example, though we might refer to a British culture, it has within its basic makeup distinct Scottish, Welsh, and English cultures, and within each of those cultures there are distinctions between regional areas. Therefore culture acts at different levels and for different reasons. The function of education in relation to culture was considered by Chinoy (1967) as a principle way in which the preservation of culture is transmitted to society as a whole. Durkheim (1956) observed that education was a primary method of enabling society perpetually to recreate itself. Singh (1993, p. 35) comments that

> By passing on from one generation to another established beliefs, knowledge, values, and skills, education contributes to continuity and the development of an organised social life. Thus "culture" and "education" are inter-related processes of social organisation and social structure within society.

Yet in a multicultural society we must consider whose culture is being transmitted from generation to generation. While there are those who contend that schools should develop in their pupils a sense of cultural heritage and national identity which is essentially (and traditionally) "British," as Nicolas Tate of the School Curriculum and Assessment Authority (SCAA) commented recently (Pyke 1997), others believe that it is important to show recognition of other cultures (Taylor 1992). In providing such recognition through educational processes children will have the opportunity to operate from a wide range of cultural bases (Verma 1984).

Where recognition of other cultural forms is not taken into account then the child from a minority ethnic group may find the difficulties of transition to school compounded (Wright 1993). For that would involve another transition from their own ethnic culture to a dominant culture. There are additional problems associated with having to learn at school via a second language while maintaining their mother tongue (Rex 1986). They stand to experience all the bewilderment and confusion as Schutz's (1971, p. 30) "stranger," where "the whole hitherto unquestioned scheme of interpretation current within the home group becomes invalidated."

In many schools the experience of transition at this stage is unalleviated by "in-between" phases. The reception class used to be considered a bridge between nursery and school, but has increasingly become the point at which children start their studies of the National Curriculum, which Blenkin and Kelly (1994) see as having "destroyed the concept of infancy," and failing to differentiate between the educational requirements of children from five to seven years of age and those of 16 year olds (p. 3). The transition thus is starker, and the National Curriculum has become part of the problem rather than an aid to its resolution as embodied in its rationale. This is even more the case for bilingual learners, as the National Curriculum is distinctly mono-ethnic as far as these children are concerned (Reid 1982).

In this paper we discuss the induction of a group of bilingual/bicultural children into the world of school and into the role of pupil. The research was part of a two-year study of how young bilingual children adapted to school (Woods, Boyle, and Hubbard 1997). The qualitative methodology involved the researcher, Mari Boyle, observing teaching and learning in classrooms; interviewing teachers, parents, and children; and studying school documents and children's work (Boyle 1996). The lower school in which the research took place served a multiethnic community, the main ethnic groups being Pakistani and Indian with a growing number of families from Bangladesh, and smaller numbers of African-Caribbean, Arab, Italian, and white English families. The school had a staggered entry system whereby groups of children start at the beginning of each new term depending on whether they have reached their fifth birthday by the first day of each term. In the autumn term of 1994, when the research began, a group of 17 children started school as Year 1 children (meaning that these children, by law, had to follow the National Curriculum). In the spring term an additional 10 children joined the class, and two started later in the term when they returned from extended stays in Pakistan. The children in this second cohort were classed as Reception class, having turned five after September 1. Much of the data reported here was collected at the beginning of this spring term. All of the children in the class had been born in England, though proficiency in English varied from child to child. All of them, with one exception, had attended the nursery unit attached to the school. There were two class teachers for this mixed R/Year 1 class: Elaine who taught in the morning and Chris (the head teacher) who taught in the afternoon. In addition, Hardip, a non-teaching assistant fluent in Urdu and Punjabi as well as some Bengali, was available during the morning sessions. A related research project was undertaken by Nick Hubbard in the nursery unit of this school at the same time. Data referring to the nursery experiences of the children is taken from Hubbard (1998).

We argue that, while all children face certain problems equally in transferring from home to school, the concept of "normal pupil" implicitly embraced by the school is embodied within a traditionally English model, leaning toward Anglo-centrism, with profound implications for identity for children from minority ethnic groups.

MARKING NEW IDENTITIES

Establishing the identity of "pupil" entails demarcating it as different from that of "child." In the attached nursery unit the latter prevailed. The difference is well illustrated by procedures at the beginning of the day. In the nursery the children would come into the unit with their parents who helped them to hang up their coats. This provided parents with an opportunity to talk with the nursery staff about their children and was all very informal. The children would then have free choice over which activity they wanted to do. There was no change of role involved. The presence of their parents and the lack of formal rules and ritual preserved the identity of child. By contrast, at the school, parents, though at first encouraged to bring their children into school to meet the teacher and settle their children, were asked to leave the children in the playground before school started once the children had become used to the start of the school day. The apparent reason for this is a practical one, the main entrance to the school being too small to cope with parents and children all coming in at once. This also cuts down on the amount of contact that the teacher has with parents. So the school design, intentionally or unintentionally, helps to separate out children from parents, and aids the transition to the school's concept of pupil.

At the start of the spring term the new Reception children quickly became used to this routine. They even began to reinforce it themselves. One mother appeared to be having more difficulty adjusting to starting school than her son, Adam, reminding us that this is a key transition for mothers as well as their children. She continued to deliver her son to the classroom door, despite Adam's obvious embarrassment. He would rush to take his coat off as quickly as possible and then jump on to the mat to be with his peers, rather than stay with his mother. Eventually the class teacher asked Adam's mother if she could simply leave him in the playground with his friends at the start of the day. She did this, but then began turning up at dinner time to give him his packed lunch. Adam seemed very uncomfortable with this. He would collect his dinner quickly and run off to be with his friends rather than stay to talk to his mother. As time went on the visits became less frequent.

Having achieved separation the pupil's identity became designated in the ritual of "registration." Bernstein (1977, p. 54) has described the symbolic function of ritual as relating the individual "to a social order, to heighten respect for that order, to revivify that order within the individual and, in particular, to deepen acceptance of the procedures which are used to maintain continuity, order and boundary and which control ambivalence towards the social order." Registration might be seen as operating in this way, and is an essential part of becoming and being a pupil. It is a check on one's being there; it marks the child's identity as one of a number of pupils who are all the same in that respect; it is a reminder of this at the start of every session; and it establishes an underlying formality to proceedings.

The first requirement of the day was for the children to sit on the carpet and await the register, whereas at nursery the children were used to free choice when they arrived. For some of the new entrants this caused confusion. Their mode of coping with this situation was at first to sit very quietly, mainly near the back of the carpet, and to listen to and observe what the older children said and did. When it came to their turn to answer their names for the register, the new children were at first prompted by the class teacher (and later by their peers). It was an indication of one of the ways in which the children needed to become quickly accustomed to how they would now be addressed at school compared with the way in which either staff at the nursery or their parents at home might address them. The teachers were careful to try to pronounce children's names correctly, though avoided using pet names or nicknames which might be used at home. Some children were puzzled by this as they were unaccustomed to being referred to in this manner. Guvinder, who was used to being called "Guvi" at home, for example, appeared a little perplexed by being given his full name on his first day at school. Similarly two of the boys had the same first names, Ahmed, and so to make the distinction they were always referred to by their full names—Ahmed S. and Ahmed H. The latter child was particularly confused by this, and in the first few days during registration, other children around him would give him a slight nudge when it was his turn to answer. The children also had difficulty in pronouncing their teachers' names.

Many of the children incorporated "taking the register" into their play, thus internalizing this part of the role and their relationship with the teacher. One of the children would take on the role of the teacher, sitting in the teacher's chair and using an old red diary which had been provided. Names would be called out and "marks" given. On the odd occasion when Mari took the register, the children insisted on her carrying out the activity in the correct manner:

> Damian (to Mari): It's Ali first then me.
> Sofia: Ali first.
> Damian: Can you do surnames?
> Mari: Okay, I'll do surnames. Damian asked me to do surnames
> Sofia: Ali first.
>   [Children began talking with each other, eventually settled down]
> Mari: Right, Ali Iqbal.
> Ali: No!
>   Children: Yes. No, it's Master! [several of the children arguing about
>   the right way to do this]
> Mari: Master Iqbal, sorry.
> Damian: Everybody's Master.
> Ali: Yes Miss Boyle.
> Sofia: And the girls are Mrs.

This is a very English format of addressing people—"Master," "Miss," and "Mrs." The children also often replied "good morning" or "good afternoon," rather than, for example, "As-Salamu-Alaykum" ("peace be upon you"), which many of the Muslim children were accustomed to use. But it was important to get things right. The children knew the correct color of pens to be used, and after the register had been taken, hands were immediately raised to guess how many children were present in the class, with the children vying for the opportunity to write the number on the easel board. The children knew the routine well, including the newer children, and they giggled at Mari's mistakes with names.

The daily repetition reinforced the children's new identities as proper pupils within the existing framework of things. There were few concessions to their own cultural forms. Status accrued to pupils with mastery of the rituals, as illustrated by the comparison with the neophyte researcher in the "register game."

CHILDREN PLAY, PUPILS WORK

The new identity was consolidated in the process and structure of activities, and divisions of space and time. One of the most conspicuous changes for the "new starter" came with the marked separation between "work" and "play." Play predominated in the nursery, though in the children's final term the nursery teacher began to use more teacher directed activities in order to develop some of the skills the children would need for school (Hubbard 1998). Much of this directed activity, however, was carried out through games or story reading, and the distinction between play and work was less obvious than in school.

In school, work and play were differentiated in three main ways. First, the classroom was divided into two main areas: the carpeted area was reserved for whole-class activities (including registration and story time) and play; the tables were where the children sat to complete specified curricular work. The area in which the children were allowed to play was considerably smaller than the area designated for work. Second, though our teachers proclaimed a basic belief in child-centeredness, and operationalized it on occasions, work activities (in order to accommodate the National Curriculum) were largely teacher-directed, while play was child-directed, with children being given free choice within the limits of the materials available to them to develop interest and learning in whatever direction they chose. Third, work in most instances was required to be completed before the children could play. In this way, play became a marginalized activity in the classroom as "work" began to dominate increasingly more and more of the school day. The diminution of opportunities for play in the children's experiences at school meant that there was a corresponding reduction in their ability to bring their cultural and linguistic knowledge to bear on the activities with which they were involved, making those activities potentially less relevant for them. For example, children playing in the home corner would role play their home experiences and appeared more comfortable using their mother tongue than during work-related activity. We have demonstrated elsewhere (Woods, Boyle, and Hubbard 1997; Jeffrey and Woods 1996) the connections between relevance to pupils' background cultures, control of learning processes and ownership of knowledge, and the particular significance of this for bilingual children.

By the summer term of the first year the dominance of work and its relation to time was exemplified through the topic of "time lines," introduced by the teacher as part of the history curriculum. As an example, the teacher used the school day. On a line which spanned the classroom were the divisions of the day—register/work/playtime/work/dinnertime/register/work/assembly/story time.

An article was placed with each section to symbolize the activity, and for the work sections math and writing books were used. Although the time line was created to develop the children's historical skills, it served also to reinforce the centrality of work and appropriate divisions of time and space in the school life of the normal pupil.

Side by side with this construct, another was being constructed for the Muslim children at the Mosque, which they attended between three to six evenings per week. Teaching methods here showed a marked contrast with those of the school. The sole aim of lessons was to teach children to read the Qur'an. The teaching methods employed in these classes were not observed by the researcher, though in talking with both the children and the parents they seemed to reflect very much the pattern of listen-repeat-practice-test, noted in Qur'anic classes in many countries (Wagner 1993; Gregory and Mace 1996) as Mobeen, one of the children, explains:

> You learn to read something by heart....First, you read your holy book, then you read another thing it's got in the Mosque and you have to read it on the day and you have to read that by heart...to the person that is the Mosque man.

Urdu and Punjabi are mutually comprehensible languages, and written Urdu is based on the Arabic script. Mobeen explained that the children must first learn to read Arabic and then Urdu, though many of the Pakistani Muslims at the school speak Punjabi as a mother tongue. The child therefore has to learn the cultural expectations of themselves as pupil both in their native culture and the English state school culture. Other children commented on different expectations regarding rituals at the Mosque such as the need to take off their shoes, cover their heads, wash their hands, feet, and faces before beginning their lessons, and separate tuition for boys and girls. We were unable to compare how far one expectation of pupilhood impacted upon the other, though one parent at least commented she and her children were able to maintain both their identities without difficulty:

> I'm Pakistani, but I live in Britain, and a lot of my way of life is the way most British people live it. But then again I've got my own separate life as well. And for example the children at school, that's totally different, and they go home and it's totally different for them, but it's so easy for them to be in the two situations and it's because it comes naturally to them because it's not been any different from the day they were born, so they just accept it.

This separation of identities depending on context was perhaps one way of maintaining a strong Pakistani identity distinct from a British identity. But the complete separation suggests bifurcation rather than mutual enrichment, and a problem of ambivalence for bilingual children.

APPEARANCE AND IDENTITY

Stone (1962) has pointed to the importance of appearance in the establishment, maintenance, and alteration of the self. Hence the importance of a school uniform in some schools—it is a prominent feature of the discourse of "normal pupil." Our school did not have any school uniform, children being allowed to wear whatever they (or their parents) chose, though many of the children were wearing new clothes or new shoes bought specially for their first day of school. The new clothing acts as a material symbol of the new status. The children wanted to look smart and tidy for their first day at school (or perhaps their parents wanted this), and for some children age labels on jumpers or an increase in shoe size indicated that they were growing up. A number of children while dressing and undressing for P.E. would comment that their jumpers had labels on them marked "aged 5-6 years," or that they were now wearing a size nine shoe.

Yet, though there was no official school uniform, there were peer pressures, among the boys at least, to wear Westernized forms of dress. Thus, Shiraz, a boy who liked to wear shalwar kameez—a common form of dress in India and Pakistan and an accepted style of fashion for the girls in particular—was sometimes teased by his fellow male pupils, as his mother pointed out:

> He gets very easily upset, like just now as we were walking in this morning he decided himself that he was going to wear his shalwar kameez, which is what he wears at home at the weekends, especially when it's hot, he doesn't like wearing trousers when it's hot, and he's often said that some of the children take the micky, and I'm always saying to him that as long as you know who you are, and you know that is part of being you, and if people want to take the micky then that's fine, let them as long as you don't let it get to you.

Shiraz was asserting his cultural identity in spite of peer pressure that he should dress in more Western styles—jumpers, t-shirts, and trousers—as many of the boys did. In an exercise based on "My special clothes," a number of children mentioned new Eid clothes they had been bought, often shalwar kameez, but also jeans, Batman clothes, Power Rangers t-shirts, and jumpers. These replies were from the boys in the main who had a greater opportunity to wear Western-style clothing compared to the girls who, even when wearing Western-style dresses, would either wear pyjamas or leggings to cover their legs.

Equal, if not more significance, attaches to undressing. This was another new experience for the Reception group, and is a good illustration of the ambivalence thrust upon them, for they felt both shame and pride—the former a product of their own cultural experiences, the latter coming from mastery of skills involved in induction into the new culture.

> Field notes 11/01/95, 10:05: Children got changed for P.E.; some of the younger children needed a lot of help with undressing. The children were asked to put their clothes neatly next to their name labels. The teacher mixed the children so that the newer children were placed next to an older child so that they could follow what they should do. This was the second P.E. lesson the children have had this term, and most of the newer children seemed happy enough to take off their clothes, though Guvinder and Ahmed H. needed more encouragement, and

Ahmed H. particularly needed help getting undressed. Because of the time taken to get undressed the P.E. lesson was very short, about 10 minutes.

Before their children start school, parents are advised to dress them in clothes that they can easily take off and put on themselves. Clearly this is a skill which some children had not mastered when they started. But there is also a cultural significance to undressing for P.E., as many of the children are Muslim and Sikh. Communal undressing is generally considered not acceptable, particularly for Muslims, and more especially for girls (Sawar 1994). Yet difficulties with undressing for P.E. lessons are often considered to be problems more often associated with secondary schooling. Even some of the parents interviewed for this research felt at this age it was not so important because, as one father commented, "they're too little." A mother thought it "not a problem" for the moment, but when they were older she would "certainly be happier if they have all-girls' swimming sessions. P.E. and stuff doesn't really bother me, but swimming I wouldn't be too happy with it."

However, by the time the children had moved into their second year at school, both boys and girls were hiding behind book shelves and tables to gain a little privacy, and most now brought shorts and t-shirts to change into, where they had previously only worn vests and knickers (see also Wright 1993). During the summer term of their second year, the embarrassment factor rose further, as the children went swimming, and therefore had to strip completely. It was noted that children frequently "nipped" into the toilets to change, rather than having to undress in front of their peers. Wilkins argues that there is potential harm for all children, regardless of religious or cultural background, from enforced communal changing:

[C]ompulsory group nakedness constitutes a gross infringement upon the civil liberties of a child and is a prospect no adult would willingly contemplate (Wilkins cited in Sawar 1994, p. 13).

While this may be the "quintessential humiliation for the pubescent child" (p. 13), it would appear that even younger children are experiencing some humiliation. In some ways, therefore, this induction into P.E. could be creating problems for both teachers and pupils in their later school careers.

Being forced to undress is a well-known technique of "mortification" (Goffman 1968, p. 24). "Stripping people of their clothes strips them of part of their 'selves'" (Woods 1979, p. 152), and, in this case, is another device for preparing them for their new identity of "pupil." Yet the induction was certainly very successful, and worked through status acquisition rather than degradation. As with registration, the children soon became skilled at getting dressed and undressed for P.E., and requested far less help when dealing with the intricacies of buttons, bows, and jumpers that were inside out. For many of the children the ability to dress and undress seemed to signify another mark of accumulating status, a sense of achievement, a growth in independence, and competitions quickly developed to see who could be ready first. In this way, pride in becoming a proper pupil was mingled with personal shame.

LEARNING THE RULES

Part of becoming a pupil is understanding school rules, many of them implicit (Woods 1990). Much use was made of older Year 1 children to induct their peers into their new roles. To the new recruits, Year 1 children had the authority of time served and were sufficiently close to them in age and ethnicity to help both steer a way through the introduction to school, and bridge the gap between the two cultures of home and school.

This is illustrated in the children learning how to move around the school. It was a crucial issue, since they were expected to move frequently from room to room, from the classroom to the hall for Physical Education, dinners, and assembly, from the classroom to the library, from the classroom to the playground, from the main teaching area to a second teaching area, and from their classroom to other teachers' classrooms to convey messages. Both teachers relied on the Year 1 children to show the Reception children about the school, pairing children off to go and collect the register from the office or to take messages to other classes, placing a Year 1 child as the leader of the line when the class went as a whole to other parts of the school. In this way the teachers and Year 1 children were able to lessen any anxieties the Reception children might have had in getting lost. Three weeks into the new term the class teacher asked Ahmed H. (a child identified as having special educational needs), one of the new entrants, if he could collect the register from the office. Asked if he wanted anyone to go with him, he shook his head and enthusiastically sped off in the right direction. After some minutes the teacher became concerned as to where he was, and was about to send another child to look for him, when he returned with a triumphant smile on his face, waving the register in front of his teacher. He was successful. Later, the researcher found out from the secretary that although he had found the office correctly, he was not sure which register was for his class, and had to wait to be shown. On other occasions when Ahmed H. had been with one of the older children, they had habitually picked up the correct register, and though he was confident of finding his way to the office, he still needed some help once he arrived. Similar problems were encountered when the new children were asked to take messages to other teachers in the school. Although they could find their way around the school having been shown on previous occasions by the older group, once there, messages became confused. On one occasion one of the children was brought back by a pupil from another class so that the older pupil could find out what the message had been.

Teachers also used older children in the class to make a point about acceptable pupil behavior. For example, the Year 1 children were often told to put their hands up when answering questions, followed by "You should know that by now," or were expected to behave "more sensibly" because they had been at school longer than the Reception children. When Year 1 children were creating too much noise, especially when teachers were working with the Reception group, they were reminded that "You know how to work quietly." In this way the teacher was often reinforcing the rules of the classroom with the Year 1 children, while at the same time providing a model for the Reception group. For the Reception group this also allowed them the opportunity of "sussing" out the teacher (Beynon 1985). This involves detecting "each [teacher's] managerial expertise and a clear definition and demonstration of the parameters of the control s/he seeks to establish" (Beynon 1985, p. 37). The Reception group was able to do this through observation of the teachers' reactions to the Year 1 children. It also raised the status of the Year 1 group. They were given more responsibility in class and more independence as they were frequently allowed to simply "get on" with their work while the teacher concentrated on developing work with the Reception group. Additionally, for those children for whom English may present difficulties with understanding what is expected in the classroom, modeling on the Year 1 children, was one way of coping with the new expectations of themselves as pupils. Simera, for example, spoke very little English. She was frequently observed waiting to see what other children were doing before she would join in, such as lining up, or going to their tables to start work, or putting their hands up in response to teachers' questions. She soon worked out why they were doing this, so followed suit. When she was asked for answers, she would immediately redden in the face, her eyes would drop to the floor, and her hand would cover her mouth. For a time she stopped raising her hand to answer questions, and positioned herself as far from the teacher as she could get. It was not until her second term at school that her confidence in these situations was such that she began to raise her hand once more, though if asked for an answer, she would still cover her mouth with her hand, and speak in a quiet voice.

In these ways children acquired the cultural resources to fulfill what was expected of a "normal pupil" (Holt 1969; Hammersley 1977; Tuckwell 1982). The concept of "normal" or "good" pupil was reinforced periodically throughout the two years of this study, often in quite an overt fashion. In the summer term of the children's first year at school one of the boys in the class, Ahmed S., broke his leg on the playing field of the school. Following the incident the head teacher conducted a special school assembly discussing rules for safety in the playground. In class the teacher discussed with the children rules for class behavior. Many of the suggestions were made by the children, and a list was drawn up by the teacher to which the children provided illustrations. The list was then displayed on the wall adjacent to one of the classroom doors, where the children lined up at least twice a day. The list consisted of the following rules:

- No kicking
- No pushing
- No hitting
- Don't pull hair
- Be kind
- Share
- Do your work quietly
- Put your hand up
- Be helpful
- Play together
- Put things back where they belong
- Don't run in school
- Push your chair in

These rules cover the various behavioral aspects of the "good" pupil. The first four reflect very much the complaints the children voiced regarding playtime. "Be kind, Share, Be helpful" epitomize the caring ethos of the school promoted particularly by the head teacher (Boyle and Woods 1996; Woods, Boyle, and Hubbard 1997). Such caring behavior was also frequently rewarded by teachers placing children's names into the Golden Book. This was a system whereby children's names were recorded in a special book for good work. The names were later read out in a special assembly each week and the children awarded certificates of merit. Other statements relate to the manner in which the pupil should "work."

ADAPTING TO NEW CULTURES

The school incorporated many of the cultural differences of the children into the everyday aspects of school life while establishing its own basic Anglicized framework. We have seen how this applied to dress. Elsewhere, options were provided in school dinners for the Muslim children who ate only Halal meats, Hindu children who refrained from beef, and those children who had vegetarian diets. Like the issue of choice of clothing, diet was not considered a problem as such, though some aspects regarding meal times linked to religious practices had caused problems in the past. One parent, for example, reported her child's confusion when, at lunch, she was required to hold her fork in her left hand, when at home, they always used the right hand only. This issue was quickly resolved when pointed out to the head teacher.

Aspects such as this can cause major problems for some children (Siraj-Blatchford 1992), and while the school sought to accommodate as much of the children's culture and traditions in school as possible, there were many areas of the children's lives which were influenced by the wider English social culture. For example, the children did some written work on their favorite foods in their second year. Popular repasts were "Easter egg and jelly and grapes," "hamburger and chips," "chips and beans," and "pizza."

The school celebrated the major religious festivals of the children including Christmas and Easter which the children talked about though at a purely secular level, and the gift-giving traditions of the festivals were clearly noted. As Christmas loomed, cards were exchanged, visits to Santa arranged, and who was getting what on Christmas morning was eagerly discussed. Similarly at Easter there was animated talk around the variety of Easter eggs available in the shops. Eid and Diwali were also talked about by the children but limited within their own religious groups indicating that there was less cross-cultural celebration from the Islamic and Sikh traditions compared with that of the Christian tradition.

The children's reading habits indicated further Anglicization. Few of the children chose library books which either told Asian stories or were linked with Pakistan, India, or Bangladesh. Asria was the only child who regularly chose books which showed images of Pakistan to take home with her. Furthermore, some of the children were predominantly English speaking. Imran, for example, was born in England and is of Indian origin. He attends the local Sikh temple regularly throughout the week, where he learns about his religion and culture, and how to read and write Punjabi. Yet he clearly saw himself as an English speaker. When asked how his mum told him stories, he replied, "She reads them from a book....She reads them in my voice [English]." At another stage, Imran was sitting reading a dual-text storybook. Asked if his parents ever told him stories in Punjabi, English, or in both languages, he replied, pointing to the English script in the book, "This," and said that he only spoke English at home.

We might consider many of the examples of Anglicization as being almost inevitable, choices of food, clothing, the celebration of festivals, television, film, and other media; all of these would be difficult to avoid. Indeed, aspects such as book reading might be viewed very positively. Fox (1993) and Wells (1987) emphasize how beneficial it is for children to have a literature-rich world before starting school. Nevertheless, it was found that many of the parents in the case study school were cautious of how far the dominant Western culture, prevalent in the school, influenced their children. Anglicization appeared to have the greatest impact on the use of mother tongue by the children. Mother-tongue maintenance had been a concern of many parents when their children first started nursery (Hubbard 1998). One of the parents of this focus group was worried about her son's lessening use of Punjabi:

Shiraz does [speak Punjabi], but he doesn't speak it as well as he used to, 'cos it's a lot easier for him to express himself in English, which I'm not quite so happy about. [...] With me it's fine, I speak English so they can say whatever they want, but they need to be able to communicate with their friends and all their relatives who don't speak English...I think that's very important, because they're not always going to be with somebody who speaks English, and they really do need to, because that's a big communication barrier between grandparents and the children, or maybe there's even aunts and uncles or any other member of the family.

A parent of a nursery unit child commented:

That's our identity, that's our inheritance, otherwise if we didn't have the culture, the language, what are we then? We'll be deprived of everything, we're not going to have anything, we're not going to have our identity. So our identity is very important to us—the way you dress, the way you live your daily life...—it's very, very important.

But parents differed in their views on language. Guvinder's mother, who had been born in England, believed that the mother-tongue language would be "caught," as her children are surrounded by the language every day outside of school. To her learning English well was of paramount importance:

Me and my husband we sort of argue, because I'm not talking Punjabi to them....I didn't prefer them to learn that language anyway, because they gonna talk it any way, catch it from us, but the base thing is English, 'cos then they can go off and study, and learn.

Guvinder's mother was confident of her children's ability to speak Punjabi. She felt they spoke Punjabi better than many of the other children from the area, and was very impressed by the way her children had picked up the correct accent—"I think they come from abroad [laughs], the way they talk Punjabi." She articulates some of the problems of young bilingual children and their parents. In Guvinder's case, it appears that he is making the most of his bilingualism/biculturalism—though his father, whom we were not able to interview, might not agree. It might, of course, be argued that some parents are being inducted into an Anglicized model of parenthood to some extent.

Yet there were children in the group for whom English still provided many instances of misunderstanding, both in trying to understand the teacher and for the teacher to understand them. We have illustrated how Simera, for example, learned to cope with much of what she did not understand by simply copying her peers. Other children such as Asria and Ahmed H. were more willing to make use of the little English they had in order to be understood. Where this failed they would often rely on Hardip, the bilingual non-teaching assistant, for translation. In this way Hardip became an invaluable asset in the classroom, though this was more in support of the Anglicized model rather than their own cultures. We noted that while the school was happy for children to use their mother tongue in class, this was not actively promoted. The language-rich environment the children were in was not fully exploited and English became the common language of the classroom. In this way the discourse of the "normal" pupil was allowed to fuel its own development. It is not surprising, therefore, that Shiraz's mum noticed her son's declining use of Punjabi at home. Clearly, merely tolerating children's use of home languages in school is not an effective method of maintaining mother tongue and ethnic culture. Much of the children's ethnic cultural identity in consequence was being challenged at school as they went about the task of constructing the culture-specific pupil role and discourse, articulated in English. This stood in sharp contrast to their experiences in their community through their attendance of Mosque and Temple, and their daily interaction with parents and extended families.

CONCLUSION

Starting school for these bilingual children represented a radical move from child to pupil, but a special kind of pupil, internalizing the rules and rituals as defined within a traditional English society. To some degree, it was essential for them to do so, though ideally, if the parents' ambivalence and fears of diminished identity (Hubbard 1998) were to be allayed, a balanced framework where the strengths of both cultures were celebrated would appear to be preferable. To some degree this was the case, at least on the surface.

In the school which Wright (1993) researched, induction was confrontational: the "Asian pupils (particularly the younger ones) were perceived as a problem to teachers because of their limited cognitive skills, poor English language and poor social skills and their inability to socialise with other pupil groups in the classroom" (p. 52), and teachers showed "open disapproval of their customs and traditions" (p. 28). Our school was quite the opposite: such disapproval was entirely absent, and induction was not confrontational. The teachers were sensitive and caring, they celebrated the children's cultural traditions in assemblies and on special occasions, and sought to make their teaching relevant to the children's own constructions of meaning. At the level of conscious interaction they engaged with the issues in committed fashion. At a deeper level, however, the children's own culture and language were becoming marginalized by default, as teachers were constrained to "make pupils" according to culturally specific role models derived from tradition, institutionalization, and the demands of the National Curriculum and assessment. Even the notably caring ethos of the school was ethnically specific. For while it may in itself be beneficial for all pupils (Noddings 1992), it involved a deficit model of the home environment (Woods, Boyle, and Hubbard 1997), which again inhibited teachers from taking full advantage of the children's backgrounds. The children's immediate launch into the National Curriculum and the implicit bias in favor of the English language as opposed to mother tongues, gave further structure to the passage into Anglicized cultural norms.

The process of these children starting school may seem smooth enough on the surface, but underneath, we would argue, are being sown the seeds of division rather than harmony; ambivalence and ambiguity rather than accommodation and incorporation. Ethnically diverse children are having to deal, not only with the transitions from family to school, and from primary to secondary socialization, but also in certain respects from their own ethnic culture to English culture. This is by no means complete. The picture is complex, there is a mix of cultures, individuals differ, and lives are lived out at different levels. Nor are these teachers clearly seen to be doing anything wrong. In many respects they are achieving high standards with unreasonable pressures and inadequate resources and they received an excellent report from their Ofsted inspection—though the fact that these inspections are conducted within an Anglicized, managerialist framework emphasizes the point being made here (Jeffrey and Woods 1998; Woods, Boyle, and Hubbard 1997).

Courses of action more consonant with a culturally diverse society involve cultural diversity being positively encouraged within schools in a way that reflects the equal status of cultures within the pupils' identities. If this is not done at the launch of the pupil's career, and sustained thereafter, monoculturalism becomes fixed and identities diminished. Where the opposite situation is to be sought, that of a truly multicultural society, in which every culture is to be maintained with equal status, we have to review models of childhood and pupilhood that have become engrained within the system. This is not just the teachers' responsibility, but that of all those who devise and enforce policies within which teachers have to work.

ACKNOWLEDGMENTS

The authors are grateful to Nick Hubbard, Bob Jeffrey, Geoff Troman, Alexander Massey, and Geoffrey Walford for their comments on previous drafts of this chapter.

REFERENCES

Berger, P.L., and T. Luckmann. 1967. *The Social Construction of Reality: A Treatise in the Sociology of Knowledge*. Harmondsworth, UK: Penguin.

Bernstein, B. 1977. *Class, Codes and Control*, Vol. 3: *Towards a Theory of Educational Transmissions*, 2nd edition. London: Routledge and Kegan Paul.

Beynon, J. 1985 *Initial Encounters in the Secondary School*. Lewes, UK: Falmer Press.

Blenkin, G., and V. Kelly. 1994. "The Death of Infancy." *Education* 3(October): 3-9.

Boyle, M. 1996. "Talking with Young Children: Partners in Research." Paper presented at the Ethnography and Education Conference, Oxford, UK, September 9-10.

Boyle, M., and P. Woods. 1996. "The Composite Head: Coping with Changes in the Primary Headteacher's Role." *British Educational Research Journal* 22 (5): 549-568.

Burns, T. 1992. *Erving Goffman*. London: Routledge.

Chinoy, E. 1967. *Society: An Introduction to Society*. New York: Random House.

Durkheim, É. 1956. *Education and Sociology*, trans. by S.D. Fox. New York: Free Press.

Edwards, A., and P. Knight. 1994. *Effective Early Years Education: Teaching Young Children*. Buckingham, UK: Open University Press.

Fox, C. 1993. *At the Very Edge of the Forest*. London: Cassell.

Goffman, E. 1961. *Asylums: Essays on the Social Situation of Mental Patients and Other Inmates*. Garden City: NY: Doubleday: Anchor Books.

Gregory, E., and J. Mace. 1996. *Family Literacy History and Children's Learning Strategies at Home and at School*. Final Report of ESRC, Project R 000 22 1186.

Hammersley, M. 1977. "School Learning: The Cultural Resources Required by Pupils to Answer a Teacher's Question." In *School Experience*, edited by P. Woods and M. Hammersley. London: Croom Helm.

Holt, J. 1969. *How Children Fail*. Harmondsworth, UK: Penguin.

Hubbard, N. 1998. "Child-Meaningful Learning in Multi-Ethnic Nursery Schools." Unpublished MPhil Thesis.

Jeffrey, B., and P. Woods. 1996. "The Relevance of Creative Teaching: Pupils' Views." In *Children and Their Curriculum: The Perspectives of Primary and Elementary School Children*, edited by A. Pollard, D. Thiessen, and A. Filer. London: Falmer Press.

Jeffrey, B., and P. Woods. 1998. *Schools Under Inspection: The Impact of Ofsted Inspections on Primary Teachers and their Work*. London: Falmer.

Noddings, N. 1992. *The Challenge to Care in Schools: An Alternative Approach to Education*. New York: Teachers College Press.

Pyke, N. 1997. "British Pride Cures Racism, Tate Argues." *Times Educational Supplement* (May 23): 3.

Reid, D. 1982. "Linguistic Diversity and Equality." In *Language, Culture and Young Children*, edited by P. Pinsent. London: David Fulton.

Rex, J. 1986. "Equality of Opportunity and the Ethnic Minority Child in British Schools." In *Multicultural Education: The Interminable Debate*, edited by S. Mogdil, G. Verma, K. Mallick, and C. Modgil. Lewes, Sussex, UK: Falmer Press.

Sawar, G. 1994. *British Muslims and Schools*. London: Muslim Educational Trust.

Schutz, A. 1971. "The Stranger." In *School and Society: A Sociological Reader*, 2nd ed., edited by B.R. Cosin et al. London: Routledge and Kegan Paul.

Singh, G. 1993. *Equality and Education*. England: Albrighton Publications.

Siraj-Blatchford, I. 1992. "Why Understanding Cultural Differences is Not Enough." In *Contemporary Issues in the Early Years*, edited by G. Pugh. London: Paul Chapman.

Stone, G. P. 1962. "Appearance and the Self." In *Human Behaviour and Social Processes*, edited by A. M. Rose. London: Routledge and Kegan Paul.

Taylor, C. 1992. "The Politics of Recognition." In *Multiculturalism and the "Politics of Recognition,"* edited by A. Gutmann. Princeton: Princeton University Press.

Tuckwell, P. 1982. "Pleasing Teacher." In *The Nature of Special Education*, edited by T. Booth and J. Statham. London: Croom Helm.

Tyler, E. B. 1871. Quoted by Chinoy, E. 1967. *Society: An Introduction to Society*. New York: Random House.

Verma, G. K. 1984. "Multi-cultural Education: Prelude to Practice." In *Race Relations and Cultural Differences*, edited by G. K. Verma and C. Bagley. Beckenham: Croom Helm.

Wagner, D. A. 1993. *Literacy, Culture and Development. Becoming Literate in Morocco*. Cambridge: Cambridge University Press.

Waterhouse, S. R. 1991. *First Episodes: Pupil Careers in the Early Years of School*. London: The Falmer Press.

Wells, G. 1987. *The Meaning Makers: Children Learning Language and Using Language to Learn*. London: Hodder and Stoughton.

Woods, P. 1979. *The Divided School*. London: Routledge.

Woods, P. 1990. *The Happiest Days? How Pupils Cope with School*. London: Falmer Press.

Woods, P., M. Boyle, and N. Hubbard. 1997. "Child-Meaningful Learning: The Experiences of Bilingual Children in the Early Years." Final Report to the ESRC.

Woods, P., B. Jeffrey, G. Troman, and M. Boyle. 1997. *Restructuring Schools, Reconstructing Teachers*. Buckingham: Open University Press.

Wright, C. 1993. "Early Education: Multiracial Primary School Classrooms." In *Educational Research in Action*, edited by R. Gomm and P. Woods. London: Paul Chapman.

FANTASY FOOTBALL LEAGUE:
BOYS LEARNING TO "DO BOY" IN A
SPECIAL (SEN) SCHOOL CLASSROOM

Shereen Benjamin

INTRODUCTION

"What that class needs is a few girls." Such was the observation of one of my teaching colleagues in the summer of 1996 as she described to me the group of ten- and eleven-year-old boys that was to become my class the following autumn. In the outer London special school where we were working, boys outnumbered girls by a little under two to one, and there were no girls of a similar age on roll. As the only all-boy group within the school, the class had established a reputation for "difficult" and hetero/sexist attitudes and actions. I felt considerable trepidation as I contemplated spending my working days in their company. At the same time I felt a degree of intellectual curiosity about how we would work together, and about how we would negotiate working relationships

Studies in Educational Ethnography, Volume 1, pages 115-136.
ISBN: 0-7623-0436-7

from our differing positions within the complicated web of power relations that characterize classroom life. Out of this curiosity, and out of my commitment as a feminist teacher to education for social justice, was born the interventionist research project on masculinities that became the focus both of our classroom work during the following spring term and of the dissertation that I was to spend the summer writing. Explicitly intended as a mutually educative enterprise, the project was designed with the twin aims of enabling me to learn about the boys, and of intervening to make conditions of egalitarian change available to them.

Unlike my colleague quoted above, I did not start out with the belief that boys were naturally, necessarily, and irredeemably problems, or that the presence of girls was the only way that the group could be "made teachable". My perception was that the boys were learning to construct their identities as boys through performing and reconstituting versions of hegemonic (especially macho and competitive) masculinities in ways that seemed to reproduce hetero/sexist power relations. In designing the project, one of my concerns was to learn about how the boys used the space of the school, and, more specifically, our classroom, as a stage upon which to enact particular masculine performances, and to understand how my role of teacher functioned as part of this process. My other concern was to use this understanding, as it evolved, to design and evaluate pedagogic approaches intended to enable the boys to learn about, to contextualize, and to interrogate their own constructions of masculinities.

The class in question was a group of seven working-class boys of varying ethnic origins. To use the current educational discourse of "needs" and "difficulties" through which particular individual differences are cast as problems, the boys presented between them a complex conundrum of mild physical disabilities, medical and neurological conditions, communication disorders, learning and developmental disorders, sensory impairments, and variously described "emotional" and "behavioral" difficulties. I describe the boys as "disabled" for, although I recognize the limitations of the term and its implications of deviance, deficit, and a bipolar division between "able" and "disabled," it is at present the term best able to encapsulate a particular constellation of oppressive structures and practices in which the boys' experience was embedded. These boys were already on the margins—categorized, excluded, and aware of their relegation to the bottom division.

The classroom project on masculinities had two distinct stages. During the first, preparatory stage I was concerned with establishing an understanding of the boys' existing constructions of masculinity. I embarked on as systematic a process of field notes and classroom and playground observations as was possible within the constraints of time and energy to which classroom teachers are subject. In addition, I found some of the conceptual and research tools associated with personal construct psychology useful (e.g. Bannister and Fransella 1986; Beail 1985; Salmon 1995). I interviewed all of the boys individually in a process adapted from repertory grid technique (Beail 1985). The boys were invited to construct narratives based on images of men in a range of situations. I went on to interview three of the boys at greater length based on their responses in the first interview. Having elicited this information about how the boys were learning about and constructing masculinity, I went on to design the second stage of the project—classroom work intended to enable the boys to interrogate some of the discourses of masculinity that had emerged in their accounts and to explore alternative discourses and discursive practices. In 14 classroom sessions over four weeks, spaces in which the boys could learn about and experiment with counter-hegemonic discursive positionings were created through discussions, singing, drawing, role-play, and puppetry. Each of the sessions was taped, and I kept field notes and a research diary.

In my interviews with the boys two broad and overlapping discourses emerged as central to their constructions of their identities as boys. These discourses were reflected in nearly all of the narratives created by the boys and they would refer to them when seeking to establish meanings for real and imaginary actions. Observing the boys in both classroom and playground, it seemed that the actions of the boys were generally consistent with these two discourses. Stephen Ball (1990, p. 2), summarizing Foucault, writes that,

> [d]iscourses are about what can be said and thought, but also about who can speak when, and with what authority. Discourses embody meaning and social relationships, they constitute both subjectivity and power relations....Words and concepts change their meaning and their effects as they are deployed within different discourses. Discourses constrain the possibilities of thought. They order and combine words in particular ways and exclude or displace other combinations.

My aim, then, was to enable the boys to problematize, and so to interrogate, the dominant discourses through which they were constructing masculinity, and to make counter-hegemonic—"excluded" or "displaced"—actions and options available to them.

COMPULSORY HETEROSEXUALITY—THE HUNTER/ PROVIDER DISCOURSE

One of these dominant discourses I have called hunter/provider. Within this discourse the boys constructed their future roles as earners of "family wages" through which they would be able to support a wife and children. They could be observed performing and re-constituting this discourse every playtime: through play that objectified girls (such as chasing, invading, and gift-giving) they positioned themselves as possessors and providers and positioned girls as objects in need of protection who waited for boys to lay claim to them. The three boys interviewed at length thought that acquiring a wife and children and providing for them materially were essential components of masculinity. Joe equated the term "good man" with "husband and father." Alex perceived the acquisition of a wife and children as essential to the achievement of manhood—"getting off with girls" was for him an important although transitory phase whose object was to "prove you're a normal boy." The boys were ambivalent about their future roles as providers of emotional and nurturing support, and in particular about what their domestic responsibilities might be. Ennis's initial response to a picture of a man cuddling a baby was one of disbelief—"I thought that was a woman...because men don't feed babies." He went on to contradict himself in constructing narratives in which husbands left paid work in favor of child care once their babies were born, revealing a considerable dilemma before finally identifying with the wage-earning model.

Essential to this discourse was a dichotomous understanding of gender and gendered relationships. Friendships with girls could not exist outside of the heterosexual matrix and could only be understood in terms of their heterosexualized meanings (Thorne 1993). The boys felt that their successful positioning within the hunter/provider discourse was contingent on constant demonstration, performance, and proof. This most commonly took the form of a semi-ritualized pursuit of one particular 12-year-old girl whom they had constructed as desirable, disruption, and derogation of those girls they had constructed as undesirable, and conversations about "girlfriends" outside of school. Homophobic performances were also central to the boys' hunter/provider success (Epstein and Johnson 1994). "Doing boy," to draw on the notion of gendered identities as performative (Butler 1990), involved active participation in ritualized displays of homophobia. These included "contamination" games in which the chaser would be "gay" and would pass "gayness" on to whichever player he caught, and verbal abuse that targeted boys who displayed vulnerability or who touched other boys in anything other than a rough and tumble game or fight.

The hunter/provider discourse and the daily performances through which it was re-constituted reflected, to a large extent, the established norms of the school. The pervasive, commonsense understanding—hegemony even—that pervaded staffroom, classroom, and playground was that boy/girl relationships were a natural and inevitable part of growing up. Heterosexuality operated as an unquestioned and unre-marked/unremarkable norm (Epstein and Johnson 1994, p. 195). Intriguingly, most staff members (including, as it transpired, myself) managed not to hear most homophobic abuse. The commonsense view was that children were not capable of homophobia (despite the fact that the oldest "children" at the school were 18 years old) and that "anti-gay" remarks by particular pupils were a function of individual "difficulty" rather than a manifestation of the school's (and society's) culture and pupils' subcultures.

Interrogating the hunter/provider discourse, then, involved problema-tizing with the boys the social construction of gender, the "naturalness" of heterosexual familial relationships, and the pervasiveness of homophobia. This was difficult territory for all of us, myself and the boys. They were being asked to examine critically some of the core notions around which they were constructing their identities and to explore positionings that they had been investing in derogating. From my position of structural authority, I was asking (and expecting) them to learn about unfamiliar ways of doing and being boys, and all of this in the public space of the classroom. Politically, I too was in potentially treacherous waters. A complicated set of micropolitical manoeuvres among staff and governors had erupted in the school two years previously. One of the results of this had been press coverage suggesting, among other things, that "political correctness" was running out of control and that pupils were being subjected to homosexual propaganda. The micropolitical reality behind these and other fairy-tale allegations had not been articulated or resolved at the time and the resultant pain of deeply felt but silenced fears, hurts, and hostilities had continued to fester. In consequence, the act of raising any issues connected with social justice in general and sexuality in particular was fraught with difficulties—there was much that was unsayable. In addition, the fall-out from section 28 of the local government act (Sanders and Spraggs 1989) continued to make itself felt in promoting, legitimating, and giving focus to this climate of fear. The dilemma of wanting on the one hand to act in a collegial, collaborative way, and on the other hand of working with the need to prevent most colleagues from knowing what I was really doing, was one that I could not resolve satisfactorily.

In the initial sessions I was surprised by the boys' perception of gender as something learned rather than biologically determined. I had expected the concept of social construction to be beyond their understanding. This extract from my research diary shows how easily they apparently took to it as an abstract theory and were able to operate it in making sense of their lived experience:

> Our first activity is to brainstorm the differences between girls/women and boys/men. There is some hesitation at first, with Jake the first to contribute. He gives three suggestions which I write on the board, then the others begin to offer ideas. At first all the differences they suggest are biological ones. After 10 of these, they begin to add perceived "learned differences." I write these in a different color. Ennis asks if he can "say something rude." I remind him that all suggestions are acceptable in a brainstorm. He says, "boys want to have sex with girls." I have to remind myself of the brainstorm rule, and write it on the board, overcoming my desire to challenge his statement on the spot. The boys giggle at this use of playground language in the formal world of the classroom. There is excitement and unease at this blurring of the boundaries. We continue. After 25 suggestions the board is full and the boys are becoming overexcited. The suggestions range from "boys have penises" and "girls have curly hair" to "women smoke more" and "men work more than women." Alex has dutifully said that "men can be sexist." Some of the boys want to contest some of the statements on the board. I tell them we will be doing that a bit later. I ask the boys if they can work out why some of the writing is in red and some in green. They work out that the green writing is "about bodies." I use the term "biological difference." They seem comfortable with this concept. They find it harder to work out a common factor for the red writing. Joe listens carefully to what the others are saying, then remarks, "They are things you learn when you grow up." We examine the red statements to see if this definition fits. It does, and I use the term "learned difference." This concept too seems to make sense to them.

> We move on to challenge some of the statements on the board. I invite the boys to contest any suggestion that they believe, through personal experience, to be untrue. The statements offered by Michael (the boy at the "bottom" of the unofficial class hierarchy) are the first to be contested. I decide to let this subcultural

manoeuvre go unchallenged for the present. I put a mark by any statements that are contested. The boys do this activity with relish, and are able to explain, by giving examples, why they are contesting particular statements. Toward the end of the activity they draw on their experience of films and television, in addition to "real-life" experience, to challenge some of the biological statements. Eventually only two statements remain uncontested: that "girls have vaginas" and that "women wear bras." All the suggestions pertaining directly to men and boys have been contested (1) (Research diary, session one).

This was the first of the classroom sessions, and accordingly my first intentional intervention into the boys' constructions of masculinities. At this stage my concern was to help the boys to notice, talk about, and learn about phenomena that had previously been unnoticed and unremarked aspects of their daily realities. The brainstorming technique, and my use of different colors to direct the boys toward particular responses, were useful in these early sessions, where we were establishing a basic shared understanding and a working vocabulary. As the boys' perceptions and understandings became more complex and nuanced, and they became more adept at asking questions of themselves and each other, other pedagogic strategies were to become more appropriate.

The boys appeared, then, to understand that the apparently unitary category of "masculinity" is in fact variable, and seemed to be saying that there are no common denominators applying to all men and boys. However, learning to understand this conceptually did not automatically enable them to interrogate the hunter/provider discourse. In other words, knowing the theory (of masculinities as infinitely varied) did not enable them to do the practice (of performing masculinities outside of the hunter/provider hegemony). They needed to learn to use other tools besides conceptual understanding to help them investigate their complicated investments in particular masculinities.

Nowhere was this more evident than in interrogating macho imagery. In the initial interviews the boys had displayed the ability to recognize such imagery instantly, and would readily name particular representations as "Macho Man." In an early session the boys used some of the pictures in Anthony Browne's *Willy The Wimp* (1984) to make explicit their perceptions of Macho Man. Through discussing the book's suitability or otherwise for younger children, they were able to identify with ease some of the dangers in macho imagery, and talked freely about the interrelationship of macho stereotypes with bullying and with drug abuse. The boys were also able to use a video clip from the Gladiators to explore the concept of Macho Man as a particular type of masculine performance, and to discuss the ways in which such performances are gendered. This conceptual work appeared to multiply the contradictions within the boys' accounts of themselves and their aspirations, and I was concerned that they might, through resistance and as a defense, be learning to intensify their positionings within macho masculine hegemony. The confusions within which the boys were trying to locate themselves were highlighted when we looked at their investments in the Macho Man model:

We begin by looking at the Macho Man picture from *Willy The Champ* by Anthony Browne. "Who's this?" I ask. "Macho Man" they chorus in reply. I decide to revisit yesterday's conversation about which of the older students they see as macho. I ask the question, "Who tries to be macho?" To my surprise six hands are sheepishly raised (Adrian is not present today). Later, I wonder if my use of the word "tries" influenced their response; maybe they feel that those older boys cited yesterday have already achieved Macho Man status while they themselves are still trying. Alex says, half jokingly, "I admit it, I do sometimes." "Sometimes but not all the time," adds Ennis. Tim stands up and takes up an exaggerated macho pose, complete with puffed-out chest and menacing frown. "That's how I do macho," he states, and adds a karate kick. The boys laugh. The atmosphere in the room is good-humoured.

I ask what the attraction is, why they sometimes want to be seen and to see themselves as macho. They find this question easy and are full of ideas. Their answers are mainly to do with peer-group relations and heterosexualized relationships with girls, ranging from "you'll be in a gang" and "people won't laugh at you" to "you'll have loads of girlfriends" and "girls will have sex with you." Social acceptance and inclusion, physical strength, and the power to secure and retain (objectified) girlfriends seem inextricably interwoven....Tim brings another buzz-word into the discussion by suggesting that macho is "cool." There follows a heated debate about what "cool" really means, and the issue of power is raised directly for the first time. I ask in what ways Macho Man is powerful. This has a somewhat circular effect, and they recapitulate some of the reasons they have already given for their attraction to Macho Man. I point this out, and ask, "So is it attractive to be powerful?" The boys agree that it is, and recast some of their earlier answers (Research diary, session three).

Given that five of the boys have physical limitations that make any approximation of a "macho" body impossible for them, their identification with tough, physically powerful imagery and their desire to achieve a "perfect" body had the quality of a fantasy defense against an untenable daily reality: the reality of growing up as a disabled boy in a culture that equates physical strength and perfection with (masculine) power and desirability.

Throughout the early sessions homophobia and the heterosexual imperative were the invisible specters in the background. They were unspoken yet implicitly pervaded everything the boys said and did. I had made my position on homophobia clear to the boys in our first days together by imposing a ban on homophobic language which I enforced through disapprobation and punishment. I thought the boys were likely to say what they believed I wanted to hear unless I found a way to change the dynamic. To do this, I used the song "So Strong" by Labi Siffre. This song was familiar to the boys and was one they especially liked singing. Although they had learned it almost a year earlier, I had never explained to them its associations with lesbian and gay rights. During the eighth session, we sang the song together and began to discuss some of its lyrics:

> The boys suggest that the "brothers and sisters" are children who are being made fun of, and that "they" are Macho Men, frightening the children. I explain that Labi Siffre, the writer of the song, is a black man in his fifties, and ask if this makes a difference to their interpretation of the song. It does. They now think the "brothers and sisters" are black people and that "they" are racists and white supremacists. The boys know about the civil rights movement, and make the link between Labi Siffre's age and his potential position within such struggles. They do this with alacrity; we have discussed racism often enough for this to be reasonably safe territory. I then add, "He's also gay." There is a stunned silence for a few seconds. Ennis repeats disbelievingly, "Gay?" The silence continues. It is as if the boys are completely thrown off balance by hearing the word used non-pejoratively and in the classroom. I break the silence by asking if this information makes any further difference to their interpretation of the song. Joe says with some anger, "There's nothing wrong with being gay." Ennis repeats this after him. I repeat my question. Joe suggests that the "brothers and sisters" are gay men. "And lesbians" adds Ennis. Joe goes on to suggest that "they" are people who call lesbians and gay men rude names. "What, like poofter and bender?" asks Tim. I write the word "homophobia" on the board and explain its meaning. The atmosphere in the room remains highly charged. Alex and Jake are resolutely staring at the floor. Alex is near to tears. Michael has disengaged and is fiddling with the books on the book rack (Research diary, session eight).

The force and emotion with which the boys responded to this session surprised me, and left me with questions about the ethics of working in this way. While I had known that asking the boys to interrogate some of their most fundamental identifications would be painful for them, this session made plain to me some of the ethical considerations of demanding, from my position of structural power, that they do this, and giving them no opportunity to withdraw.

I decided to continue the work with an unfamiliar song, one in which they had no prior investment. "Old Joe's House" by Si Khan tells the story, through the eyes of a child, of an old man in a small Dixieland town whose male partner committed suicide in his youth after the town found out about their relationship. In the song, Old Joe retreats behind the unopened curtains of his house and is never seen again. I considered that the subject matter of the song was sufficiently emotive to promote frank discussion, while being situated at enough distance from the boys' lived experience to create a degree of safety. I sang the song to the boys. They listened carefully and were able to make sense of its story. The discussion that followed moved quickly into their own direct experiences of homophobia:

Tim:	That's bad—um—um—'cause when you like—you call someone a bender and that, it's 'cause you wanna make fun of them, right, it don't mean like you want them to kill theirselves—when you call them bender...
Ennis:	Like if Adrian jumped off a sewer I would never be seen again.
SB:	Remember—suicide means killing yourself. Not quite the same thing as jumping off a sewer.
Joe:	Would that still happen?—er—do people still kill theirselves if, like, someone says homopho- pho- makes fun that they're gay, like if someone calls them bender, is that homophobia, or was it—like—was it just in the olden times like when Old Joe was a boy?
Tim:	That's bad, man. 'Cause when Darren, like, when Darren is playing football, yeah, and he—someone don't pass him the ball... [inaudible] um—and misses it, he like says bender, he says it all the time, and he gets other people to say it.
Adrian:	And gaylord.
Tim:	And gaylord, right, and it isn't olden times no more.
Ennis:	And gaylord he calls them.
Joe:	Gaylord. Is that homophobia?
SB:	Do people think that calling someone gaylord is homophobic?
Ennis:	I thought a sewer was a river.
SB:	Let's stay with what we're talking about. We're talking about homophobia.
Ennis:	It makes you gay.
Adrian:	It ruins lives.
Tim:	Calling names. Names what hurt.
Alex:	Like when Darren—he—when him and me used to be best mates, yeah—we did, before Adrian come to this school, yeah—

we was best mates and then Adrian come and um—Adrian and me was mates and then Barney left, and Darren he didn't have no mates—um—except I still would've been his friend...

Adrian: He was jealous—at first, yeah, when Barney was still here he wasn't jealous, then Barney left, and also, like—he didn't grow none, he's—um—still small, and he got jealous...

Joe: Before I come to this school—

Alex: And he was jealous of our relationship and he wants to split us up—like, like when we're playing football, yeah...

Adrian: On the playground and Alex he falls over, yeah, Darren he says, "Go on, then, go and cry to your boyfriend, to Adrian he's your boyfriend"—

Tim: He does...

Alex: He says Adrian's my boyfriend for two years—and other people say it 'cause they're scared of him...

Ennis: I'm scared of him.

Alex: —to split us up, our friendship, and I don't want him to do it no more... (Transcript, session nine).

In this part of the discussion, homophobia, rather than homosexuality, is constructed as the problem, the deviant and unacceptable "other." Prior to the extract Joe had aligned himself firmly with me in problematizing homophobia by asking questions that were transparently about eliciting information, with no hint of a subtext. His undisputed position at the top of the group's established hierarchy meant that the other boys were given implicit permission to do the same. With homophobia discredited, the boys were able to talk about their feelings, and in particular, their feelings for each other with an unusual degree of openness. Ennis is the first to make an identification with the central—homosexual—character in the song, although at the time I missed the implication of his statement about Adrian, and responded only to his misunderstanding of the word "suicide." The boys go on to distance themselves from the practice of homophobia by positioning a slightly older boy with a reputation for toughness and "bullying" (Darren) as the source and instigator of what they and I know to be the routine use of homophobic abuse during the boys' football game every breaktime and lunchtime. As Adrian and Alex's story progresses, not only do they distance themselves from the practice of homophobic abuse, they also begin to place it within a discursive framework. As they tell their story they consider how and why Darren had wanted and been able to use the hunter/provider discourse to position them as vulnerable and himself as powerful. It is interesting to observe how, as the story unfolds, Adrian and Alex move into a lexicon more commonly associated with (hetero)sexualized romance. Through borrowing the terms "relationship," "jealous," and "splitting up" with their romantic connotations, they are able to verbalize strong homosocial feelings, challenging the core of the hunter/provider discourse and taking up positions outside it.

COMPETING AND CONNECTING—THE "EVERYONE LOVES A WINNER" DISCOURSE

In his study of Mike Tyson, Tony Jefferson identifies a "hyper-masculine" discourse which he calls the "will to win" (Jefferson 1996, p. 162). When a similar discourse emerged during my interviews with the boys, I initially named it "winner takes all," since the boys talked at length about the material rewards of "winning." Alex described the opulent lifestyle that he saw as the justifiable reward for success on the football pitch, contrasting this with the abject poverty of "failure." There was, for him, no intermediate position. For all of the boys the "winner" indeed gained everything—money, acclaim, and security—while the "loser" was left with nothing. However, closer listening to the tapes revealed another element to their accounts. Their motivation for wanting to acquire the benefits of winning—in personal construct terms, their superordinate constructs—were about the possibilities for meaningful relationships and the power to control those relationships to which the status of winning would give them access. Inclusion was a priority mentioned repeatedly. Conflating football success, financial success, and inclusion, Joe remarked that, "If you score the most goals, everyone will want you to be in their team and you'll earn loads of money and have a big house and car." Respect was also part of the overall picture. Ennis said that, "When you're the best in the team no one will laugh at you and call you names...because they'll want to be your friends."

Football stardom was at the heart of the boys' construction of the everyone loves a winner discourse. This was very disturbing, since six of them are likely to be precluded from achieving significant football success due to the nature of their disabilities. Ironically, Jake, the only one of the boys not to face such a challenge, was also the least invested in football stardom as the route to adult fame and fortune. Through their investment in winning, configured by the discursive practices of the "football business," the boys appeared to be making fantasy identifications with the ideal of the physically powerful and dextrous male body—a body that could never be theirs. Although similar to their identifications with Macho Man, there were no contradictions for the boys here. Macho Man was a complicated hero—powerful and attractive, but also frightening and a bully—and in the space of that contradiction the boys were able to parody and deconstruct. The football star was, by contrast, an uncomplicated hero, an all-encompassing fantasy with a closure that left no room for fissures or disjunctures (Davies 1993; Barker 1997). Personal power, manifested in control of relationships and evidenced by inclusion, seemed to depend, for the boys, on how convincingly they could perform identifications with this heroic image.

Since football was the major discursive referent in the everyone loves a winner discourse, I knew I would have to raise the subject with the boys. I was very aware of the gulf of class and gender that might well be exposed between myself and them: the potential for "othering" was enormous. I wanted to help the boys interrogate their investment in football stardom but without imposing on them the potential humiliation of having their most cherished dreams and heroes subjected to the questioning gaze of authority. It was while I was puzzling over how best to work with these tensions that football "arrived" in the classroom in a way I could not ignore:

The boys tumble into the classroom full of triumph, pride, and hearty congratulations. Ennis, Joe, and Alex have all scored goals in the big boys' football game and the class is basking in reflected glory. I abandon the session I had planned on role models and relationships—they are clearly wanting to talk about football.

I tell them we are going to cover the board with words about football. They cheer. Everyone wants to talk at once. We go round and round the circle, taking one idea from each boy in turn. Soon the board is covered, apart from a space I have left blank at the top, with 52 words about football. The boys have found this exciting and motivating, and would have gone on for hours had I let them. I draw their attention to how easy they have found this activity, and how much they know about football. I ask how they come to know so much. "Because we love football!" Tim bursts out, a huge smile of delight on his face. Other suggestions follow. I write them in the blank space at the top of the board. I use red for reasons such as "because our Dads teach us" that are to do with direct experience, and blue for reasons such as "reading football magazines" that are to do with cultural imagery...

I suggest to the boys that a group of girls might have found it much harder to write a list of words about football, and ask if they agree. They go through the red and blue writing, and find two points emerge; that girls have less experience of playing football in "real life," and that images of football, whether on television, in magazines, on bags and stickers, and other paraphernalia, are almost exclusively male. I ask what the underlying message is. "That football is a game for boys and men," says Joe. Alex wants to contest this. "Girls can play football if they want. Kate played with us last week," he argues. I ask what Kate's part in the game had been. "She wasn't very good, she couldn't kick the ball." Ennis joins in with, "Girls aren't tough. If you tackle them they will fall over and then they will cry."..."They're no good at football because they don't practice," adds Michael....I pose a question about why girls might think that football is not a game for them. Ennis replies hesitantly, "It's always men on the telly, so they think football's a boys' game." "It's not. I don't like football," argues Jake....Tim introduces the idea that football is important. Some of the others pick this up, reflecting on how we are surrounded by images of football. Alex is dubious and the others try to convince him. Jake expresses his frustration at the ubiquity of football images from which he feels that he, as a non-football-loving boy, suffers (Research diary, session four).

This session narrowly avoided, largely due to Jake's contributions, constructing the discursive practice of football as a site of male privilege equally accessible to and enjoyed by all men and boys, and one in which girls and women are defined by their "lack." The tension here between investigating gendered differences and promoting a dichotomized view of those differences was one that surfaced throughout the work. Bronwyn Davies writes that,

> Binary thought is absolutely fundamental to the male/female dualism....There are a whole range of binarisms that are created in the discourses we have access to, many of which are linked to what we understand as male and female....As long as we are capable of holding the binarisms intact, there is always precisely the risk that those ways of being that threaten or disrupt the binarisms will be understood as transgressive, rather than as, say, a multiplicity to be celebrated (Davies 1994, p. 10).

In the everyone loves a winner discourse, football could only be understood and configured in terms of binaries; principally male/female and winner/loser. Did Jake's contributions threaten or disrupt these binaries? In taking up, at this point, a position outside of the everyone loves a winner discourse—through asserting a lack of interest in football—Jake risked being marginalized and derided. The fact that he was taken seriously by the boys may have contradictory interpretations. Perhaps the boys were willing to problematize the dualistic assumption that all boys love football. Or, conversely, perhaps the discourse was so firmly established, and the boys' positions in it so solidified, that they could understand Jake's position as sufficiently deviant and marginal as to pose no serious threat.

During a later session the boys used examples from football to explore the relationship between their disabilities, their hunger for winning, and their responses—fight and flight—to situations in which they could not win. In the following extract Tim has described a scenario in which he became angry during a football game and was sent off:

Tim: See, I thought we was—we was going towards one goal only we wasn't, it was the other team, and this bloke, right, he was massive, yeah, and I—um—tackled him 'cause I thought he was going the wrong way, yeah, only like he wasn't and—and—and I thought they was laughing so I nutted him.

Michael: [laughs]

Tim: and—like—I got sent off, and—and I got lost.

Alex: Didn't they know you couldn't hear?

Tim: I can hear. I can—they just shouted too loud and they was all bigger than me and I forgot my drink.

Ennis: That's sad. You must've been really angry. I would've...

Tim: [signs—had enough]

SB: You've said enough, Tim? Has anybody else got an example of a time when they haven't been winning? Doesn't have to be football. All those other times—say like playing a Maths game?

Ennis: When you have to go back to the start.

Joe: When we played Elmside and—and we like—we got the first goal and it was half-time, they started swearing at us...

Alex: If they—if they sweared at me...

Joe: I would swear back.

Ennis: Yeah.

Alex: I wouldn't. I'd just turn my head away and say, "See you."

Ennis: See you later alligator.

Michael: That's rude. Miss, he's being rude.

Alex: 'Cause if you sweared back at them they'd only do it more.

SB: They'd carry on swearing?

Ennis: Yeah, and then there'd be a big fight [makes fighting noises]. You'd get in trouble.

Joe: When people cuss your Mum and that, you have to swear back or they pick on your friends. I would stand up for them I would— I would stand up for my friends like if Darren picked on Alex and I would stand up for him—'cause—'cause you don't want your friends to get hurt like, and I don't care getting in trouble.

Tim: Like—um—say if Darren was picking on me, would you get
        him?
Joe: Yeah.
Ennis: I would get him. All of our class would get him (Transcript, ses-
        sion eleven).

The boys resisted my attempt to move the discussion into my territory—the Maths game—and kept it firmly within their world of the
football pitch. As the discussion progressed, its focus shifted toward the
performance and control of friendship. The position of "winner"
seemed to imply, for the boys, a powerful position within a relationship.
It conferred the power to attract and retain friends, as well as connoting
the physical power to hurt or prevent hurt. In the everyone loves a winner discourse the goal (in more than one sense) was inclusion. When, at
the end of the above extract, Tim anxiously seeks reassurance that he is
part of the group and entitled to its protection, Joe is able to take up the
most powerful discursive position: the power to make a decision about
somebody else's exclusion or inclusion within the group is, in that
moment, his. Conversely, the position of "loser" was equated with the
absence of power and consequent loss of control. Not winning appeared
to mean, for the boys, dependence and vulnerability. For the "loser"
inclusion within a group was contingent on other people's decisions and
liable to be withdrawn for reasons they could not understand or influence. The boys apparently associated the position of loser with (male)
physical weakness and with disability: Tim's denial of his hearing loss
toward the beginning of the extract may have represented an unwilling-
ness to take up a subordinated discursive position.

Winning and losing appeared to operate as hard and fast distinctions—binarisms—for the boys. I found it hard to enable them to construct intermediate positions between the total power and control—
domination—of winning and the total absence of power and control—
subordination—of situations in which winning was impossible. The
boys' feelings associated with winning and losing were intense and, I
felt, potentially explosive. During the session cited above some of the
boys suggested using role-play, which was a technique we had often
used together. We discussed the risks that might be involved, and
decided to use the less exposing medium of puppetry.

Using a group of furry animal puppets, each of them named and "gendered" (concerns about anthropomorphism suspended for the duration),
we developed a way of working in which one boy would "be freeze

frame," with the power to stop and restart the action, and at least one boy would observe and comment. In this extract a situation in which one of the puppets cannot win is being constructed:

Alex:	Tommy and Gilly, Gilly she always gets catched in "Bulldog" and Fozzie he won't let her catch him and Wilma—Wilma she feels sorry for Gilly.
Ennis:	She's only a baby giraffe.
Alex:	Gilly she doesn't win. And she keeps getting catched....Can I be Gilly?
SB:	Right, you're Gilly. Joe, you're Tommy?...
Jake:	I'm Fozzie. I don't wanna be Wilma no more today.
Ennis:	Yeah—[cheers] I'm Wilma—I'm Wilma - um—don't be naughty, Wilma. [throws puppet repeatedly]...
Michael:	Action!
Alex:	[makes panting noises] Wait—wait for me!
Jake:	Quick! Don't let her get you! [chants] you can't run, you can't run!
Alex:	You have to go slower! Wait for me!
Ennis:	Hey man, she's only—um—only—only a baby giraffe.
Michael:	Freeze frame!
SB:	Gilly?
Alex:	I'm sad 'cause I can't catch no one and they can all run too fast and—too fast and like its not fair 'cause I ain't got no chance and—um - I don't wanna play no more but if I stop they'll laugh at me and I'll be sad.
SB:	Fozzie?
Jake:	It's my game and when I say don't let Gilly catch you—they've got to do it 'cause it's my game and, like, if they let Gilly—and they let Gilly catch them I won't let them play no more. 'Cause it's my game and I'm in charge.
SB:	Wilma?
Ennis:	Man, I'm sorry for Gilly. She's only a baby giraffe. Man, they're—they're mean to her. She won't never catch them unless—um—she won't never do it.
SB:	Tommy?
Joe:	Fozzie, he's too much bossy. If he be's mean, I don't wanna play with him...
Michael:	Action!
Ennis:	Gilly! (as if talking to a baby) Gilly—come on—you can catch me—come on Gilly.
Jake:	Hey! It's my game! Don't let her!
Joe:	I'm not playing with you 'cause you be's mean to Gilly...

A resolution in which the excluding character is himself excluded (at the instigation of the other "male" character) is enacted by the boys. The situation is then re-created, but this time, "Wilma" is excluding "Tommy."

Joe: Ow! My ankle man! I can't run good! You lot—slow down—I can't run good!

Ennis: Nobody let him catch you! It's my game!

Alex: [chants] Can't catch me!

Jake: And it's my game. You can't get me!

Ennis: It's my game. 'Cause I say don't—don't let Tommy get you. 'Cause it's my game.

Jake: And I said too.

Michael: Freeze frame!

SB: Tommy?

Joe: My ankle hurts—um—my ankle really hurts, man. And them lot they're bad, yeah. They make fun of me 'cause like my ankle hurts. They're bad.

SB: Wilma?

Ennis: It's my game—um—and if I let them catch Gilly—no, Tommy—it won't be my game no more and Fozzie he will take over if they catch Tommy. 'Cause it's my game.

SB: Gilly?

Alex: I don't like having to be mean to—mean to Tommy. But if I let them catch me, Fozzie he won't let me play no more.

Ennis: It's my game!

Alex: Wilma she won't let me play no more.

SB: Fozzie?

Jake: It's my game only I'm letting it be Wilma's game, but if she lets people catch Tommy it's my game again. It's my game really.

Ennis: No!...

Michael: Action!

Joe: My ankle—um—my ankle hurts. I'm going to Nurse (Transcript, session eleven).

The boys constructed dominant and subordinate positions in the everyone loves a winner discourse differentially for "male" and "female" characters. In the first part of the extract, when a "male" character is nominated as the one in charge, this role is ceded to him without question. When, in the second part, leadership is supposedly transferred to a "female" character, it is hotly contested by Jake and overlooked by Alex. Positioning a female character as powerful within the everyone loves a winner discourse appeared problematic for the boys. When, in the first part, a "female" character is positioned as vulnerable, this is by virtue of age: Ennis repeatedly confirms that she is "only a baby." When she is included within the game she is positioned within a mothering discourse, with another "female" character taking the role of mother. The vulnerability of the "male" character in the second part, however, is attributed to a temporary physical infirmity, one which is minor and transitory and which need have no lasting impact on the identity of the sufferer. Joe resolves the problem by positioning his character within a medicalized discourse. He actively withdraws his character from the game, saving him from the humiliation of conditional inclusion and passive dependence on a more powerful character. In subsequent puppetry work the boys continued to find it humiliating to perform vulnerability while in a "male" role, and would go to considerable lengths to avoid doing so. It appeared as if they believed that their survival as boys was dependent on how effectively they could suppress any display of, or identification with, vulnerability.

And yet, just occasionally, the boys did manage to construct alternative positions. In the following extract we have been talking about how we respond to other people "losing." The boys have worked in pairs on a role-play in which the same scene is played, at first with an unhelpful response, then repeated with a more supportive one:

> Each pair decides to show their role-play to the rest of the group. Without exception they ham up the first take, portraying reactions that are far more extreme than any they would expect to find in real life. Jake spills the tea, for which he is thrown out of home, Joe is executed for scoring an own goal, and Ennis is imprisoned for missing a penalty. Each of these scenes elicits laughter—it would be too painful to enact them in any other way. The second takes are much more realistic, and are characterized by kind words, nonabusive physical contact, and the chance to try again (Research diary, session seven).

The boys clearly did have considerable resources—in this instance demonstrating humor, care, empathy, and compassion—that they were able to use, when they felt safe enough to do so, in positioning themselves outside of the everyone loves a winner discourse. I deeply regretted the fact that I was carrying out the project in my own classroom and in isolation from my colleagues, since a concerted effort by all of us might just have had an impact on the pupils' subcultural world (Troyna and Hatcher 1992) and made the school playground a safer place in which to perform gentler masculinities.

BOYS CONSTRUCTING AND
RECONSTRUCTING MASCULINITIES?

Throughout the duration of the project the boys reproduced versions of hegemonic masculinities in the classroom and in the playground. They were routinely involved in taking up positions within hetero/sexist, homophobic, macho, and competitive discourses through which they would seek to perform and demonstrate their hold on high-status masculinities and to distance themselves from lower-status ones. However, there was also plenty of nonreproduction, of the creation of new meanings, during the classroom work. Through collaborative participation in activities that involved them as whole, complex people, and that engaged with the realms of fantasy as well as cognition, the boys were able, at times, to question their existing constructions of masculinity and to experiment with alternatives; to use the "scaffolding of counter-discourses" (Epstein 1993, p. 146) to build their own constructions.

The boys in this project were simultaneously engaged in "doing boy" and "doing pupil"; I was their class teacher as well as researcher. We were all embedded in, although differentially positioned by, the school and its own constellation of cultural practices. In our relationships we were expected to enact particular structural and institutional norms, and the matrix of power relations was perhaps more complex than if I had been able to assume a "least adult position" (Thorne 1993). We were in a deeply paradoxical situation. I was asking the boys to identify with me, an authority figure, probably perceived by them as middle class, in resistance to a constellation of hegemonic and working-class masculinities that I had identified as oppressive. The boys could and did develop a variety of ways of working "with me" and "against me," but whichever way they chose to act, they could not avoid being involved in resistance. Arguably, though, it was the close, contested, often intense but ultimately trusting relationship that exists between a primary classroom teacher and her class that created conditions of sufficient safety for the boys to be able to engage in the often painful task of interrogating and reconstructing their identities as boys.

For me, their teacher, the process was one of educative insight into the worlds of "my" pupils, enriching and challenging my perceptions of life and learning in our classroom. Through observing, reflecting upon, and intervening in the boys' learning I was able to begin to develop a practical and theoretical understanding of the ways in which the boys constructed their masculine identities and of the complexities of my part, as their teacher, in this. Through incorporating some of the values, techniques, and insights of ethnography into a piece of action research, I was able to move beyond those technicist interpretations of the "teacher-researcher" that have been robustly (and, in my view, rightly) critiqued (Siraj-Blatchford 1995), toward a model of critically, intellectually, and politically engaged practitioner-research.

It is impossible for me to say whether the project will have lasting effects for the boys, and since I left the school on completing the classroom-based work, I cannot document even short-term effects. My hope is that the act of deconstructing existing meanings and exploring new ones will have made the boys aware that alternatives to hegemonic masculinities do exist, and will have given them some tools with which to question and experiment in their identity work as they continue learning to "do boy."

NOTE

1. The boys used evidence from films and TV programs featuring elements of trans-gendering to contest the statement that "boys have penises."

REFERENCES

Ball, S. 1990. "Introducing Monsieur Foucault." In *Foucault And Education*, edited by S. Ball. London: Routledge.

Bannister, D., and F. Fransella. 1986. *Inquiring Man: The Psychology Of Personal Constructs* (3rd ed.). London: Croom Helm.

Barker, M. 1997. "Taking The Extreme Case: Understanding A Fascist Fan Of Judge Dredd." In *Trash Aesthetics: Popular Culture And Its Audience*, edited by Cartmell, Hunter, Kaye, and Whelehan. Milton Keynes: Pluto.

Beail, N. 1985. *Repertory Grid Technique And Personal Constructs: Applications In Clinical And Educational Settings*. London: Croom Helm.

Browne, A. 1984. *Willy The Wimp*. London: MacRae.

Butler, J. 1990. *Gender Trouble: Feminism And The Subversion Of Identity*. London: Routledge.

Davies, B. 1993. *Shards Of Glass: Children Reading And Writing Beyond Gendered Identities*. St. Leonards: Allen and Unwin.

Davies, B. 1994. *Poststructuralist Theory And Classroon Practice*. Victoria: Deakin.

Epstein, D. 1993. *Changing Classroom Cultures: Anti-racism, Politics And Schools*. Stoke-on-Trent: Trentham.

Epstein, D., and R. Johnson. 1994. "On The Straight And Narrow: The Heterosexual Presumption, Homophobias And Schools." In *Challenging Lesbian And Gay Inequalities In Schools*, edited by D. Epstein. Buckingham: Open University Press.

Jefferson, T. 1996. "From 'Little Fairy Boy' To 'Compleat Destroyer': Subjectivity And Transformation In The Biography Of Mike Tyson." In *Understanding Masculinities*, edited by M. Mac an Ghaill. Buckingham: Open University Press.

Kahn, S. 1994. "The Curtains Of Old Joe's House." In *My Heart: A Retrospective*, edited by S. Kahn. Toronto: Rounder Records.

Salmon, P. 1995. *Psychology In The Classroom: Reconstructing Teachers And Learners*. London: Cassell.

Sanders, S., and S. Spraggs. 1989. "Section Twenty-Eight And Education." In *Learning Our Lines: Sexuality And Social Control In Education*, edited by C. Jones and P. Mahoney. London: The Women's Press.

Siffre, L. (1992). "Something Inside So Strong." On L. Siffre *So Strong*. China Records.

Siraj-Blatchford, I. 1995. "Critical Social Research And The Academy: The Role Of Organic Intellectuals In Educational Research." *British Journal of Sociology* 16 (2).

Thorne, B. 1993. *Gender Play: Girls And Boys In School.* New Brunswick, NJ: Rutgers University Press.

Troyna, B., and R. Hatcher. 1992. *Racism In Children's Lives: A Study Of Mainly-White Primary Schools.* London: Routledge.

LEARNING ABOUT SEX AND DOING GENDER:
TEENAGE MAGAZINES, GENDER ENACTMENTS, AND SEXUALITIES

Mary Jane Kehily

INTRODUCTION

It is not uncommon for teen magazines to get bad press. They have been variously viewed as poor quality dross for the undiscerning masses (Alderson 1968) and as "ideology purveyors" producing and reproducing a culture of femininity which provides young women with limited and limiting ways of making sense of their experiences (McRobbie 1978a, 1978b, 1981, 1991; Tinkler 1995). Magazine scholarship has explored the enduring popularity of magazines for women and the ways in which the magazine can be seen to provide a space for the construction of normative femininity (McRobbie 1996). Through this extensive

Studies in Educational Ethnography, Volume 1, pages 137-166.
Copyright © 1998 by JAI Press Inc.
All rights of reproduction in any form reserved.
ISBN: 0-7623-0436-7

literature it is possible to trace key themes in feminist scholarship more generally; a concern with issues of power and subordination, a consideration of the pleasures of femininities and, more recently, a recognition of the "failure" of identity and the impossibility of coherence at the level of the subject. Studies of magazines have been marked by two distinct methodological approaches; textual analysis focusing on the magazine and its associative meanings, and audience ethnography exploring the ways in which readers make sense of the text. Studies of magazines aimed at a female readership initially pointed to the many ways in which the stories and features of the magazine format could be bad for you, directly connecting the femininity represented in the pages with the oppressive structures and practices of patriarchal society (McRobbie 1978a, 1978b; Winship 1985; Coward 1984; Tinkler 1995). Further work has suggested the complexity and agency involved in reading practices where pleasure and fantasy can become strategies for the organization and verification of domestic routines and lived experience (Radway 1984; Hermes 1995). Psychoanalytically inflected studies point to the internal fracturing of the psyche and the conceptualization of subjectivity as a site of struggle, suggesting that ideological messages can never be fully conveyed. Valerie Walkerdine's (1990) study of girls' comics explores the relationship of cultural products to the psychic production and resolution of desire. Walkerdine's analysis of "Bunty" indicates that reading practices involve formations of fantasy where desires take shape and conflicts can be resolved. From this perspective the consolidation of heterosexual relations can be seen as a product of the complex interplay of conscious and unconscious dynamics involved in the constitution of femininity.

From the perspective of educational research, it is possible to detect a disjuncture between education and popular culture. Earlier studies of pupil culture describe incidents where magazine readership is regarded as an inherently counter-school activity. Viv Furlong's (1976) study of interaction sets in the classroom recounts an example of girls' reading "comics" which are subsequently removed by the teacher. Similarly, in Fuller's (1984) study of black girls in a London comprehensive school, the reading of magazines in class is generally understood, by teachers and pupils, as an "illegitimate activity" (1984, p. 83) to be ranked alongside chatting and avoiding work as strategies of opposition which could be utilized by pupils at certain moments to register their intolerance of school routines. These incidents are suggestive of the ways in which dominant educational discourses have traditionally eschewed "the popular" as intellectually impoverished and unworthy of critical attention. By contrast, the official school curriculum has occupied a reified status which, simultaneously, bespeaks erudition, refinement, and self-improvement while concealing the "inherited selections of interests" (Williams 1965, p. 172) which constitute it.

Educationalists have documented the ways in which the "new" sociology of education of the 1960s began to ask critical questions about educational values and the role of the school (see, for example, Hammersley and Woods 1976; Whitty 1985 for a discussion of these themes). This emergent body of work was directly concerned with children's learning in relation to issues of social class and educational achievement and drew upon ethnographic methods to explore such themes. As Hammersley and Woods (1976) articulated it,

> Instead of school achievement being taken to be the product of some mysterious "intelligence," people began to ask, What exactly are pupils required to learn in school? The obverse of this was also posed at the same time: Is there something else besides the official curriculum that is learned? (p. 2).

Here there was an acknowledgement that "learning" extended the boundaries of the official curriculum and that it may have inadvertent effects; what is learned by pupils is not necessarily what is intended by teachers and educational policymakers. Hammersley and Woods further suggest that what pupils learn, as gleaned from research of the period, can be seen in terms of conformity to school values. Through participation in school routines, pupils "learn" to conform or resist the official culture of the school as elaborated in the identification of pro-school and anti-school groupings in studies such as Rosser and Harré's (1976) *The Meaning of Trouble* and Willis's (1977) "Learning to Labour."

This chapter focuses on "conformity" and "learning" of a different sort. I would like to suggest that the "hidden curriculum" can also be seen in terms of the regulation of sex-gender categories. Within the context of school much informal learning takes place concerned with issues of gender and sexuality; the homophobia of young men, the sexual reputations of young women, and the pervasive presence of heterosexuality as an "ideal" and a practice mark out the terrain for the production of gendered and sexualized identities. Furthermore, such social learning is overt and explicit rather than "hidden." Specifically, this chapter explores the ways in which magazines aimed at an adolescent female market can be seen as cultural resources for learning about issues of sexuality. In focusing on magazine readership in school I am interested in investigating the following research questions: In what way is the school a site for learning in relation to issues of gender and sexuality? What do young people learn about gender and sexuality in this context? My analysis suggests that, through engagement with popular cultural forms, young people produce sex-gender identities which provide an arena for the negotiation of peer-group friendships and the consolidation of heterosexual relations. My conversations with young people in school suggest that they are critical readers of popular culture who engage with text in productive ways. They are aware of the ways in which sexual issues are presented to them through the magazine format; this awareness contrasts and occasionally overlaps with sexual learning in more formal contexts such as sex education classes. The comments of young people I spoke with suggest that they have developed a range of strategies for reading, discussing, and negotiating these media messages.

METHODOLOGY

This chapter emerges from an ethnographic school-based study which aims to explore issues of sexual learning in relation to young people. In particular, I consider how secondary school students relate to, utilize, and experience issues of sexuality. In this research I seek to explore the ways in which sexuality can be seen to be shaped and lived through pupil cultures where school students actively ascribe meanings to events within specific social contexts. The study aims to look at two key areas in the field of sexuality and schooling; first, the construction of sexual identities within pupil cultures and second, how the school and its students shape the domain of sexuality through the curriculum and the social institution of the school. Teenage magazines and the place they occupy within the lives of school students can be seen as one feature of this study. The research draws upon and uses a wide range of ethnographic research methods informed by feminist methodology, which acknowledge the importance of reflexivity to the research process (Harding 1987; Hollway 1989; Stanley and Wise 1993). This methodological insight is particularly appropriate for a study which uses students and teachers personal accounts as the basis for collecting and analyzing data within a domain which is already constructed as "private," sensitive, and controversial. Specifically, I use participant observation, group work, and semi-structured interviews with teachers and pupils over a one-year period.

The school is a mixed secondary school for pupils age 11-16 in a large town in the East Midlands area of England. This paper draws upon data collected during the participant observation of a 10-week sex education course for a Year 10 class (age 14-15). During this period a taperecorder was used to generate transcripts of lessons and discussions with students. This data was supplemented by note-taking before and after the sessions. The sex education course forms part of a broader personal and social education program for all pupils in the school. Following the sex education course I conducted group work discussions with boys and girls from the Year 10 class I observed. Although the school students were predominantly white and working class, there were some African-Caribbean students and a small number of middle-class students. This chapter will consider, first, the place of magazines in the lives of students and, second, the ways in which reading practices are gender differentiated. Finally, the methodological approach of the chapter combines the use of ethnographic evidence with textual analysis of magazines to explore the ways in which teen magazines provide a site for sexual learning. The chapter suggests that the relationship between school students and magazine readership involves a complex enactment of gendered identities where young people read the material and the messages within the social context of friendship groups and personal experiences.

MAGAZINES IN CONTEXT

Recently, in the British context, there has been some debate concerning appropriate reading material for adolescent girls. Teenage magazines such as *More!* and *Sugar* have been at the center of this controversy. Media attention in the form of news items on television and in the tabloid press have suggested that these teen magazines are too sexually explicit for young women. Concerns over the "corruption" of adolescent girls have found voice in governmental debates and legislative proposals with a Member of Parliament, Peter Luff, declaring that the magazines "rob girls of their innocence".[1] Concerns expressed at this level can be seen, in part, as the articulation of a broader "moral panic" relating to teenage pregnancy, single motherhood, and the provision of state benefits.

During the research period I found that young people frequently used popular cultural forms as a resource and a framework for discussing issues of sexuality. Plots from the soaps such as *Brookside* and *Eastenders*, characters such as Hannah in *Neighbours*, episodes of *Byker Grove*, and TV personalities such as Barrymore were cited and used as reference points in discussions of sexual relationships, physical attraction, parental constraints, and homosexuality. These cultural references acted like roadmaps whereby students could negotiate the hazardous terrain of sexual taboo. They also provided a frame, or way of looking at sexuality, where students could juxtapose their personal experiences to media constructions. Teen magazines can be seen as part of this broader social context; they are a popular, mass produced, and publicly shared media form which speaks to young people in particular ways and enables them to talk back. In this way teen magazines can be seen as a cultural resource for young people which they can, at different moments, "talk with" and "think with."

All of the young women I spoke to, and some of the young men, were regular readers of magazines aimed at an adolescent female market. The young people frequently mentioned magazines such as *Bliss*, *Mizz*, *More!*, *Sugar*, *Just Seventeen*, and *Nineteen* with *Sugar* being the most popular and *More!* the most controversial. The young women were aware of the magazines as playing a part in a developmental process which was guided by age and gender.

> Sophie: I think that *More!* is for older girls really. Like the younger ones [magazines] where you've got, you've got ponies and stuff.
> Naomi: And pictures of kittens.
> Sophie: Yeah, there's like Girltalk and Chatterbox and you go up and you get *Shout* and then you get *Sugar* and *Bliss* and then it's like *Just Seventeen*, *Nineteen*, and then it's *More!* and then it's *Woman's Own* and stuff like that. So you got the range.

The "going up" that Sophie refers to can be related to the gendered experience of moving from girlhood to adolescence and into womanhood where particular magazines may be seen as cultural markers in the developmental process. The reproduction of a specific class-cultural femininity is naturalized within the magazines as an appeal based on age and gender. Angela McRobbie (1978a, 1978b, 1981, 1991) has commented on the ways in which *Jackie* magazine of the 1970s introduced the girl to adolescence by mapping out the personal terrain, "outlining its landmarks and characteristics in detail and stressing the problematic features as well as fun" (1991, p. 83). McRobbie's analysis of the multiple ways in which *Jackie* worked demonstrates that the different features of the magazine are involved in reproducing a culture of femininity cohering around the concept of romance. From this perspective *Jackie* can be seen as preparatory literature for a feminine, rather than a feminist career; the search for a "fella," the privileging of "true love," and an induction into repetitive beauty routines which can be seen as an introduction to domestic labor. Penny Tinkler (1995) in her study of popular magazines for girls during the period 1920-1950 similarly suggests that these magazines actively "construct girlhood" by according significance to age, social class, and girls' position in the heterosexual career.

Martin Barker's (1989) research suggests other ways of looking at these magazines which problematizes the feminist assumption that *Jackie* is "bad for girls." His analysis indicates that a knowledge of the history of the production of magazines can contribute to an understanding of the ways in which magazines can be seen as specific cultural products, produced within a context of technical and social compromises and constraints which change over time. Factors relating to the physical production of magazines such as machinery, resources, artistic input, and marketing, complexify notions of "reproduction" where to see *Jackie* as ideological purveyor of a culture of femininity overlooks many other factors which make the magazine what it is. Barker's reading of *Jackie* postulates that the magazine has an agenda that is based on "living out an unwritten contract with its readers" (1989, p. 165). The "contract" is premised on active engagement of the reader with the magazine—the magazine invites a reader to collaborate by reading in particular ways:

> The "contract" involves an agreement that a text will talk to us in ways we recognise. It will enter into a dialogue with us. And that dialogue, with its dependable elements and form, will relate to some aspects of our lives in our society (p. 261).

Barker points out that the contractual understanding between magazine and implied reader is reliant on social context. The act of reading can be seen as a process capable of creating feelings of mutual recognition and familiarity between the reader and the features of the magazine. Barker's reading of Jackie and other magazines develops a textual analysis which emphasizes the interactive engagement of the reader with the magazine, where both parties are involved in a conversation premised on shared social experiences and expectations. By contrast, Joke Hermes's (1995) study of the readership of women's magazines develops an analysis based on interviews with women who identify themselves as readers of women's magazines. Her audience research indicates that the reading practices of women is mediated by the context of their everyday lives. The "pickupable" and "putdownable" quality of magazines fits in with daily domestic routines women describe and participate in. This contributes to the magazines' popular appeal as an appropriate companion for women in moments of "relaxation," signifying the demarcation of personal space within a busy day. I am indebted to feminist scholarship on magazines and the insights of Barker and Hermes where the use of different methodological approaches contributes to our understanding of magazines and acts of readership. Barker (1989) and Hermes (1995) suggest that the reading of magazines can be seen, respectively, as a contractual understanding between reader and magazine and an integral part of everyday routines in the lives of women. The ethnographic study I conducted suggests that the reading of magazines by students in school is shaped by the context of school relations where gender displays are enacted collectively through friendship groups and peer relations.

SCHOOL-BASED READING PRACTICES AND GENDER DIFFERENCES

Group work discussions with young women and young men in school indicates that gender plays a key role in shaping the attitudes and practices whereby young people read magazines. This theme is further elaborated by researchers in this field where there is an acknowledgment of the significance of gender to reading patterns and levels of literacy among school-age students (see, for example, Alloway and Gilbert 1997; Davies 1997; Millard 1997). Within this literature the investments in particular reading practices by young woman provides a point of contrast with the nonparticipation of young men. Many young women I talked with spoke of magazine reading as a regular collective practice. Within the context of the school day this involved the reading of magazines in breaks and lunchtime as well as in certain lessons such as drama, English, and personal and social education where the magazine features and format could inform discussions and classroom activities.

MJK: Do you read the magazines together?
Ruth: We used to, all the time.
Amy: Sometimes we do.
Ruth: When we've got a magazine we do, we have a good laugh.
Joanne: Like if one person buys it and brings it into school, we all look through it together, so we don't buy four separate copies.
Amy: Some of them make you laugh though, don't they?

For these young women reading magazines can be seen as a shared, school-based activity which female friendship groups draw upon as a resource for humor. Here the "contract" between the magazine and the reader which Barker refers to has been extended to the friendship group where readership offers the group the opportunity for dialogue at the level of collective experience. McRobbie (1981) has commented on the way in which girls' collective reading of *Jackie* may be oppositional, citing an example of a group of girls truanting from lessons to do a *Jackie* quiz in the toilets. Within the school context such activities can be seen as a point of resistance to the organizational structure of the school day where magazine reading serves to disrupt and fracture everyday routines rather than fit in with them. However, as Walkerdine (1990) has pointed out, not all acts of resistance against school authority have revolutionary effects: they may have "reactionary" effects too. In this case young women locate themselves within a class-cultural dynamic where they actively choose reading magazines and "learning" femininity as an alternative to attending lessons (see also Nava 1984).

By contrast, the reading of magazines did not appear to occupy a similar social space among male peer groups. In a group work session with boys, the absence of magazines for young males which speaks to them of social/sexual issues appears to generate feelings of emasculation and suspicion.

MJK: Do you wish there was a boys' magazine?
Blake: Nah, you'd get called a sissy wouldn't you? [all laugh]
Christopher: Well there are some like *Loaded* and there's *Q* and *Maxim* as well with things like football, sex, and clothes.
Blake: You're an expert you are! [all laugh]
MJK: If there was a magazine like that for your age group—what about that?
Andrew: Yeah, I wouldn't mind buying a magazine like that sometimes but I wouldn't, like the girls do, buy it every week, that's just too—I wouldn't like that. I'd only buy it when there was

something in it like an article or something. You know, sometimes like when you get into a situation and you don't know
what you're doing it would help then if there was a magazine
to tell you what to do then.

The responses of the boys indicates that their reading of magazines is
more of an individual than the group activity it is for girls. The boys
indicate that reading magazines risks being regarded as "sissy," a derog-
atory term suggesting such practices could be less than manly. Eric
Rofes (1995) documents the painful experiences of "sissy" boys in the
American school system where bullying and abuse become part of a
process of othering, establishing differences between dominant and subordinate groups of males (see also Haywood 1996; Mac an Ghaill 1996;
Kehily and Nayak 1997 for a further discussion of masculinities and the
production of heterosexual hierarchies in educational settings). Rofes
notes that, "sissy boys have become contemporary youth's primary
exposure to gay identity" (1995, p. 81). The shared laughter of Blake,
Andrew, and Christopher at Blake's connection of magazine readership
for males with being a "sissy" indicates that there is group recognition/
surveillance relating to gender appropriate behavior for young males.[2]
Here, the reading of teen magazines comes dangerously close to falling
beyond the bounds of publicly acceptable behavior for male peer
groups. Christopher's awareness of magazines aimed at a male readership and his willingness to name and discuss them, is viewed by Blake
as a form of "expertise" which generates more laughter. In the context
of male peer groups in school, Christopher's "knowledge" may be hazardous to the presentation of a socially recognized male identity.
Andrew's comments specifically see magazines as a manual or reference book to be consulted as and when necessary to solve particular
individual problems. His expressed distaste for regular readership "like
the girls do" is suggestive of the resonant interplay of internal anxieties
and external policing where there may be a fear of dependency and a
need to display an emotional self-sufficiency based on investments in an
imagined masculine ideal.

Hermes (1995) notes the enjoyment of gossip magazines among certain gay men where a camp fantasy world of appearances, trivia, and
"bad taste" is celebrated. Here pleasure in subversion turns the reading
of gossip magazines into a "performative art" (Hermes 1995, p. 137)
and establishes points of difference between gays and dominant culture.
This social practice contrasts sharply with the group of boys in school

who articulate their ideas within a dominant culture of masculinity where an unspoken desire to assert themselves as heterosexual structures the discussion. The boys' attempt to distance themselves from the perceived reading practices of girls may be voicing an internal fear of camp, where to embrace magazines in the same way as girls may create internal anxieties about becoming gay/female or "sissy" as Blake puts it. The comments of the boys in relation to magazine readership is suggestive of the complex dynamics involved in the relationship between cultural forms and the constitution of gendered subjectivities. For the young men in this group there is a collective investment in forms of masculinity premised upon heterosexual desire and the enactment of a gendered identity defined as against females and gay men (Connell 1989; Mac an Ghaill 1994; Nayak and Kehily 1996). In this exchange the concern to demonstrate competence, self-reliance, and an independence from cultural products become signifiers for a particular, publicly displayed, and socially validated form of masculinity.

Treatment of homosexual themes by teen magazines such as *More!* and *Sugar* do little to challenge the homophobias present within pupil sexual cultures. A "real-life drama" in *More!* publicized on the front cover as, "My gay friend Ian stole my man!" illustrates some of the ways in which homosexuality is positioned as a deviant and marginal practice, existing at the fringes of a centered and normalizing heterosexuality. Tina tells her story of meeting her "soulmate," Jules, and discovering he is gay by reading his diary:

> I'll never forget the hideous, sick feeling that swept over me. As I turned each page, details of their secret liaisons leapt out....It described "rolling around together" and kissing. Thank God there were no descriptions of full sex.

Tina's description of the gay relationship between Jules and Ian reveals a strong sense of repulsion and disgust. The "hideous, sick feeling" experienced when gay sexual practices are inferred contrasts sharply with the normalization of heterosexual penetrative sex, visibly displayed on other pages of the magazine. Tina's narrative can be read teleologically, pathologizing Jules's homosexuality and problematizing their relationship in the light of her discovery. The realization that Jules "simply was gay" engages Tina in a reconstruction of their past where a low sex drive, lack of excitement during sex, sexual conservatism, and an absence of jealousy become signifiers of a latent homosexuality.

Tina's account moves toward narrative closure with her reflections on meeting her new partner, David:

> It was the best thing that ever happened to me. I'd forgotten what it was like to have sex more than once and not just in the missionary position. But I asked David early on, "Are you sure you don't prefer men?" It's an odd question to ask, but I never want that to happen to me again. Now I feel lucky I didn't marry Jules, have two kids and find out the truth when I was 40.

Tina's good fortune is seen as an escape from the inadequacies of gay masculinity where to marry someone who also enjoys same-sex relationships would ultimately be a regrettable error and a waste of a life. The presence of homophobias in pupil cultures and teen magazines is illustrative of the different ways in which sexualities are regulated. Gendered differences in reading practices and the associated meanings generated collectively by boys and girls in school reveal that teen magazines are more likely to be a cultural resource for sexual learning among young women than among young men. This has implications for classroom practice and, particularly, the ways in which personal and social education programs relate to young men.

SEXUAL LEARNING—PROBLEM PAGES

Problem pages in magazines can be seen as an interactive space specifically set up for producers of the magazine and readers to engage in dialogue. Rosalind Coward (1984) comments on the spectacle of public confession to be found in problem pages which encourage readers to view these pages as a distinct sub-genre of sexual fiction producing culturally specific ways of knowing oneself:

> problem pages are themselves a historically specific symptom of the way in which sexuality and its emotional consequences have been catapulted to the foreground in our culture as the true expression of our intimate selves (p. 137).

The incitement to share problems, particularly sexual problems can be seen as constitutive of a sexualized subjectivity, a technology bringing into being a discursively produced "deep" self that can be situated within a field of social regulation (Foucault 1976). My research findings suggest that young women self-regulate their use of magazines to enable discussion and informal learning of sexual issues. Problem pages in particular are read and discussed collectively by young women in school.

They are viewed as a "laugh," not to be taken seriously, and, simultaneously, as a way of framing personal problems, emotional concerns, and "boy trouble." Boys and girls in school shared a skepticism and enjoyment of problem pages, often mentioning the problem page as the first page they turn to when they open a magazine. The following extract demonstrates the ways in which young women distance themselves from the problem page and, at the same time, find the feature compelling.

> Rebecca: Yeah, the agony aunts, they're good.
>
> Sophie: They're good because a lot of people enjoy reading that sort of page, if you buy a magazine you go straight to the problems for the information.
>
> Julia: Yeah!
>
> Rebecca: Yeah you read the problem but not the advice. [all laugh]
>
> MJK: Why is the problem more interesting than the advice?
>
> Rebecca: I don't know, it just is.
>
> Sophie: Some people find it really—fascinating.
>
> Julia: Yeah if the problem is to do with you then you read the advice but otherwise you just go on to the next one (problem).

Rebecca, Sophie, and Julia suggest that the "fascination" of the problem page lies primarily in reading about a problem where the "information" to be gleaned is contained within the problem as the reader expresses it rather than in advice given by the experienced agony aunt (see Lee 1983, pp. 80-91 for an interesting discussion of the difficulties of being an "agony aunt"). However, if the problem is "to do with you" and can be seen as an articulation of your own situation in some way, then advice may be read. McRobbie asserts that the problem page in *Jackie*, known as the "Cathy and Claire" page, "sums up the ideological content of the magazine" (1978a, p. 29) by giving girls culturally loaded messages in the form of guidance to be heeded by the sensible girl. Barker's analysis of the "Cathy and Claire" page found most advice to be "specific and commonsensical" (1989, p. 160) where girls are encouraged to take a close look at themselves, their reasons for writing, their personality, and self-confidence. He suggests that the significance of the "Cathy and Claire" page revolves around girls being asked to engage in a personal reevaluation, to look in at themselves in different ways and to see their feelings and emotions from other perspectives. My ethnographic evidence, however, suggests that the advice is of marginal interest and the focus of appeal for young people in schools is in the problem itself which may be read in friendship groups and discussed critically in terms of pleasure, humor, empathy, and disbelief:

Andrew:	Some of them (problems) are pretty terrible, I reckon some people just write for fun. When you're reading them—they can't possibly be for real.
Christopher:	You can't take them seriously.
Tim:	Yeah, you can't take them seriously.
Andrew:	You can't imagine someone not knowing stuff like that.
MJK:	So you think that some people, they haven't got a problem really but they just sit down and...
Andrew:	Yeah, just write in for a joke, see if it gets published or not, just for something to do.

The views of the boys express a disdain of ignorance, "you can't imagine people not knowing stuff like that" which is working with a sense of amusement and "fun" where writing to problem pages can be seen a practical joke to relieve boredom and generate humor. In this exchange Andrew, Christopher, and Tim position themselves as knowledgeable and discerning readers able to detect the "for real" problems from the wind-ups. Problems which do not appear credible are not worthy of being taken seriously. Viewing the problems with a sense of disbelief which can be explained in terms of ignorance or tomfoolery enables these young men to establish a distance from the feature and the problems. The incredulity of the boys was also shared by many of the girls I spoke with:

Clare:	They (the problems) look as though they're made up.
Ruth:	They do, some of them are really silly.
Joanne:	Sometimes it's like really serious 'cos we have them in Drama when you're reading it and some of them are just, you know, really serious.
Amy:	You wouldn't say that kind of thing or put it in a magazine or even write it...
Joanne:	If you're desperate you would.
Ruth:	Yeah!
Clare:	Yeah!
Amy:	You know, they don't sound real.

Clare: Half the time I think they're made up, people do it for a laugh and then they (the staff at the magazine) take it seriously, or the editors make them up.

Ruth: At the start of, like, *Sugar*, when *Sugar* first came out there was a problem page in it and, like, how d'you know where to write to 'cos the magazine hasn't come out yet.

Clare: Well maybe they just make up the first ones.

In this discussion the group of girls work through their feelings of disbelief, empathy, and deception which contribute to the contradictory appeal of problem pages. The "silliness" of some problems and the "seriousness" of others combine to create distrust of the feature, grounded in evidence that new magazines have problem pages in their first issue before a readership has been established. The deception involving readers and editors fabricating problems is punctured at one moment when Joanne asserts that if you were "desperate" you would write to a problem page. This is echoed by the affirming voices of Ruth and Clare. Joanne, Ruth, and Clare are responding to Amy's point that some problems as printed in magazines transgress certain boundaries by speaking the unspeakable, "You wouldn't say that kind of thing or put it in a magazine or even write it." The responses of the other girls indicate that, in cases of extreme distress, you would talk about taboo subjects. This understanding that the magazine can assist in difficulties by placing them "out there" simultaneously gives girls' license to discuss these issues among themselves. From this perspective problem pages can be seen to open up areas for discussion by giving young women access to a particular discourse; ways of talking about issues and emotions, giving experiences a vocabulary within the language of the felt. My discussions with young men and women indicate that young people collectively negotiate their responses to problem page features within the context of friendship groups. Here, friends act as mediators and regulators of "problems," determining whether they should be dismissed, humored, taken seriously, or discussed further. The activities of young men and women in this respect indicates that, within the context of the school, peer group relations play an important part in the social regulation of sexual discourse, offering a sphere for conveying sex-gender identities. The gendered dynamics of these exchanges illustrate the distancing displays of young men in relation to cultural products and sexual problems while young women appear more open to discussion in this area.

SEXUAL LEARNING AND CULTURES OF FEMININITY

The problem pages, like other regular features of the magazine such as the stories and fashion pages, present points of continuity for readers, providing them with a familiar format and set of expectations:

Sara: I find *Sugar* good value.

Laura: I like *Sugar*, I get *Sugar*.

Catherine: *Just Seventeen*, I get that every week.

Sara: In every issue of *Sugar* there's always something about sex, something involving sex.

Catherine: There's like good stories in there as well about "I was terrorized by a flasher" and stuff like this. Someone with really bad problems will write in and they get really helped and next month they write back and say "Thank you" and a bit of their little note will be in there saying "Thank you" and stuff like that.

Here, the agreement that *Sugar* is "good value" and a good read is supported by Sara, Laura, and Catherine. A salient feature of every issue is "something involving sex" as Sara puts it. This "something" could be expressed in the problem page or in stories such as I was terrorized by a flasher. The comments of the girls suggest that problems and stories are read alongside one another and conform to their expectations of the magazine speaking to them about sex. The problem page in particular provides a direct link between the magazine and the reader by creating a cozy, interactive environment where intimacies can be shared. Catherine's comments suggest that individuals can be "helped" by the problem page which provides a linear trace of events through the problem, advice offered, and expressions of gratitude.

Teen magazines containing features on sex and readers expecting to be informed and entertained by the sexual content of the magazine can be seen as part of the contractual understanding that Barker (1989) refers to. However, the young women I spoke to indicated that this source of sexual knowledge is viewed critically by individuals and mediated by friendship groups. *More!* magazine in particular aroused controversy among the young women:

Clare: But that *More!* really goes into it. I mean some of the stories are, you know, you wouldn't want to tell anybody about 'em. Like, if you look in those other magazines they say, "My boyfriend did

> this and what can I do?" and a story and there's other stories you
> would want to tell your friends at your age. But that *More!* mag-
> azine, it's more, you know, for seventeen year olds to read 'cos
> it goes too into depth with them.
>
> Amy: In fairness to *More!* though, it aims at a higher age group, so,
> like, it's younger peoples' fault if they read it, or their mom and
> dads' fault.
>
> MJK: But you'd find, like, things in, say, *Sugar*, you'd all talk about
> among yourselves?
>
> Clare: Yeah.
>
> Amy: Yeah we would.
>
> Ruth: Yeah.
>
> Amy: But you couldn't do the same with *More!* magazine.
>
> MJK: Because of embarrassment?
>
> Amy: It is yeah. You say, "Oh I saw this in this magazine" and then
> everybody starts laughing at you.
>
> Clare: Yeah, it just goes over the top really.

In this discussion Clare, Amy, and Ruth suggest that *More!* breaks the
contract between magazine and readers by being too sexually explicit.
By printing stories "you wouldn't want to tell anybody about" *More!* is
placed beyond the collective reading practices of these young women.
The embarrassment of the young women suggests that their reputations
may be tainted by reading and embracing *More!* magazine. Amy's comments, particularly, indicate that to repeat features to friends may result
in embarrassment and humiliation, "everybody starts laughing at you."
This collective action which relies on humor to deride and "other" a
member of the group is illustrative of the ways in which these young
women negotiate some subjects deemed appropriate for discussion and
successfully marginalize others. This active engagement with issues
arising from the reading of magazines suggests that female friendship
groups provide a site for the enactment of a particular culture of femininity. This culture of femininity may, at moments, work to expel other
cultures of femininity such as those contained in the pages of *More!*
magazine and external to the friendship group. In this context the "too
in depth" and "over the top" features of *More!* transgress the boundaries
of legitimacy defined by these young women as suitable for their age
group and feminine identities. Cindy Patton has commented on the ways
in which identities carry with them a "requirement to act which is felt as
"what a person like me does" (1993, p. 147). Clare, Amy, and Ruth indicate that female friendship groups adopt a collective "requirement to

act" in relation to issues of sexuality which appears to be anchored in an agreed notion of "what girls like us do." This action can be seen to be concerned with the establishment and maintenance of a particular moral agenda which marks out the terrain for discussion and/or action. Female friendship groups, in moments of collective action, "draw the line" (Canaan 1986, p. 193) to demarcate the acceptable from the unacceptable. In these moments female friendship groups incorporate spheres or practices they feel comfortable with and displace practices that do not concur with their collectively defined feminine identities. In Canaan's U.S. study concerning middle-class young women and sexuality, young women who do not "draw the line" incur a reputation as "the other kinda girl" (1986, p. 190), the sexually promiscuous and much denigrated female figure whose lack of adherence to conventional morality serves as a "cautionary tale" for young women to be ever vigilant in the maintenance of their reputation.[3] The collective activity of female friendship groups in relation to the reading of teenage magazines can be seen as part of a constant and sustained engagement in the production of school-based femininities. These processes involve the continual negotiation and delineation of acceptable and unacceptable behavior/action which bespeak and thereby bring into being feminine identities. The collective investment in particular feminine identities as expressed by the young women I spoke with reveals the associative link between magazine reading and identity work as mutually constitutive acts in their everyday social interactions in school. The creative energy involved in the constitutive enactment of a particular femininity is suggestive of the labor involved in the production of sex-gender identities and can be seen as an attempt to fix and consolidate continually shifting social and psychic locations.

MORE! IS TOO MUCH

Recently McRobbie (1996) has commented on the ways in which contemporary teenage magazines such as *More!* embrace and display an intensification of interest in sexuality. She notes that this sexual material is marked by features such as exaggeration, self-parody, and irony which suggest new forms of sexual conduct for young women:

> this sexual material marks a new moment in the construction of female sexual identities. It proposes boldness (even brazenness) in behaviour....Magazine dis-

course brings into being new female subjects through these incitations (pp. 177-178).

My ethnographic evidence suggests that this "new moment in the construction of female sexual identities" is actively resisted by the young women I spoke with. A closer look at the content of *More!* magazine may offer an insight into practices and behaviors which were points of concern for the young women. A regular feature of *More!* magazine is a two-page item called "Sextalk." This includes an assortment of information about sex such as answers to readers questions, sex definitions, sex "factoids," short "news" items, and "position of the fortnight"—a line drawing and explanatory text on positions for heterosexual penetrative sex such as "backwards bonk" and "side by side." The following are examples of a "sex definition" and "sex factoid" from two issues of *More!*:

Sex Factoid:

Once ejaculated, the typical sperm travels five-and-a-half inches an hour—that's about twice as fast as British Rail! (*More!*, Issue 198, 25 October-7 November 1995)

Sex definition:

Penis Captivus

The act of holding his penis tightly in your vaginal muscles during sex (hold it too tight and he can develop a castration complex). (*More!*, Issue 208, 13-16 March, 1996).

The combination of "fact," definitions, drawings, and advice found in "Sextalk," expressed colloquially and with humor, points to a departure from the ideology of romance as expressed in teen magazines such as *Jackie* (McRobbie 1981; Winship 1985) and a move toward the technology of sex where consensual procedures organize and monitor human activity (Foucault 1976). From a Foucaultian perspective the proliferation of sexual material in teen magazines can be seen to demarcate a terrain for social regulation where the exercise of power is productive rather than repressive. Ways of having intercourse, things to try, things to ask "your man" to try, ways of looking and thinking in relation to sex, privilege heterosexual penetrative intercourse as the cornerstone of sexual relationships. In the "Sextalk" feature of *More!* magazine sexual activity is demystified through line drawings and instructive text, presented and discussed in ways that encode heterosexuality. This can be interpreted as the creation of a site where heterosex can be learned, desired, and manipulated, where sexual experimentation and pleasure leads to a particular expertise. The link between sexual knowledge and pleasure established in the "Sextalk" feature privileges sexual identity as a way of knowing our "inner" selves and, of course, "our man." In this feature the magazine appropriates a discourse of sexual liberation as articulated in 1970s sex manuals such as the Alex Comfort collection, *The Joy of Sex* (1974). Here, the language, style, and diagrammatic mode of instruction suggests to young women that the route to sexual emancipation lies in the "doing it" and talking about "doing it" of male-female fucking. Many young women I spoke to regarded *More!*'s up-front, "over the top" approach to sex as embarrassing, disgusting, and "too much" (Lara). The responses of many young women I spoke with indicate that *More!* literally is "too much"; its sexual excesses denote that it is not be taken seriously and requires regulation at the level of peer-group interaction. Some young women reported that their parents had banned them from buying *More!*, while another said she had bought it once and "binned it" (Joanne). In discussions I conducted with young women, the regular feature "position of the fortnight" was spoken about in ways which fused embarrassment with a moral discourse of censorship and self-censorship:

      Catrina: Oh, I saw that, totally...
       Laura: Yeah. [all laugh]
        Sara: Yes, well.
    Catherine: I don't think we should say anymore about that!
         MJK: Are we talking about position of the fortnight? [all laugh]
         All: Yeah.
       Laura: My sister has one and it had like the best positions or something.
         All: Ughhh. [muted laughter]
         MJK: What do you think of that then?
    Catherine: I think there should be age limits on that kind of thing.
       Laura: There should be a lock on the front!

In this discussion the embarrassment of the young women can be seen in the half sentences, laughter, and exclamations of disgust which reveal a reluctance to name and acknowledge the topic they are speaking about, "I don't think we should say any more about that!" My attempt to name and explore the issue in the question, "Are we talking about position of the fortnight?" produces more laughter and embarrassment which further suggests that *More!* transgresses the bounds of the speakable for these young women. Catherine and Laura's expression of censorship, "I think there should be age limits on that kind of thing" and, "There should be a lock on the front!" may indicate that appropriation of a moral, parental discourse, in this case, offers an unambiguous way of othering "position of the fortnight" illustrative of their distaste of the feature. For Catherine and Laura, explicit details of sex or as they put it, "that kind of thing" is clearly not their kind of thing—a matter they feel comfortable with or wish to be associated with. In this exchange the young women discursively position themselves as untouched by the sexual material of *More!* and resistant to the possibility of new female sexual subjectivities/behavior referred to by McRobbie (1996). The moralism of the young women and expressions of disgust in relation to issues of sexuality finds points of resonance with Freudian analysis where childhood is seen as a period of (relative) sexual latency producing mental forces of shame, disgust, and claims of aesthetic and moral ideals which impede the course of the sexual instinct (Freud 1905). In the transition from childhood to adulthood these negative associations can be expressed and reconciled in the consolidation of heterosexual relations. The adverse reactions to the sexual content of *More!* can be seen to produce a moment of collective psychic and social positioning where young women take refuge in childhood approaches to sexuality rather than the older and potentially threatening domain offered by *More!* Of course, this does not mean that young women do not enjoy talking about sex or engaging in sexual activity. Rather, it suggests the power and agency of female friendship groups where, at certain moments, a collective approach to sexuality can be shared, regulated, and expressed.

THE JIGSAW PUZZLE OF SEXUAL LEARNING

In other moments, however, the young women I spoke with did discuss issues of sex and sexuality in positive and affirming ways. In these discussions they suggested that some teen magazines such as *Sugar* and *Just Seventeen* were a useful source of information on sexual matters. Their comments in these examples indicate that magazines can serve as a supplement to formal sex education classes in school and other forms of communication on sex such as leaflets and discussions with parents and peers. Rachel Thomson and Sue Scott (1991) comment on the ways in which young women in their study pieced together information from different sources in their search for sexual knowledge:

> The young women we spoke to reported learning by "picking things up" and "just catching on"...[young women] would frequently search for sexual references in any available sources such as popular sex manuals, "Jackie Collins" books and most commonly in magazines aimed at young women (Thomson and Scott 1991, pp. 27-31).

Hermes (1995) suggests that women read magazines through a range of different repertoires where acts of readership engage them in ways of making sense of their experiences in relation to the contents of the magazine. The repertoire of "emotional learning and connected knowing" is identified by Hermes as a way of dealing with emotions, validating experience, and developing understanding. In the following example, young women "connect" knowledge gained in a sex education class with pictorial advice in a magazine. In this case the sexual learning relates to a demonstration on the use of condoms:

MJK: What did you think of the putting the condoms on?

Ruth: That was good that was...

Clare: It was good actually 'cos, like, I didn't know how to put it on. [laughs]

Ruth: At least you got a chance to try.

Joanne: It was in the magazines as well.

Ruth: You can see what they're like in real life rather than just pictures.

Joanne: Yeah, it was in that magazine wasn't it? The *Sugar* magazine and what to do, so if you did in class you'd know you can do it yourself, you build up a better picture.

In this example, school-based sex education and commercially produced magazines can be seen to work together in a productive way, "building up a better picture" by providing advice that young women find helpful. Hermes (1995) suggests that the repertoire of connected knowing offers the potential for developing understandings which can give women feelings of increased strength. This is both real and imagined as women are preparing themselves for difficulties and entertaining fantasies of becoming a "wise woman." The critical approach of young women in school suggest that magazines and acts of readership play a part in the connections and renouncements made in relation to sexual learning. Their comments indicate that popular cultural forms are continually mediated and negotiated collectively by female friendship groups. In such moments issues of sexuality can be opened up through shared reading and discussion and closed down through derisive laughter, evasive maneuvres, and moral appeals. The actions and behavior of young women indicate that they are discerning and self-regulating in relation to sexual matters and magazine readership. Their discriminating approach could be a valuable resource in sexuality education programs where the use of teen magazines offers the potential for common ground between teachers and pupils' sexual cultures.

"NOT THE THING BOYS DO": CONNECTIONS AND DISCONNECTIONS

The responses of young men, however, to areas of potential "connected knowing" tell a different story. Here, the use of teen magazines in formal spaces such as sex education lessons produces embarrassment for boys and a reluctance to enter into the discourse of popular culture. Researchers have commented on the disruptive behavior and nonparticipation of boys in school-based sex education programs and the ways in which such programs fail to meet the needs of young men (Lupton and Tulloch 1996; Measor, Tiffin, and Fry 1996; Sex Education Forum 1997). During my time in school I observed a personal and social education lesson involving an activity where pupils were asked to create problems and share advice for a fictitious problem page. This activity sees girls as active and willing participants while boys attempt to enact a cool detachment from the imaginative exercise of writing and discussing "problems." Of the seven "letters" read aloud by pupils, six were written by girls, with girls playing a more prominent part in the discussion of all "problems." A follow-up discussion with a group of girls reveals their awareness of the boys' unease and discomfort. They explained it in the following terms:

> Joanne: The boys were dying of embarrassment! [all laugh]
> Ruth: Yeah, I know, maybe 'cos we read the magazines, they don't read them. Like for us there is a problem page in every magazine, girls magazine, but they don't have them in the boys magazines,

like football magazines and that—you don't see a problem
page—so that's probably why.

The comments of the girls indicate that they have a familiarity with
problem pages which boys do not share. This gives the young women a
vocabulary to articulate social/sexual problems based on collective
experience and mutual recognition. The laughter of the girls suggests
that they take pleasure in their shared knowledge and in the obvious
embarrassment of the boys in the class. Researchers have commented
on the ways in which young women actively use sexuality and an exaggerated femininity as a strategy to resist, challenge, and embarrass
teachers and boys (Anyon 1983; Lees 1986; Skeggs 1991; Kehily and
Nayak 1996). Here, sexual knowledge developed within female friendship groups can become a way of disrupting dominant power relations
when used in more formal contexts such as the classroom.

Follow-up discussion with a group of boys suggests that their lack of
dialogue around certain issues may be part of a struggle to perform a
coherent masculine identity where boys' negotiation of speech boundaries differs from girls:

MJK: Have you all—among yourselves—have you spoken about
        things on the [sex education] course?
James: Not really.
Andrew: No, not like that.
MJK: You don't, why not?
Blake: 'Cos we already know it. [all laugh]
Blake: I do anyway.
MJK: Well, that doesn't mean you can't talk about it does it?
Blake: True, true.
MJK: So why is it that you don't talk about relationships and sex?
Blake: Not the thing boys do.
Andrew: Not the things boys do.

Here, Blake offers two reasons for the absence of such discussion
among boys; they "know it already" and it is "not the thing boys do."
Andrew's reiteration of this point indicates that the boys' invest in a
masculine identity premised on assumed knowledge and the conceal-
ment of vulnerabilities. Here, denial and effacement can be seen as necessary repetitions for the presentation of a particular version of
masculinity. Julian Wood (1984) and Chris Haywood (1996) note the

ways in which boys sex talk commonly manifests itself as a loud public display of sexism and bravado. For a boy, to talk about sex in other ways, such as sharing a problem with other boys, seeking and giving advice, may risk being regarded as transgressive male behavior. Blake's performance within the group as the lad who knows all about sex and says so receives social recognition from the other boys in the form of shared laughter; the display of sparse words and implied sexual knowledge/action, "we already know it," is endorsed. In this exchange Blake, Andrew, and James demonstrate that sexual knowledge becomes a burden to be assumed and works with a collective desire to suppress anxieties, doubts, and areas of ignorance in pursuit of an imagined masculine ideal. The discussions I conducted with girls and boys in school may suggest that sex-gender identities are played out within different cultures variously defined as "masculine" or "feminine" (see Thorne 1993). My argument, however, is not for the establishment and maintenance of different cultures of femininity and masculinity in school. Rather, it is that cultural products have the power to tap into social and psychic investments producing gender-differentiated displays, repetitions, and practices. Here, it is the meanings and associations given to teen magazines by groups of boys and girls that produce gender displays resonant with "doing" gender as, simultaneously, an imaginary ideal and an everyday practice. In the examples cited, acts of readership offer a sphere for the enactment of sex-gender identities which are mediated and regulated collectively by people like us. In such moments teen magazines can be embraced or repelled, believed or doubted, discussed or censored, incorporated or othered.

CONCLUDING COMMENTS

This paper has focused on the ways in which teen magazines provide a site for learning in relation to issues of sexuality. Ethnographic evidence suggests that young people in school use popular cultural forms as a resource and framework to facilitate discussion, thought, and action within the sexual domain. Young women, in particular, enjoy teen magazines and view them as cultural markers in an externally constructed developmental process demarcated by age and gender. For young women, collective reading of teen magazines offers an opportunity for dialogue where femininities can be endlessly produced, defined, and enhanced. The responses of young men, however, indicate that reader-

ship of teen magazines takes on a different gendered significance where
boys express a reluctance to engage in regular readership or acts of collective readership and view such practices as emasculating. The relationship between reading practices and gender difference indicates that
of acts of readership offer a sphere for producing and conveying
sex-gender identities in school. Here, peer group relations play a part in
the mediation and regulation of reading practices, where embracing
magazines and repelling them can be viewed as a gender display
intended to purvey a particular masculinity or femininity. The processes
involved in the production and consolidation of school-based masculinities and femininities suggest that cultural products have the power to
tap into social and psychic investments, producing gender differentiated
enactments, repetitions, and practices. Here, it is the meanings and associations ascribed to magazines by groups of boys and girls which produce public demonstrations of doing gender. The performative
expression of these displays suggest that gendered identities operate,
simultaneously, as imagined ideal and everyday practice in the lives of
young women and men in school (see Walkerdine 1990 and Butler 1990
for further discussion of the ways in which gender can be seen as "performance").

The sexual content of contemporary teen magazines can be seen as
part of a "contractual understanding" (Barker 1989) between the magazine and its readership where readers expect to be informed and entertained by sexual issues. In acts of collective readership, young people in
school negotiate and regulate sexual discourse in ways that affirm their
gender identities. In such moments sexual issues can be discussed or
censored, laughed with or laughed at, incorporated or othered. The
energy and agency of young people in relation to issues of sexuality suggests that the protective discourse and moralizing agenda mobilized by
Peter Luff, M.P. may be insignificant and superfluous to the lives of
many school students. Features in *More!* magazine such as "Sextalk"
and "real life dramas" illustrate some of the ways in which teen magazines work within the boundaries of normative discourse where preju-
dice and stereotyping pertaining to same-sex partnerships remain
unchallenged while heterosexuality is presumed (Epstein and Johnson
1994) organized and acclaimed in pictures and text. The discourse of
sexual liberation appropriated by the "Sextalk" feature works within
clearly defined, dominant sexual categories and does not extend beyond
straight sex. This has implications for the use of teen magazines as

resources for sexual learning, particularly in relation to sex education programs, where different strategies may be needed to discuss certain issues and to encourage the participation of young males.

NOTES

1. Newsnight report, BBC 2, 5/2/96. Peter Luff, M.P. tabled a private members bill in the British House of Commons which called for a party political consensus on parental duties and responsibilities with regard to adolescents and the censorship of teenage magazines as suitable for specific age ranges. Teen magazines are also the subject of a Radio 4 phone-in program, Call Nick Ross, 6/2/96.

2. See Thorne (1993) for a discussion of gender appropriate categories and the possibilities and constraints for "gender crossing" among boys and girls.

3. See also McRobbie and Garber (19820, Griffin (1982), Lees (1986, 1993), Cowie and Lees (1987) for a discussion of the ways in which young men draw upon patriarchal discourse where misogynist labeling and a concern with female sexual reputations become key markers for the construction of young women's identities.

4. Thorne's (1993) analysis points to the limitations of viewing boys and girls as occupying different cultures. This approach, she suggests, exaggerates gender differences, overlooks intra-gender variation, and raises questions about whose experiences are represented in educational research.

REFERENCES

Alderson, C. 1968. *Magazines Teenagers Read*. London: Pergamon Press.

Alloway, N., and P. Gilbert. 1997. "Boys and Literacy: Lessons from Australia." *Gender and Education* 9(1): 49-59.

Anyon, J. 1983. "Intersections of Gender and Class: Accommodation and Resistance by Working Class and Affluent Females to Contradictory Sex-role Ideologies." In *Gender, Class & Education*, edited by S. Walker and L. Barton. Lewes: Falmer Press.

Barker, M. 1989. *Comics, Ideology, Power and the Critics*. Manchester: Manchester University Press.

Butler, J. 1990. *Gender Trouble, Feminism and the Subversion of Identity*. London: Routledge.

Comfort, A. (ed.). 1974. *The Joy of Sex, A Gourmet Guide to Lovemaking*, London: Quartet.

Canaan, J. 1986. "Why a 'Slut' is a 'Slut': Cautionary Tales of Middle Class Teenage Girls' Morality." In *Symbolising America*, edited by H. Varenne. Lincoln: University of Nabraska Press.

Connell, R.W. 1989. "Cool Guys, Swots and Wimps: The Interplay of Masculinity and Education." *Oxford Review of Education* 13: 291-303.

Coward, R. 1984. *Female Desire*. London: Paladin.

Cowie, C., and S. Lees. 1987. "Slags or Drags?" In *Sexuality: A Reader*, edited by *Feminist Review*. London: Virago.

Davies, B. 1997. "Constructing and Deconstructing Masculinities through Critical Literacy." *Gender and Education* 9(1): 9-30.

Epstein, D., and R. Johnson. 1994. "On the Straight and the Narrow: The Heterosexual Presumption, Homophobias and School." In *Challenging Gay and Lesbian Inequalities in School*, edited by D. Epstein. Buckingham: Open University Press.

Foucault, M. 1976. *The History of Sexuality*, Volume 1, trans. R. Hurley. Harmondsworth: Penguin.

Freud, S. 1905 [1977]. "Three Essays on Sexuality." In *On Sexuality*, Pelican Freud Library 7, trans. J. Strachey. Harmondsworth: Penguin.

Fuller, M. 1984. "Black Girls in a London Comprehensive." In *Life in School, the Sociology of Pupil Culture*, edited by M. Hammersley and P. Woods.Milton Keynes: Open University Press.

Furlong, V. 1976. "Interaction Sets in the Classroom: Towards a Study of Pupil Knowledge." In *The Process of Schooling, A Sociological reader*, edited by M. Hammersley and P. Woods. London: Routledge & Kegan Paul.

Griffin, C. 1982. "The Good, the Bad and the Ugly: Images of Young Women in the Labour Market." Centre for Contemporary Cultural Studies Stencilled Paper, no. 40, University of Birmingham.

Hammersley, M., and P. Woods (eds.).1976. *The Process of Schooling, A Sociological Reader*. London: Routledge & Kegan Paul.

Harding, S. (ed.). 1987. *Feminism and Methodology*. Bloomington: Indiana University Press.

Haywood, C. 1996. "Out of the Curriculum: Sex Talking, Talking Sex." *Curriculum Studies* 4(2): 229-249.

Hermes, J. 1995. *Reading Women's Magazines*. Cambridge: Polity.

Hollway, W. 1989. *Subjectivity and Method in Psychology*. London: Sage.

Kehily, M.J., and A. Nayak. 1996."'The Christmas Kiss': Sexuality, Story-telling and Schooling." *Curriculum Studies* 4(2): 211-227.

Kehily, M.J., and A. Nayak. 1997. "Lads and Laughter: Humour and the Production of Heterosexual Hierarchies." *Gender and Education* 9(1): 69-87.

Lee, C. 1983. *The Ostrich Position, Sex, Schooling and Mystification*. London: Unwin.

Lees, S. 1986. *Losing Out: Sexuality and Adolescent Girls*. London: Hutchinson.

Lees, S. 1993. *"Sugar" and Spice*. London: Penguin.

Lupton, D., and J. Tulloch. 1996. "'All Red in the Face': Students Views on School-based HIV/AIDS and Sexuality Education." *Sociological Review* 44(2): 252-271.

Mac an Ghaill, M. 1994. *The Making of Men.*, Buckingham: Open University Press.

Mac an Ghaill, M. 1996. "Deconstructing Heterosexualities within School Arenas." *Curriculum Studies* 4(2): 191-209.

McRobbie, A. 1978a. "'Jackie': An Ideology of Adolescent Femininity." Occasional paper, Centre for Contemporary Cultural Studies, University of Birmingham.

McRobbie, A. 1978b. "Working Class Girls and the Culture of Femininity." In *Women Take Issue*, edited by Centre for Contemporary Cultural Studies. London: Hutchinson.

McRobbie, A. 1981 "Just Like a 'Jackie' Story." In *Feminism for Girls: An Adventure Story*, edited by A. McRobbie and T. McCabe. London: Routledge & Kegan Paul.

McRobbie, A. 1991. "'Jackie' Magazine: Romantic Individualism and the Teenage Girl." In *Feminism and Youth Culture: From "Jackie" to "Just Seventeen"*. London: Macmillan.

McRobbie, A. 1996 "'More!': New Sexualities in Girls' and Women's Magazines." In *Cultural Studies and Communications*, edited by J. Curran, D. Morley, and V. Walkerdine. London: Arnold.

McRobbie, A., and G. Garber. 1982. "Girls and Subcultures." In *Resistance through Rituals: Youth Subcultures in Post-war Britain*, edited by S. Hall and T. Jefferson. London: Hutchinson.

Measor, L., C. Tiffin, and K. Fry. 1996. "Gender and Sex Education: A Study of Adolescent Responses." *Gender and Education* 8(3): 275-288.

Millard, E. 1997. "Differently Literate: Gender and the Construction of the Developing Reader." *Gender and Education* 9(1): 31-48.

Nava, M. 1984. "Youth Service Provision, Social Order and the Question of Girls." In *Gender and Generation*, edited by A. Mc Robbie and M. Nava. London: Macmillan.

Nayak, A., and M.J. Kehily. 1996. "Playing it Straight: Masculinities, Homophobias and Schooling." *Journal of Gender Studies* 5(2).

Patton, C. 1993. "Tremble, Hetero Swine!" In *Fear of a Queer Planet, Queer Politics and Social Theory*, edited by M. Warner. Minneapolis: University of Minnesota Press.

Radway, J. 1984. *Reading the Romance: Women, Patriarchy and Popular Literature*. Chapel Hill, NC: University of North Carolina Press.

Rofes, E. 1995. "Making our Schools Safe for Sissies." In *The Gay Teen, Educational Theory for Lesbian, Gay and Bisexual Adolescents*, edited by G. Unks. London: Routledge.

Rosser, E., and R. Harré. 1976. "The Meaning of Trouble." In *The Process of Schooling, A Sociological Reader*, edited by M. Hammersley and P. Woods London: Routledge & Kegan Paul.

Sex Education Forum. 1997. *Supporting the Needs of Boys and Young Men in Sex and Relationships Education*. London: National Children's Bureau.

Skeggs, B. 1991. "Challenging Masculinity and Using Sexuality." *British Journal of Sociology of Education* 11(4).

Stanley, L., and S. Wise. 1993. *Breaking Out Again*. London: Routledge.

Tinkler, P. 1995. *Constructing Girlhood, Popular Magazines for girls Growing Up in England 1920-1950*. London: Taylor & Francis.

Thomson, R., and S. Scott. 1991. *Learning About Sex: Young Women and the Social Construction of Sexual Identity*. London: Tufnell Press.

Thorne, B. 1993. *Gender Play, Girls and Boys in School*. New Brunswick, NJ: Rutgers University Press.

Walkerdine, V. 1990. *Schoolgirl Fictions*. London: Verso.

Whitty, C. 1985. *Sociology and School Knowledge, Curriculum Theorty, Tesearch and Politics*. London: Methuen.

Williams, R. 1965. *The Long Revolution.*, Harmondsworth: Penguin.

Willis, P. 1977. *Learning to Labour, How Working Cclass Kids get Working Class Jobs*. Farnborough: Saxon House.

Winship, J. 1985. "A Girl Needs to Get Streetwise: Magazines for the 1980s." *Feminist Review* 21.

Wood, J. 1984. "Groping Towards Sexism: Boys' Sex Talk." In *Gender and Generation*, edited by A. McRobbie and M. Nava. London: Macmillan.

Magazines Cited

More! Issue 198, 25 October-7 November 1995, publisher EMAP Elan.

More! Issue 206, 14-27 February 1996, publisher EMAP Elan.

More! Issue 208, 13-26 March 1996, publisher EMAP Elan.

LEARNING THE ROPES:
ETHNOGRAPHIC ACCOUNTS OF
WITHIN SCHOOL TRANSITIONS

Gwen Wallace, Jean Rudduck, and Julia Flutter

The "Making Your Way Through Secondary School" project began in September 1991, and was supported by the British Economic and Social Research Council. We followed about 85 secondary school students until they finished their 16+ examinations. Subsequently, a small sub-sample (24) was investigated as they moved into different post-compulsory schooling experiences.

At the start of our main study the students were aged 12 and in three classes of three, very different, English secondary schools. The schools were chosen from our local knowledge because of their differences and because their head teachers had confidence in the schools and their futures. The largest school of 1,400 students had some legacy from its former status as a selective grammar school but, at the time of the study, was serving a diverse, relatively balanced social class intake under the leadership of a new head. The smallest school had fewer than 700 stu-

Studies in Educational Ethnography, Volume 1, pages 167-184.
ISBN: 0-7623-0436-7

dents, had falling rolls, and was sited on the fringe of an urban area. It served an ethnically diverse community where a high percentage of households was affected by long-term unemployment. The third school drew from a white, working-class population in a former coal-mining area, with high current unemployment (see Rudduck, Day, and Wallace 1996; Harris, Rudduck, and Wallace 1996; Wallace 1997; Wallace, Rudduck, Flutter, and Harris 1998).

We generally interviewed the students three times each year in December, March, and July. We also interviewed heads and key teachers regularly, attended some key meetings with parents, read relevant documentation, and took note of the schools' changing organizational patterns. The main study ended in the summer of 1995 when the students were 16. Our major (and enduring) organizing concept drew on Goffman's (1961) "two-sided" definition of "career"; one side linked to the development of self, self-identity, and sense of future, and the other concerned with the progress of the individual through institutional time and with her or his movement within the hierarchical structure of the institution.

Significant in our findings has been the way students experience the everyday transition from class to class, teacher to teacher, subject to subject and from classroom to lunch queue, outside grounds, and back to classroom (Rudduck, Harris, and Wallace 1994). However, even more significant, and less well documented, is the annual within-school transition as students in one year grade move on to the next. We were particularly struck by the way each year of secondary schooling presents students with new challenges in terms of differently structured patterns of expectations and events (Rudduck, Day, and Wallace 1996; Shaw 1995). Students who have an overview of this process, "learn the ropes" more quickly than those who do not.

Briefly, our work suggests that in spite of the novelty of new teachers and new subject-based timetables, in year 7 learning takes second place to the social excitement of adjusting to the "big" school. The powerful social and peer pressures continued well into year 8. Indeed, we found the way students perceived their particular tutor group tended to develop into the shared self-perception (reinforced by teachers' comments) that they were reluctant learners and a "bad" class to teach. There were some notable accounts of disorder and a sense of the fragmentation of student experiences. However, year 8 was also noteworthy for summer camps and outings: events anticipated well in advance and long-recalled after-wards in socially shared myth and anecdote.

Year 9 was more academically demanding as teachers placed more emphasis on student responsibility for their futures. For our students it would have been the first year of the nationally imposed standardized assessment tests (SATs) had not teachers successfully boycotted them. More traditionally, it was the year of "options," when, with a growing sense of individuality and guided by staff, students self-selected them-selves into their subjects for their 16+ examination and non-examina-tion courses and split into differentiated groups.

The final two years were a relative treadmill for those who were moti-vated toward "getting the grades." Portfolio building for coursework assessment, work placement experiences, and repeated revision for tests and examinations placed many students under quite severe stress. Oth-ers (mainly boys with a reputation for "dossing around," but some who had consistently vowed to "work harder" but without success), aban-doned the struggle altogether and dropped out of school.

The title of our project "Making Your Way Through Secondary School," prompted one head to quip that it "conjured up an image of cut-ting your way through the jungle with a machete" (Rudduck, Day, and Wallace 1996, p. 144). However, looking at our data, we see the students as strategically, if differentially, engaged with the organizational struc-tures which have been and are being woven around the schooling process. There is evidence from other work that this engagement with institutional expectations begins in primary school. Pollard (1985) argues that class-rooms are places where, "a working consensus...a collective, interdepen-dent adaptation by the teacher and children to survival problems which are, in different ways, imposed upon them both" (p. 161). In this chapter we use the interview data to show how, as active participants in the dynamic interplay of changing policies, the "survival problems" in sec-ondary schools differ from one classroom to the next and, most particu-larly from one year to the next. Successful adaptation turns on student (and teacher) capacity to "learn the ropes" before they can navigate the rocks!

EARLY EXPERIENCES: LEARNING TO COPE WITH THE "BIG SCHOOL"

Compared with earlier studies (see, for example, Delamont and Galton 1986), there was little evidence of the dissonance and pain associated with primary to secondary school transfer. Rather, our students' reflections on year 7 (aged 11-12) and their descriptions of year 8 (aged 12-13) suggested to us that they were more aware of the differences in school size and space, and more involved in their changed social relationships than they were impressed by changes in the pace and level of their academic work:

> If you are a first year and you are going through a door people just push you out of the way and go through first. But if you're a second year they tend not to, they wait a little bit (Y8 M).

> It's more spacey and you've got different teachers for every subject (Y8 F).

> Some of the third years I don't like and I'd prefer them to leave. They're a bit bossy. I don't think I'll do that but I'd prefer not to be under them (Y8 F).

> When you're walking through the corridor and there's a load of fifth years in the corridor [they] trip you up, pushing you over, banging you and everything (Y8 M).

Students often complained of the emphasis on apparently meaningless rules, routines, and procedures. Harris (1994) notes the continuing restrictions on "their time, space and movement" (p. 63) in what Silberman (1971) called a "congested social environment" where "there is little space or means available...to exert real autonomy over what happens to them" (Harris 1994, p. 63; Delamont and Galton 1986; Metz 1978).

In contrast, students' comments on lessons suggested a dependent relationship with teachers and focused on the relative strictness or weakness of the teacher and the relative interest or boredom they evoked.

Although some students found school work more demanding and felt they were already out of their depth, for some the lessons repeated work done in primary school and they were bored with the repetition. Students varied in the way they perceived these differences. Some had a broad overview of the concept of "ability" and were aware that the school already operated, or would be operating policies which put them into different ability "sets." Others saw the differences as arising from different learning experiences (Harris and Rudduck 1993; Rudduck, Day, and Wallace 1997). Different teachers were seen to approach the matter in different ways:

> He gave 9 x 9 to me and I says 81. And he goes to somebody else, "What's 7 times?" or some'at like that. And they said someat that was really stupid like 59

or someat. And do you know what he did? He didn't go, "Oh well, you are meant to do it like this and this," he just gave them a sheet and said, "Every time you need to, look it up on the sheet!" (Y8 M).

Say if you wanted some help or something, you won't be able to get it because the teacher's too busy and then he starts shouting his head off telling everybody to be quiet (Y8 M).

I think at the moment most of them [school subjects] are quite easy but I think it might be a bit harder next year when we're in sets because the teachers concentrate more on you not on the people who are below you, which they do at the moment. I think a lot of our teachers aim the work at our level and then try and make the others catch up with us, instead of us going down to them, which is good. 'Cos in French we're still doing the right work that we would have been doing if we were in another class with people about as good as us. In science it's just boring, but we still do the work that we should be doing. And then in maths it's good because we get different booklets so whatever level you are at you can work at your own pace (Y8 F).

Boredom could be relieved by the variety inherent in the movement between different teachers and different subjects but this also produced a fragmented structure to the school day. The discontinuities presented particular problems for some students and these could be exacerbated by a combination of staff absenteeism, inexperienced staff, and staff on short-term contracts. One class had two different teachers for math and three different teachers for English. Indeed, while there were regular routines to each day, such as lesson changes, punctuated by bells and breaks—routines which gave some sense of overall pattern—there was no overall coherence to students' learning experiences in terms of the formal curriculum (Rudduck, Harris, and Wallace 1994).

There was also much "teasing" between groups of boys and girls within each form. Focused on an individual it was experienced as bullying. More often it took the form of verbal harassment between factions, often with sexual and racial overtones.

We have gone as far as to suggest that this Year 8 may be an academically fallow year (Harris and Rudduck 1994; Rudduck, Chaplain and Wallace 1995; Wallace 1997). Hargreaves (1996) has also emphasized the dominance of social aspects of schooling in year 8. While schools varied in the way they saw good pupil behavior as a prerequisite for academic progress, we found evidence that the lack of intellectual challenge could provoke form groups into a collective, anti-boredom (rather than anti-school) peer identity, particularly when faced with inexperienced or temporary teachers:

> They seem to have given us all the naff teachers this year. Nobody wants to teach us. We got told that nobody wanted to teach us (Y8 M).

> We don't do what we're told; never (Y8 F).

> I think we need stronger teachers that won't break under us (Y8 M).

Yet the prospect of being setted by abilities worried some students:

> It'll make me feel stupid. It'll make me feel less intelligent than everyone else because I'll be in a lower set for maths (Y8 M).

Nonetheless, while we found some instances where students during year 8 felt they were not getting the best learning experiences, we also found contrary views. Some teachers were liked because, "they explain things well and they speak to you nicely" (Y8 M). Or similarly, "they don't stand there shouting at you when you do something wrong, they tell you how to do it properly" (Y8 M). Such views were clearly colored by individual student responses to teachers' interactional styles (Midgeley, Eccles, and Feldlaufer 1991).

Most memorably, year 8 was the year of summer outings or camps which took students' out of school for about a week of what (in recall) appeared a relatively relaxed environment in residence together. These experiences were recalled even after students had left school at 16 and much else had been forgotten. At their best, they enabled staff and students to get to know one another informally as "real" people—a process which yielded dividends in school on their return. However, students sometimes recalled events which suggested inadequate standards of organization and supervision, including times when, for example, food was badly cooked and inequitably distributed.

We found almost all students were unable to articulate long-term goals and ambitions at this stage, although, toward the end of the year a few looked back with regret on their lack of intellectual effort and declared it was a temporary phenomenon. They anticipated the differences that work for GSCEs would bring:

> What's the point [of working harder]. At the moment I don't get anything from it. At GCSE I do but in [year 8], no (Y8 M).

> In [Year 9] it's going to get a lot harder. We'll be the first year to get the new cur-
> riculum and there's SATs [Standard Assessment Tests] so there's going to be a lot
> more tests. Generally I think I'm going to prefer next year (Y8 F).

However, most students had little idea of the shape of the next, or following years and could only surmise:

> I'm lost about that. I don't even know what SAT stands for (Y8 M).

NEGOTIATING YOUR PLACE: SATS 'N OPTIONS

As we have argued elsewhere, the annual transitional ritual of "moving
up" offers 11-13 year olds the chance to make a fresh start (Rudduck,
Harris, and Wallace 1994).

In contrast, years 9 (ages 13-14), 10 (ages 14-15), and 11 (ages 15-16)
form a structured buildup to the 16+ examinations. Year 9 carries a tradition of giving students "options" on some of the courses they studied.
These date from around the early 1970s when they were seen as a way
of increasing student motivation, a consideration of particular importance at a time when the school leaving age was raised to 16 for everyone. Much more limited than in their early conception and constrained
by budget restrictions and the pressures of the National Curriculum,
"options" still carry connotations of personal choice and responsibility.
Providing it is not in the National Curriculum, there is also the chance
for a student to drop his or her "worst" subjects and maybe try something new. Everything depends, however, on the kinds of options available and the way they are organized into groups of alternatives.

We found differences between schools which, to some degree,
reflected their traditional cultural and socioeconomic base, their local
authority policy, and internal micro-politics as well as their market position. Students in the best-resourced school, for example, had a wide
range of GCSE options. Against this, our third school offered only nine
courses altogether (Harris, Ruddock, and Wallace 1995).

Within each school, divisions were also opening up between those
who had begun to see the future in terms of GCSE grades and who saw
the importance for their careers of getting down to work, and those who
were still "messing about." There was evidence of a gender divide, with
the girls accusing some of the boys of causing trouble. Estimates of the
amount of disruptive behavior varied from school to school and class to
class. Some students were more likely to complain than others:

The ones that don't mess about get carried along by the main group. I used to think it was funny but now they're getting on my nerves (Y9 F).

There was also some calculated cynicism about the extent to which the choices were student or teacher options! Some students read this as pressure on them to work harder and "be good." Some boys believed they could be denied their options if they persisted in disruptive behavior:

You've got to work hard this year to get, to be sure of getting a place into the subjects you want. Because if you misbehave then if they look at your record and say, "This boy had messed around in this lesson and he wants to go in it, we might as well not waste the place on him." So they choose the subjects for you (Y9 M).

Placed "on report," a system whereby teachers in every lesson provided formal statements on his behavior, another lad, who said the only way he could comply was by ignoring his friends and staying away from them, claimed "Well it's killing me being good; I know that" (Y9 M).

In contrast to the rhetoric of progressive liberalism that accompanied the introduction of options' systems in the early 1970s, spring 1993 was the date set for the first of the government-initiated attempts to "raise standards" by means of nationally administered Standard Assessment Tests for all 13 year olds (SATs). From the start of year 9 our cohort experienced considerable uncertainty about SATs because of a threatened teacher boycott. The English teacher in one school, firmly committed to mixed ability teaching, brought *Romeo and Juliet* to his students through a year-based production of the play which involved every student. This attempt at egalitarian treatment was undermined when, with the boycott threat unresolved, teachers had to pre-decide the "level" of test each student would take. For students in two of the schools this was the first time their teachers had formally assessed their ability "level" in English. As with other "key" events, students responded differently. Some were pleasantly surprised; others confused and even angry at finding themselves given a "level" that they believed undervalued their achievements. Yet others appeared to take little interest in the process, while some students' responses suggested they were not aware of it at all.

Some students had begun to pick up and share the discourses coming from the teachers as they realized that year 9 was the start of the build up to GCSE grades which would affect their post-school career prospects. The teachers they were getting were generally permanent staff and familiar with the examination system. An instrumental interest in results, rather than any intrinsic interest in the subject, was becoming students' main reason for working rather than messing around:

> This year, we are getting all the things right because we only have one teacher [for the subject area]. Last year we had about five, four, different ones and we couldn't keep up with them (Y9 F).

> Last year was just like making relationships with our teachers and building a standard. This year we have got to put everything we've got into it and try and get good results (Y9 M).

> I think they're slightly helping you because like if you're capable of doing somat and you want a good grade it's going to make you work harder, a lot harder. So, as in year 7 and 8 we didn't know a lot about SATs anyway then, [they] suddenly change everything. That's going to make you work a lot harder to get into it now and to get a good grade for it (Y9 M).

Pressure on budgets left two schools negotiating early retirements almost to the end of the spring term, so the options they could offer had to be adjusted accordingly. One school only finalized the subjects available after Easter. Together with the enduring dispute around implementing the SATs, the budget uncertainties left students ignorant of what the courses on offer would be and unable to make any coherent plans until the options lists were made available in late spring.

Ultimately, students' choices were made in consultation with teachers in a process which included evening meetings with parents. It was a serious business that focused school and home environments on a common issue. It also involved students in strategic negotiations for which many were ill-prepared. Some of the complexity is illustrated by the case of an Asian girl who had problems at home because her mother, who had known only Indian schooling, suffered from high blood pressure, and was easily upset. She found the system difficult to explain to her:

> My mum, [I] never told her anything about it....She had a look at it...She knows how to speak and write well and read well but she doesn't really know about this system....My dad was well educated and he really understood it (Y9 F).

One of the boys whose passion was football (and who was in frequent trouble in later years), wanted to teach physical education. His parents could offer little advice and, in spite of all the advice on offer from the teachers he claimed, "None of them know anything about being a PE teacher though" (Y9 M).

Some students had their suspicions confirmed:

> We don't have as much freedom as...the people last year did because they've mainly chosen all our options for us (Y9 M).

> I don't reckon we've got much choice, even though we have got choices they're saying, "Ah, you're going to have to do at least three of these." You do have to do art. They might as well pick them for you (Y9 M).

Although the 1993 test boycott was successful, all schools went ahead with some form of testing and used the results to aid the internal differentiation of students. Students who selected a non-examination option and who teachers deemed capable of taking a GSCE option were persuaded to change, and vice versa (see for example Harris, Rudduck, and Wallace 1996; Wallace 1997). Nonetheless, we gained the impression that students had appreciated the opportunity to discuss courses with their teachers and felt broadly content with the outcomes. One complaint in one school came from girls who found themselves in the lowest ability set for math, in the company of what some of them described as disruptive boys and a sexist male teacher. The serious issue here is that the increasing predominance of girls in top sets tends to leave those who need most help (boys and girls) in the company of those who have (for whatever reason) chosen to "doss around." The problem was exacerbated in this school because, with falling numbers on roll, it was forced to accept students (usually boys) who had been expelled from elsewhere.

In years 10 and 11 the challenge was to work under pressure and keep up with deadlines. Between the two came a week of work experience. The overall consequence was a growing sense of individuality, built around and reinforced by the institutionalized situations in which students and teachers worked. Along with the pressure to "behave" and "work hard" (in that order as far as teachers were concerned), widening social divisions within the school increasingly reflected the future prospects students were imagining for themselves.

YEAR 10: WORKING FOR A FUTURE

From the beginning of year 10 students felt the increased pressure to work. They responded in a variety of different ways:

There's a lot of pressure on you now. It's like if you don't do well you're not going to do well in GCSEs. Like if you're ill, you're right scared of missing like some math, and like, I had a problem with my right arm...so I was really useless at being in school and my mum said, "Why don't you stay at home?" and I can't because I've got my science lesson and I have a science test (Y10 F).

It comes as a shock how much you work, how much more work you're getting now than you did in year 9. And the deadlines you're supposed to meet. I don't know why, I don't know whether they get together and plan it but all the course-work deadlines come in together which can be just a bit irritating when you've got everything due in at once (Y10 F).

Behavioral expectations had also been raised, and some students were clearly concerned about potential failure:

Sometimes it's really like a weight on you....The way [teachers] start saying to, you know, [to] the ones who want to go into advanced math and advanced science, "You have to do this and this," and everyone's going, "Yeah, we want to do that." And like even if they don't [understand] they'll put on a brave front, like to show the teacher they understand it, and sometimes you have to do that...because in math you can be demoted. And this year....I was with my friends and we messed about so much I was nearly demoted out of the class. So we settled down then and it's all right now (Y10 M).

The teachers are strict and obeying all the rules set down. If you just forget your pens and pencils they can give you a detention, where they'd probably just lend you a pen last year (Y10 M).

Parents and siblings (usually, but not exclusively mothers and older sisters) often provided advice, support, or firm encouragement, and some students thrived under the pressure:

{ex}I'm getting down to working hard now. Because I used to mess around in lessons but I don't now because my brother's told me, he's been through it all so, he says if you work harder then you get good grades and that so I'm working a lot harder...Mr. D has sorted out a timetable for revision and I'm trying to keep up with that and I'm trying to do my homework on top. I do it like every day (Y10 M).

[My parents] didn't used to [put pressure on me] but like they are saying "Do your homework before you go out because your exams are coming up next year and you've got to think and learn." (Y10 F)

By the end of the year, having survived the stress, some students who had worked hard and saw themselves as doing well, had found it all worthwhile and several commented that it was big improvement on previous years:

> Well it's been quite hard at times, in some of the projects and things, but it's been good doing it because it was hard. The teachers have been helpful a lot, helping us a lot more than the years before that. It's been a good year.(Y10 M)

> Before it was, like, you used to just like copy work and everything but now you've got certain tasks to do and you've got your coursework and things like that....It's better (Y10 F).

Some boys were responding to the competitive atmosphere (Owens 1984):

> All the other years were like just nothing, like nothing to work on, and then [we] start[ed] to do coursework in year 10 and get ready for exams (Y10 M).

Another had found an overall strategy that worked for everything!

> [Cramming] works! I started off really bad, all I do like in lessons, I talk to my mates but I always get everything down that I know I need and then, before any exam. I revise my socks off and never stop all week. Now like I get right good grades, shock all the teachers, get in top sets next year. It's brilliant (Y10 M).

Some students had found other ways round their problems. Not unusually, one boy had discovered that he could get better marks in English than math and so directed his energy selectively toward doing well in the better subject:

> I'd sort of quite like a job to do with English and writing and stuff. I'm not really good enough to have a job in math, so I try harder in English (Y10 M).

However, some students were giving up. Missed work and missed deadlines could leave them with a vision of GCSE grades that were either "not worth the effort" or simply unobtainable:

> If you miss just even with like a day, you miss so much it doesn't seem worth it (Y10 F).

> Well I know like this year and next year are the most important years and I've got to cram everything in, but they're going too fast and I'm getting lost (Y10 F).

> I just hate coming to school. Everything's boring and I just can't be bothered to go....There's loads more [homework]. They leave you to do projects and stuff at home and I never have time to do them (Y10 F).

Using "self-concept as a learner" scale, Chaplain (1995) found that disengaged students "felt they had greater difficulty in particular with task-orientation and with more abstract problem solving tasks" (p. 110). In line with his thesis our evidence supports the idea that students who find themselves failing engage in "strategic withdrawal." By the end of the year, those who had failed to keep up had stopped trying:

> You get a reputation...as a trouble maker, and you just can't lose it (Y10 M).

> Teachers have just given up on me now, so I can't change nowt. Just can't wait to leave (Y10 M).

> Just everything what goes off I still get the blame for it, even if it weren't me. So they're just against me so, so be it. Just let them be like that. That's why I keep wagging and that (Y10 M).

In making this case, we are reversing the view (widely held by teachers) that it is students' cultural and behavioral attitudes that need to change before they will learn successfully. Students who disengage do so because they believe, from experience, that teachers have nothing to offer them but blame and condemnation.

Attempts to make school more vocationally orientated through work placements simply confirmed these students' worst fears. Work experience tends to affirm social and gender divisions, rather than extend opportunity and, while it motivates some students to strive for high grades, those who found themselves with negative experiences—doing what they called "skivvy jobs" (like shelf-filling in local supermarkets) were equally likely to have their belief that grades were unimportant, confirmed (Day 1995).

YEAR 11: KNOWING YOUR PLACE

Students' ability to organize and pace their coursework and build up the required portfolios was crucial to a successful conclusion to year 10. But the most crucial change for many, and one which could undermine any possibility of achieving good grades in their GCSE options, was the requirement to perform well in formal examinations. This, in turn, depended on the "mock" rerun and the judgments teachers had to make on the level of paper for which each student should be entered. Students became ever more conscious of the way time was running out and the boundaries were hardening around their beyond-school options. School learning (for both teachers and students) had become directed toward "getting the grades" (see also Harris, Wallace, and Rudduck 1995; Wallace 1997).

> It's more stressful than the previous years, especially now. Before Christmas in most lessons it were a gentle pace because we were doing a lot of study about careers as well and teachers weren't giving us quite as much work. But now like, especially around now because by Easter all coursework's got to be in in every subject, so there's a right lot of pressure to get everything done by then (Y11 M).

> It's been really hard, very hard work....Right now, I'm in between coursework and revision. I've had to start revision so I've got a bit of free time. But a month ago I would have been feeling really tired, feeling really ill and working until, all day, you know, no free time at all (Y11 F).

> I'm going to get enough GCSEs to do A level, which is what I want to do. It's just that I want to get like the best grades that I know I can. I mean the best that I can do and I don't want anything to go wrong and I don't want to get a grade that I know that I could have done better, so it's a bit scary (Y11 F).

However, some of the most hardworking students had doubts about the value of placing so much emphasis on hard work and grades:

> I've worked hard for so long, because I mean some people messed about in middle school, in first school, first couple of years at this school and I was thinking, "No. Got to work. And now...[not working] doesn't seem to have any detrimental effect at all. They seem to be just like everyone else....Sometimes I feel I've worked or so hard for so long that, if I just mess it up in these last three months, whatever, then it will all be a waste. But I don't know. I just want to do well for myself (Y11 F).

> When [some teachers] are in front of a class, GCSEs are the most important thing you'll ever do in your whole life. And if someone actually told you how important they really were, it might be easier to know what you were doing (Y11 F).

And one student, who had not worked very hard, wondered if she should have done and reflected on what might have been.

> It's just something that happens isn't it? The last four years happened, but it doesn't affect...it's not had any huge effect on my life at the moment. I wish I'd have kept working a lot harder and actually got a thirst for learning. That would have been nice because then I would have been in top sets and would actually want to pass my GCSEs...I think I just got lax. I think I just like saw how easy I could take it and just took the easy life for a couple of years (Y11 F).

It was only after the results came through that students fully realized the extent to which their results would shape their immediate futures. GCSE grade levels had already been set as prerequisites for A level courses. School sixth forms were setting higher grades for entry than the further education colleges. Competition at further education colleges, even for places on vocational courses, meant students who did not have the required grades had to repeat work for another year before getting their options. Those who had dropped out were often left with unskilled, heavy manual work found by relatives or friends, and looking for something better. One student who had first worked retreading tires with his father and had then moved to laboring for landscape gardening, talked of "going to night school," to make up the ground he had lost and "get qualifications."

For those doing A levels the pressures increased further. Looking back after a year the students we followed up reflected on the changes:

> When we went to the new [college]...having another two years to adapt and do well and hopefully succeed...it's a bit tricky. It's like you've got to establish yourself again and feel comfortable in your new surroundings which takes time....It's taken a while. It's taken nearly a year if I want to be open with each other. It's a very selective place (Y12 M).

> I didn't do so much work [for GCSEs] as I do for A levels. The depth of work and the amount of understanding you have to have. I mean we have just had exams, mid-year exams, we will have another set in December and you go for finals in June....So you never stop. (At school) you (had) long rests between exams (Y12 F).

The imagined futures moved further away and became possible university courses for some still only vaguely divined futures, "I'm sitting on the fence at the moment" (Y12 F). Some looked forward to "a year out" traveling the world. What they all found was greater isolation. What they all missed was the companionship of their friends.

DISCUSSION AND CONCLUSION

Our impression throughout was that the students were on the receiving end of a process of which they understood little. Each year was distinct from either its precursor or its successor. Looking back, students feelings echoed our views that years 7, 8 and, to some extent, 9 were more socially oriented than academic. Lessons had no apparent overall purpose beyond the immediate event. They could be good; they could be boring. They were, in any event, transient and readily forgotten. Students felt no particular sense of responsibility for what they learned. "Real work" did not begin until year 10. With help from home, from parents and older siblings, some students rapidly grasped the importance of active participation in achieving the grades they wanted. The "drop-ins" became "schoolwise." Believing that it was good grades that would get them where they wanted to go, they set about finding strategies to get the grades they wanted. Interestingly, high-aspiring girls were striving to go beyond this; to get the best grades they possibly could, because they believed this would affirm their self-belief. Others found their social lives too important to give up for lonely study, particularly where they felt "lost" or undervalued. Girls sometimes dropped out because they felt rebellious, became pregnant, or they missed work when they were needed at home to help with family problems like parental illness or to care for small brothers and sisters. The "drop-out" boys were becoming "streetwise"; networking with families and friends for unskilled jobs that aided their belief that schoolwork was unnecessary.

Yet few, if any, connections were being made between what students learned at school and the skills they would need in the world of work. Nor was there much emphasis on the alternative: learning for its own sake. The credentials were what counted. But these had to be obtained at the speed and under the circumstances set by the institution.

We have played with a number of metaphors to conceptualize the dynamics of this process. We mentioned earlier the head who talked of the process as, "finding a way through the jungle." In other papers we have viewed it as a process of following someone else's script and of navigating the rocks (Harris, Wallace, and Rudduck 1995). Neither metaphor quite captures the complexity of the student's active interchanges with a changing environment, drawing on family support systems. Here we have chosen the idea of learning the ropes. Learning the ropes (like navigation) has its origins in seafaring. The ropes were the rigging for masts, yards, and sails on schooners and other sailing ships. Learning the ropes was an essential skill if the rigging was to be set appropriately to catch the wind and navigate successfully. Top group students revealed in their responses how their rigging was in place (helped by homes, families, and resources) and they were navigating the storms with some skill. The rest could never "catch up" on the same terms. Indeed, some preferred the revelling onshore and had never left port.

As Nixon, Martin, Mckeown, and Ranson (1996, p. 112) observed, "The students want to achieve, and their parents want them to achieve, but neither understands fully the formula for achieving or the disciplines of study."

REFERENCES

Chaplain, R. 1995. "Making a Strategic Withdrawal: Disengagement and Self-worth Protection in Male Pupils." Pp. 101-115 in *School Improvement: What can Pupils Tell Us?*, edited by J. Rudduck, R. Chaplain, and G. Wallace. London: Fulton Press.

Day, J. 1995. "Confronting the World of Work." Pp. 148-159 in *School Improvement, What can Pupils Tell Us?*, edited by J. Rudduck, R. Chaplain and G. Wallace. London: Fulton Press.

Delamont, S., and M. Galton. 1986. *Inside the Secondary Classroom*. London: Routledge and Kegan Paul.

Goffman, E. 1961. *Asylums*. Harmondsworth: Penguin.

Hargreaves, A. 1996. "Resisting Voice." *Educational Researcher* 25(1): 12-19.

Harris, S. 1994. "Entitled to What? Control and Autonomy in School: a student perspective." *International Studies in Sociology of Education* 4(1): 57-76.

Harris, S., and J. Rudduck. 1994. "Establishing the Seriousness of Learning in the Secondary School." *British Journal of Educational Psychology* 63 (part 2): 322-336.

Harris S., G. Wallace, and J. Rudduck. 1995. "It's not that I haven't learnt much. It's just that I don't really understand what I'm doing": Metacognition and Secondary School Students." *Research Papers in Education* 10(2): 253-271.

Harris, S., J. Rudduck, and G. Wallace. 1996. "Political Contexts and School Careers." Pp. 32-50 in Teaching and Learning in Changing Times, edited by M. Hughes. London: Blackwells.

Metz, M. 1978. *Classrooms and Corridors*. Berkeley: University of California Press.

Midgeley, C., T. Eccles, and H. Feldlaufer. 1991. "Classroom Environment: The Transition to Junior High School." In *Educational Environments: Evaluation, Antecedents and Consequences*, edited by B. J. Frazer and H.J. Walberg. Oxford: Pergamon Press.

Nixon, J., J. Martin, P. Mckeown, and S. Ranson. 1996 *Encouraging Learning: Towards a Theory of the Learning School*. Buckingham: Open University Press.

Owens, L. 1984. "Co-operation, Competition and Individualisation: A Longitudinal Study of the Learning Preferences of Australian Primary and Secondary School Students." Paper presented at the Third Asian Workshop on Child and Adolescent Development, Kuala Lumpa.

Pollard, A. 1985. *The Social World of the Primary School*. London: Holt Education.

Rudduck, J., R. Chaplain, and G. Wallace (eds.). 1995. *School Improvement: What can Pupils Tell Us?* London: Fulton Press.

Rudduck, J., S. Harris, and G. Wallace. 1994. "'Coherence' and Students' Experience of Learning in the Secondary School." *Cambridge Journal of Education* 24(2): 197-211.

Rudduck, J., J. Day, and G. Wallace. 1996. "The Significance for School Improvement of Pupils' Experiences of Within School Transitions." *Curriculum* 17(3):144-153.

Rudduck, J., J. Day, and G. Wallace. 1997. "Students' Perspectives on School Improvement." In *Rethinking Educational Change With Heart and Mind*, edited by A. Hargreaves (ASCD Yearbook). Alexandra VA: Association for Supervision and Curriculum Development.

Shaw, J. 1995. *Education, Gender and Anxiety*. London: Taylor and Francis.

Silberman, M. L. (ed.). 1971. *The Experience of Schooling*. New York: Holt, Rinehart and Winston.

Wallace, G. 1997. "Changing Structure, Changing Experiences: How Policy Effects Reverberate through Secondary School Students' Life Chances." *Research Papers in Education* 12(3): 299-316.

Wallace, G. J. Rudduck, and J. Flutter, with S. Harris. 1998. "Using Ethnographic Methods in a Study of Students' Secondary School and Post-school Careers." In *Doing Research About Education*, edited by G. Walford. London: Falmer Press.

Wallace, G., J. Rudduck, and S. Harris. 1994. "Students' Secondary School Careers: Research in a Climate of 'Moving Perspectives'." Pp.170-183 in *Researching Education Policy: Ethical and Methodological Issues*, edited by D. Halpin and B.Troyna. London: Falmer Press.

TOWARD A "CREATIVE SCHOOL":
A CASE STUDY FROM RURAL NEW SOUTH WALES

Barry Cocklin

INTRODUCTION

We all can probably recount situations when visiting a school we had subjective feelings that students and teachers appeared comfortable with their situation, there was a sense of enjoyment, and learning was taking place. Such was my experience when I first went to Rana Primary School in September 1995. The previous semester when the principal (David Kennedy) had been seconded to the university, discovering we shared many ideas regarding education, we intended to continue contacts in the future. However, it was not until allocated supervision of two practicum students in September that I had the opportunity to spend time at Rana. From the outset, then, the research involved that extent of "luck" or "opportunity," as I had not requested to supervise these students, nor was there any prior condition that Rana would have students at that time.

Studies in Educational Ethnography, Volume 1, pages 185-206.
Copyright © 1998 by JAI Press Inc.
All rights of reproduction in any form reserved.
ISBN: 0-7623-0436-7

On my first visit to the practicum student with Upper Division (years 3-6), David said, "Don't just stand there, do something," immediately involving me working with pupils. When I visited with Lower Division (Kinder-year 2), the practicum student included me in the lesson, then, going outside for a sports session; a group of the pupils attached themselves stating "You're with us, Mr. Cocklin." In both contexts the relaxed nature of the pupils, their confidence, self-esteem, enthusiasm, and an acceptance of those who were there to assist in their learning were evident. As events showed over subsequent visits, their sussing-out skills were well developed, and this acceptance was on their conditions.

These first contacts provided critical moments influencing all aspects of the research. During the remainder of the year I visited the school as often as possible, maintaining ongoing contact with staff, pupils, and parents, also working with individuals, small groups, and teaching some lessons to Upper Division. This engagement in the context established an underpinning contribution of the ethnography to children learning. David and I also took most of Upper Division and some of Lower Division on an excursion to the university. This critical event provided them with a certain status and self-development/ empowerment through talking to a lecture of second-year teacher education students, while seeing where I worked gave a greater sense of ownership of the researcher and study. Two events indicated that the parents also adopted me into the school community. First, at the school fete they insisted that as a member I played Santa Claus, then at the end-of-year concert the parents and citizens (P&C) presented a gift of thanks for the help I had given the school. During these early contacts discussions developed the intended study in 1996 to focus on why the environment appeared to work in promoting effective learning, not only by pupils, but others as well. In short, why this context promoted a community with shared purpose. This led to an ethnography where I was integrated into the community, largely through their actions and on their conditions, producing a particular, and perhaps somewhat opportunistic, set of relationships and interactive context. At Rana, then, access was a variable process involving actions, initially unconsciously (see Woods 1998), where the school community negotiated the involvement, a situation where the researcher just "goes for it."

CONTEXT AND THE RESEARCH

Establishing community involvement from the outset, considerable lobbying from the local community saw Rana Primary School open in 1935, followed by their significant efforts in providing additional facilities such as fencing, trees, and general work around the school grounds. It has been a two-teacher school for most of its history. During the research in 1996 David taught Upper Division, and Bev Osborne, new to Rana that year, taught Lower Division, while there was also a part-time release teacher/librarian, school secretary, and school handy-person. For Term 2, a fourth year BEd (Primary) teacher student, Sally Dean, took Upper Division for an eight-week extended practicum. This involves the student as full-time teacher, releasing the classroom teacher for a period of professional development. There were 38 pupils at the start of the research, 18 (nine girls, nine boys) in Upper Division, 20 (nine girls, 11 boys) in Lower Division. Although the majority of pupils came from the local district, others, reflecting both parental and pupil choice, traveled past their local school to attend Rana Primary.

The study commenced under a general question as to: what is it that makes the school what it is, and how can this understanding be better used and translated into more effective learning for the school and its community? We sought to start with a description of the culture of the school, then, through an action orientation use these findings to examine and reflect upon the situation, effecting strategies and processes of change and development as a result (Cocklin and Davis 1996). The research began in January 1996 and was one of involved participation, where at various times I took the roles of "teacher," "friend," and "critical advocate," seeking to have a shared experience of the school in action. The pupils appeared to have little difficulty with these roles, although their actions and comments suggested that the friend relationship dominated.

The focus was on participant accounts of their lived reality as they acted to develop the experiences of schooling (see Smyth 1995). The research was predicated on the basis that learning is an unpredictable task, the investigation of which requires time spent in the context, observing, talking, and reflecting, between researcher-as-participant and those directly involved in the situation (Woods and Jeffrey 1996). All participants were informed that I would be looking at the school and their experiences, observing them, talking with them at school, and interviewing them at various times, and at the school as often as possible. The observations ranged between involved and observer-only, while unstructured interviews discussing experiences of schooling with staff, parents, and individual pupils from Upper Division and small groups from Lower Division were conducted.

As an intensive period was to be spent in the school, collaboration was the key, working with the participants rather than doing research on them (see Woods and Jeffrey 1996). This collaboration included David, as well as being a key informant, in a twofold involvement in the research process. First, through constantly discussing the research there was an ongoing reflection providing him with insight and information relevant to practice, thereby further contributing to children learning. Second, as the history of the community and school impinged upon both perceptions and the present context, he interviewed community members regarding the school's history, with a focus on

> What has happened in the past that has bonded the community and the school so closely together and how does this affiliation work to make the school the learning community it seems to be.

Data collection and analysis was within a broadly based interactionist paradigm to derive categories which were then related to an examination of the overall notions of creative teachers (Woods 1995; Woods and Jeffrey 1996) and learning communities (for example, Johnson 1995). In so doing, the study sought to celebrate the perception within the school that children learning should be the focus of education. This context and perception appeared to represent the antithesis of the technocratic emphasis which has teachers' work in danger of becoming a less reflective, more bureaucratic, deprofessionalized, deskilled activity (see Apple 1986), through the increased emphasis on a business-oriented managerialism and political control of both content and process (see Ball 1994; Pollard et al. 1994).

RANA PRIMARY

As David already knew, and my initial involvement in the school clearly indicated, certain crucial elements derived from the context and the history of the local district had a marked influence upon the school and its relationships, both interpersonal and with the community.

The Historical Context: "Community"

Although only a few kilometers outside a major rural center, the school and community are very much isolated and independent of their larger neighbor, reflecting both history and geography. Settled in the 1930s, 41 families were balloted for undeveloped rural blocks on the banks of a large river subject to occasional flooding which has precluded denser settlement and preserved the rural nature. With the Great Depression in full swing, some were among the unemployed, and all were pioneers with little more than basic tools and a willingness to turn their block into a home to sustain them. As the Depression eased, some of the men obtained work in town, leaving further development of the farm to their family, and to evening work where all the community turned out to help. This independence from the larger center, and sense of sharing and working together generally remain today, at least in part due to the descendants from the original settlers.

This history has contributed to a pattern of constructive community involvement and interaction within the school. In turn, this has promoted feelings of ownership by all stakeholders, represented in an allegiance to the school and the learning that occurs within. It was these aspects which demonstrated the ways in which context, teaching and learning, interactions, and development of the self integrated into providing an environment wherein learning was relished by all involved.

Rana School: A Community Promoting Children Learning

Those in the context described the school as a learning community. However, this term is subject to differing, and at times contested, interpretations, while also often applied as a generic descriptor to schools. As we have argued elsewhere (see Cocklin, Coombe, and Retallick 1996) it is often taken as synonymous and used interchangeably with learning organization (Senge 1990) derived from the business and managerial contexts. Here, then, I have used the term community in recognition that the discourse is not neutral and that the term "learning organization" may signify an acceptance of a dominant position for the managerialism deriving from its business origins.

The notion of community adopted in this chapter, and applied by those at Rana, is one of working together, wherein difference and even contestation are valued, and which places particular emphasis upon the everyday lived reality of the school context. This notion of community, in terms of relationships and children learning, was most akin to going with the flow which "puts the emphasis on process, and involves intuition, spontaneity, tacit knowledge, enthusiasm and fun" (Woods and Jeffrey 1996, p. 34). While many teachers will recognize elements and avow that they already do that, or something like it, the chapter will indicate essential differences between the parts and the whole. The basic premise of a learning community is one of participation by all:

> Our traditional concept that teachers teach, students learn, and administrators manage is completely altered. In a community of learners, everyone is about the business of learning, questioning, investigating, and seeking solutions. The basis for human interaction is no longer a hierarchy of who knows more than someone else, but rather the need for everyone to contribute to the process of asking questions and investigating solutions (Kleine-Kracht 1993, p. 392).

I also suggest that this community requires a bottom-up process of development involving all stakeholders. Accordingly, it was decided to seek participant views of their culture and its workings, in particular, those facets which created the environment which promoted children learning.

Our School: Ownership—From Past to Present

The point that the history of both school and district influenced the current context, as David noted, should serve to remind us that:

> The school has reaped the rewards from the historical development of the community and will continue to do so as long as it remembers its origins and feeds the needs of the community to be involved.

Rather than seeking the continuous improvement derived from the corporate sphere (see Senge 1990), which underpins much of the change rhetoric at present, within educational contexts there are elements of the school we may wish, upon critical reflection, to preserve (Hargreaves 1995).

From the oral history interviews certain characteristics of the school, and school-community relationships, emerged, particularly the strong sense of community and cooperation. One of the dominant themes was that of pride, as one of the past pupils (from 1938) recounted:

It went from one generation to the other and that went down through the school. You took a pride in your school. Because we went to the Rana School and because we were all so close we took pride in the school so that even when we grew up, the ones that didn't shift away from Rana still continued that same effort your parents had.

This ongoing contact with the school reflects both an allegiance and ownership which continues to be a particular feature of the context. At various school functions members of the local community, and past pupils, were regularly in attendance. Furthermore, during the research a number of past pupils dropped in when they had a day off from their secondary school, with some sitting in on classes, taking part in lessons, and giving assistance to teacher and pupils. This ownership and relationship with the school was illustrated by comments one parent made regarding her older children who had left the Rana district:

...they pretty much think of Rana as their school. I've got to tell them about it because they want to know what's going on—anything that's got to do with Rana they just help.

Across-generational ties continue, with a parent of two current children noting that not only were she and her mother past pupils, but it was her grandmother who "got the school going." There remains a continuity of involvement with the school, certainly among a core who have returned as parents in the P&C and support the school, but also in general from among the local community who, as one noted, "look on the school like it's our school."

From the early days there has been a sense of allegiance to and ownership of the school, which continues to the present, represented in an awareness of the school among the Rana community and reflected in the comment by all that "what we do is for the kids." The culture of the school, and its historical context, is a factor in developing this sense of community over time and through particular relationships and strategies. This is not to argue that a learning community cannot be developed within another school, rather that the starting point must be the historical context and it may require processes of reculturation (see Hargreaves 1995). We need to recognize, also, that schools are not just marked by their commonalities, but also by their differences. An environment which facilitates children learning may be in marked contrast to the uniformity of product, architecture, technology, and work practices, underpinning the McDonaldization (see Ritzer 1993; Craft 1996) of society, and aspects of the learning organizations model (see Cocklin 1997).

Our Great School

With the present dominance by political and economic imperatives in the educational debate and rhetoric (see Bates 1993; Marginson 1993), direct input from children, or their families, is infrequently valued or sought. Children are not mere receivers of information, they are engaged with teachers and community in a shared process as constructors of meaning, thus we should pay greater attention to their perceptions of schooling, in particular, those which contribute to their preparation for a future where knowledge and change are best served by autonomous, critical, and reflective learners.

The current pupils also spoke of a strong sense of pride in their school, stating that this was the best school, and as Kat remarked "I don't really want to change the school." The sense of ownership also came through strongly, expressed in terms of "our school" and their loyalty to it, for instance, when asked to sell his school to me, Mark said:

> To make you come here I'd tell you how great we are....Well, I've been to two other schools. The first one was really good, the second was a bit down in the dumps, and this one is great.

They were also very proud of the history and buildings, particularly the older block which now forms the classrooms. Some felt that the view of the school from the main road had been spoiled by the new library in front of the classroom block, suggesting it should be moved out the back to restore the focus on the school.

Others spoke of their family connections, even where the family had moved away from the district for a time:

> My Pop [Grandfather] used to go to this school and he's always said it was good and that. My Pop suggested we should go and have a look (Ben).

Summarizing the pupil attitudes toward school were comments by Bev Osborne that at Rana you have to kick the kids, and some of their parents, out at the end of the day. Throughout the research pupils stayed after school, in the classroom playing on the computers, talking with each other, or with the teachers, or playing around the grounds. Similarly, parents stayed talking with various children, each other, or with the teachers. As Bev noted, in all her prior experiences pupils were always in a rush to leave, and few if any parents entered the school grounds other than on formal visits. Parents also reported this enthusiasm for school:

> The best thing my children have learned is the fact that they like school and it's not a common thing for children to like school....It's rare that we have had to drag them out of bed. Most mornings Mark's up and dressed by 7:15, ready to go. He would walk out the door there and then.

Togetherness—A Sense of Family and Community

One important feature of the school, was the togetherness produced within the small school environment, including benefits such as space provided by the large area and small number of students, relationships in terms of making friends, and the teaching/learning situation. As Nicole comments:

> There's not much people—so there's not much bullying. We all get to learn a lot more because there's not many of us and the teacher has more time to teach us. Most of us get along very well. And so you could have more chance of getting friends in other classes. You just get to know other people in higher grades who know more.

While a number of the students noted a lack of bullying, fights did occur at Rana, it was not an idyllic setting, but rather the students focused more on the positive aspects of their interpersonal relationships.

The effects of size, and their contribution to both relationships and learning featured prominently in parent comments as well:

> I took them up to [nearby school] for a week and the kids nearly died. They didn't like it. It was too big, too much of a shock for them. They were used to having, not only me, but other parents. They were really used to having that closeness with everybody else. Then I brought them down here and that was the end of it.

It was evident throughout the study that the small size contributed to the formation of a particular set of relationships, between students, with teachers, and with the wider community. On the other hand, I would be loathe to suggest that size is the determining factor, rather that the pupil:teacher ratio needs to be given consideration in larger schools, as well as relationships and community involvement. Again, these are things which all must work toward a process of negotiation and personal and professional development, which can be neither implanted nor created over a short period of time. In current educational contexts, where the political agenda emphasizes a notion of efficiency where big is better, and issues of class size are being overlooked, we can take encouragement from the fact that teachers, pupils, and parents realize the considerable advantages in the small school environment (Cocklin 1997).

The interpersonal relationships, both in and out of the classroom, were supportive and seen by pupils as a central benefit from the Rana context:

> It's got good kids. Some [bad] behavior—well, some of them—but there's no bullies. Because everyone cooperates. Yeah, like a family thing. Some fight but not as much. We sort it out. I ask, "Who sorts it out—teachers or students?" Both (Taylor).

This concept of family was noted as a defining characteristic of Rana by parents, pupils, and teachers. During the study pupils indicated "these are my friends," reporting any changes in these groups, while many of the fights were akin to a form of sibling rivalry. As David suggested at the start of Term 3 some discipline issues had arisen over what he termed a "rivalry for position as the top dog in the school." On the other hand, Taylor emphasized the strong group loyalty noting that they "stuck up for each other," and "against everyone—in the school and out of the school." An incident at an interschool athletics carnival exemplified this support. As one of the senior girls competed in the 800 meter, a parent organized community members into a cheer squad, then, when by the final lap she could only walk, a number of her peers went out and accompanied her to the finish. This involvement and support, then, is not only among the pupils, but the community as a whole supporting all Rana children. It was also clearly evident in the general relationships at school where, for instance, if one is hurt or upset others rally around and offer help.

Overall, the general point was made by parents that:

> [Rana] seems to bring out that protective attitude. It's taught them a lot about relationships. Because they've got all the kids, they've got the teachers, then they've got the parents, then the community—everybody is so involved, and there's so many different personalities involved—it gives them a good grounding. It is like a family.

This sense of supportive community, contributed to by the historical context, was not a given. Rather, it required conscious effort and leadership, initially when David was appointed as principal:

> Second objective, I suppose, was to build up the community support again, because it had suffered a little because of the previous principal. He had come from Regional Office and hadn't been in a school for about eight years—and that was reflected in the comments by the parents—the fact that he locked himself in the office and wouldn't talk to anybody. Another objective was to get out and make the school a community school again, and reinforce some of the things that people had been saying that they wanted done.

The result of this approach and philosophy has been a continuation of parent involvement in a variety of in-school and out-of-school activities. It was also very evident that parents felt comfortable about coming to the school, even just for a look during the day, and that the commonly held view was:

> To everybody it is their school. They'll donate their time, they'll donate their energy, they'll donate their money. Everybody looks out for everybody else, too, other people's kids (parent interview)

This appeared to derive from the historical context of involvement in the school, the ongoing sense of community and ownership, but also was reinforced by both the size of the school and the actions of staff:

> Because it's a small school—you can really have a say—make a contribution. The guy we've got there promotes that type of thing (parent interview).

This was also reflected in a further variety of contexts, the school council, P&C, and parent involvement in the classroom, all of which contributed to relationships, ownership, contact, and awareness:

> ...you get to see how the school runs, you get involved in policy sort of issues, discipline codes, this sort of thing. So, you really get an idea of how the school runs...(parent interview).

The school, then, has an open-door policy, involving a process of negotiation with parents, and reflecting David's view that:

> ...the parents know that they're welcome—that it is your school and they are your kids, you've got just as much right to have a say in what happens. You know, you don't have a right to tell me what happens, but you have a right to have a say. In

the final analysis, it's my decision as to what actually happens. But most of them
take that fairly well.

As David notes, collaboration is encouraged, but this does not mean that
it is synonymous with consensus; rather the approach was one of partnership.

A Partnership

   Parents were encouraged to come in as a partnership between community and school:

> It's good. I mean, if you're having problems with the kids—or the kids are having
> problems—I have always felt perfectly comfortable with coming in. The teachers
> will help you. It's a two-way street...working with the parent....And the parents
> coming in and actually helping with the kids. So, if those [teacher and parent]
> combine and it's sort of like a run-on from home to school—and they've got a
> good working partnership. I mean, they won't always have a good partnership—
> they will disagree and that—but, if they feel comfortable to disagree and that—
> and work it out like that. I think that's the most effective way. Not only that, but
> parents are very interested in education and the educational processes. I think it's
> got to be a partnership to work (parent).

This also extends to the situation of parent involvement in teaching:

> As much as having my children at school I probably even get more pleasure out
> of helping out there;...when I help kids like Duane that is probably a really great
> thing and that's when I grow. When I see a child like Duane or one of the others
> suddenly take off I really think I had a bit to do with it (parent tutor).

The pupils appreciated this school/community linkage, and the
extended family situation which existed both outside and inside the
school, as Mark indicated these were very important:

> The community, how it is involved in the school. We just have days when the
> community comes in and walks through - they always know something about
> Rana School....It helps a lot with the students as well. The parents know the
> teachers, and they work in the school with reading and things like that.

However, there was also that extent to which they were emphatic that it
was their school and, while help was appreciated, parents needed to
acknowledge that ownership was the responsibility and perhaps right of
the current pupils:

I: So, you think there is a need for people to listen to the kids more?

Colin: Yes! Not parents being able to rule the school!

The pupils also contrasted the responsibility teachers gave them at school with joint school-community events where parents needed to do the same. As Kat remarked "Like, some parents are pains—you know the fair we had - well, they wouldn't let us do anything."

Creative Teaching: Enhancing Children Learning

Across the ethnography the approach to teaching was noted as a crucial component not only in creating but also maintaining the school as an environment promoting children learning. In this context staff, parents, and pupils all noted the contrast with 1995 and a relief principal:

> To start off with, the parents were perfectly willing to be friendly, welcoming, helpful. But it was made quite clear to them from the start that they weren't welcome at the school. In fact, the further away they stayed the better.... the kids were basically told right from the start that they...knew nothing....The kids weren't academically brilliant, but they loved going to school....But, they were turned off. There was no homework done, they had totally no interest in school. They weren't interested in anything—they were becoming disruptive....It took all their self-confidence away (parent).

Given this situation, some parents seriously considered withdrawing their children from the school. For all participants this provided a point of contrast with the current context, and a basis for their elaboration of the central contribution of teaching to children learning. It was also used to illustrate the importance of school-community relationships, particularly in situations where the community has a sense of ownership and involvement in the school.

Similarly, the pupils often used this 1995 situation to contrast their perceptions of effective teachers with those held in less regard. Here, pupils noted that "good teachers spend more time with you" (Bruce), "they help you, they tell you how to do things, you seem to work together better" (Petra), or just a general perception across both content and relationships that "They understand everything—they understand stuff" (Kylie). Pupils also noted the emotional/self-security support such teachers provided, an attribute David himself emphasized:

> That's the beauty of the school, too, the fact that they do feel happy that they can divulge their deep, intimate, dark, life secrets. And they're quite happy to share

them with you, without somebody ridiculing them—saying that's stupid. The
thing is that they do support each other—as often as possible (interview, David).

Overall, pupil perceptions were markedly similar to those documented
in the literature on creative teachers (see Woods 1990, 1993, 1995). The
pupils also reported their ability to differentiate "We can tell a good
teacher and a bad teacher in about 5 minutes" (Mark), and the influence
upon learning "Because if you don't like the teacher you won't find
yourself learning very much." (Nicole).

In view of the prominence given to teaching by both pupils and parents, descriptions of the ways in which the current teachers went about
their work enhancing children learning were sought.

The " Job" is to Teach "Kids"

The approach to teaching was clearly focused on allowing every child
to experience success:

Each school would have it's own history, and would have it's own emphasis on
different things. And Rana's emphasis is on the achievement of kids who don't
normally experience great achievement. Everyone is given the opportunity, and
everyone has to participate—we just don't have the numbers, so everyone is given
the opportunity to do something. It gives them a sense of achievement all the time
(David, interview).

The parents supported this, noting that the emphasis on working
together and participation was more beneficial than competition. The
multiage grouping contributed to this:

Being a split [multiple grades] class situation, it allows them to expand, and
progress and grow, as they feel comfortable, and I guess a lot of that stems back
to the ability of the teachers....He has come home and said I've got year 6 homework. He complained a bit and I told him he should be proud of himself because
it was a great effort. Now if he was in a structured school he wouldn't have that
flexibility and that's where I believe that our kids are fortunate...(parent interview).

Such comments provide a contradiction to that so often championed in
the political and media rhetoric where there has been an increasing pressure to return to traditions of teacher-directed, rote learning of content.
This has been accompanied by increasing controls on education and
teaching, a direction toward a uniformity of approach and content (see

Bates 1993; Woods 1995). As Woods and Jeffrey (1996) argue, teaching as an art needs, not constraint, but flexibility, the very antithesis of the McDonaldization approach.

As indicated by the data from Rana, the alternative is a focus on catering for the individual child, and involves teacher and pupil in a collaborative learning experience (see Sugrue 1997). As Woods (1995, p. 3) notes, this learning is where "pupils have control over their own learning processes, and ownership of the knowledge produced, which is relevant to their concerns." If we are to move toward an environment which enhances children learning, schools must focus on educating children:

> the job is to teach kids not get bogged down in management—and not a fixed structure—need to be adaptable and open to change—change to make learning for staff and kids more effective. And push the department line—that's what we've got to say—[laugh]—the systemic—we realize we're a political body, we have to do what we're told—in some aspects, you just can't get away from it, but there are other parts that you work within. Translating what the system wants us to do, but putting it in to the kids and community needs. You're looking at utilising those things, but around the kid's needs. But, there are things that kids need to be taught that they don't want to learn. It's their development—and sometimes their development has to be structured—it can't be free rein all the time. It's a combination of a number of factors. (David, interview)

This approach is marked by a flexibility of pedagogy within a context where it is learning together. Over a period of time the teachers could be observed working with individual pupils, groups, or the class on the floor, sitting at the pupil desks, learning together on the computer, and in front of the class, throughout delivering content, skills, and facilitating individualized learning processes. The context was dynamic, where the classroom could be best described as both teacher-centered and child-centered (Woods and Jeffrey 1996; Sugrue 1997). Children moved around the room, helping others, seeking information, discussing issues, debating with the teachers, often with a level of working noise. In the classroom there was very much an ethos of working with pupils in a collaborative learning style. The pedagogy was constantly varied and flexible, reflecting teacher philosophy, morals, values, and beliefs, influenced by children's needs and the requirements of curriculum, a focus on children learning, rather than merely encountering content. Underpinning this was constant reflection, a willingness to take risks, to experiment, where the teacher is, even if not formally, undertaking reflection-in-action (Schön 1983) where "You have to develop them [ideas/strategies, etcetera]—and you have to keep developing them. Trying them out, chucking them out, trying something different" (Bev).

The overall approach was directed toward an emancipatory praxis, one where staff sought forms of critical, self-reflective, and collaborative work to create conditions where they themselves, pupils, and parents came to develop a greater sense of control and ownership of knowledge and practice (see Grundy 1993). This was evident throughout the research where staff noted the need to be adaptable, to be flexible, to focus on the children learning, to work with all members of the school community, but within the reality where:

> ...you can't do everything to please everyone. Somewhere along the line you have to make a decision—the people I should be pleasing, should be looking after the most, are the kids—the focus is on what they should be doing, not a minority or a particular group want to do. And that's a learning curve. You can't solve all the ills of the world. And I think it's a philosophy I try to give to the kids—the fact that there's things we just cannot solve, no matter how good we think we are— you just cannot solve every problem, no matter how hard you try (David, interview).

The job, then, for such teachers is one of controlling change, where the teacher's professionalism and expertise is used to filter and manage change, and their own continuing professional development (see Woods and Jeffrey 1996). David willingly acknowledged that his teaching practice was developing and changing, that he could acknowledge past mistakes, that others would occur in the future, and his engagement in a constant process of at times adopting, others adapting, yet others resisting, the current directions and trends within education. This also involved determining priorities reflecting his overall approach, values, and beliefs for education. In particular, this involved the issue of time:

> I try and find more time for the kids—don't know how you do—if I could have someone as an offsider all the time—team teaching in the class, that would be the ideal. Where you've got two people working with the kids at once. Because there's such a variety, and such a variance of abilities, different ages, and interests—those sorts of things—that makes the class dynamic, and interesting, but it makes it a hell've a challenge because you just cannot physically cater as an individual for every single kid in the class. You do your best (David, interview).

This time also included planning and preparation, often impinged upon by the proliferation of external meetings and requirements which characterize teachers' working lives. In short, time both structures teachers' work and, in turn, is structured by it (see Hargreaves 1994). These pressures were clearly evident at Rana. With the demands of department, those of school and community meetings, the proliferation of bureaucratic recordkeeping, the constantly changing educational agenda, and their own lives outside school, the issue of time becomes an ongoing dilemma for teachers. To manage this at Rana both teachers and pupils sought to adopt a flexible approach, people-oriented, and multidimensional, where they made the time to undertake tasks, in an environment where they had ownership and control of it (see Woods and Jeffrey 1996). But, as David noted above, time for teaching, so central to children learning and self and professional development, is under threat with the potentiality of being marginalized by many of the reforms current within education. The children strongly advocated the approach to teaching adopted, and attributed it to a number of factors:

> We learn a lot more faster because of the size. Because the teacher has more time....And we've got great teachers who help a lot.

Humanism and Individualism

Two basic premises underpin the relationships with and approach to children in the school. As one parent noted, children felt comfortable approaching staff, and saw them as part of the family, due to the staff having a particular:

> Attitude. I think most parents—they don't see the need for their child to be the top but they do want their child to feel comfortable and intelligent—and they want their child to be working to the best of their ability. Some teachers haven't got that attitude—they are there to teach at the kids—they are not there to work with the kids....[the good ones have] got a lot of enjoyment, a lot of thought, into what they do for the kids—the kids are actually learning because they are enjoying it and they're interested in what they're learning. And nobody is left out. They've got a little bit more time, a little bit more thought, about ways in which to approach that child to get them to want to learn....Instead of seeing the classroom as 20 or 30 kids that you've got to teach this thing, they see it more as an individual thing. It's 20 individuals, rather than 20 kids or a class.

Certainly, the teacher/student relationships at Rana were very close. Partly, this can be attributed to the size factor, as both teachers have said in a small school you're never off duty, but it seems to have more to do with an attitude of involvement, as Mark commented: "It's them [teachers] being with the children all the time. I think it's great." At both recess and lunch the teachers are out in the playground, often joining in games and participating in activities. The relationships with the children, and the benefits this held for the teacher, were also a particular aspect noted by Ms. Dean:

> The one thing, at every other school I've been at, you don't play with the kids, you keep your distance, they're over there, you're over here sort of thing. Whereas, out there, at lunch if someone said lets play handball [we do], you could also get pleasure from being with them as children, as well as just teaching them. That was really good.

Throughout, parents and students placed particular emphasis upon these close, personal relationships as one of the defining characteristics of Rana Primary. As such, these relationships were strongly reflected in comments from the teachers about the enjoyment they derived from their teaching (see Woods, Jeffrey, Troman, and Boyle 1997). This is not to suggest that an idyllic setting existed; there were occasions when disciplinary actions were required, where parents were upset with situations, staff were under stress, and where either individual or groups of children were reminded of their obligations. However, the children reported that they expected to be told off for some of their behavior, but saw this as entirely legitimate under the circumstances, and in no way as a threat to the relationships. The context, even when David resorted to his "principal's voice," was one of classroom or individual management—a situation of negotiation maintaining individual and mutual respect and self-image. As such, this provided a firm basis for children learning. This approach is supported, too, in the literature on creative teachers (Woods 1995; Woods and Jeffrey 1996) and accounts of enhanced professionalism (Woods et al. 1997).

Creating Responsibility and Self-Confidence

Another significant issue involved the sense of responsibility the pupils were given by the teachers, both in terms of the content and issues of relationships:

> [Principal] has said heaps of things we should do—and we've been doing wrong—we've fixed all of these things—and it's become more fairer now. He says this is what we should do and this is what we shouldn't do...every couple of days we write down what we're going to do and what we're going to change of each other. It's like...well, when we write down those things it's like a commitment. I ask, " And that's a good idea?" Yeah, it's a pretty good idea. It gives you some responsibility (Petra).

At Rana school some unique characteristics exerted considerable influence upon the student perceptions of their learning. One important factor was the multiaged context allowing for teaching to stages rather than the age-grading approach. This has important consequences for both relationships and for teaching/learning, and all pupils saw this as beneficial:

> Instead of working on your own, if you've got a problem you've got another person next to you to ask to help you out with it. It's just like one big class instead of just 1,2,3....It's better to be all together (Colin).

However, and thus applicable to all contexts, is the notion of working together, including student-as-teacher and teacher-as-student. In other words, there was an interactive partnership of learning characterising the context, where both teacher and student took responsibility for their own learning. This peer support approach provided a teaching context where pupils had access across levels of ability. They were encouraged to work for their self and their learning style, at their ability, but while challenging, encouraging, and supporting them to extend themselves. Equally, teachers actively engaged in their own learning with and from the children as well.

Each child was seen as an individual, and an emphasis put on a caring and sharing relationship. The children were allowed to make mistakes, and encouraged to take responsibility for their own learning and development. Both teachers were constantly alert for all the nuances of the experiences of the children, and were not averse to providing emotional support. The emphasis at Rana was upon an individualized approach to learning, varied and interactive, contributing to creative learning where "pupils have control over their own learning processes, and ownership of the knowledge produced, which is relevant to their concerns" (Woods 1995, p. 3). This approach also appeared to contribute to a view that learning was something that would continue throughout their lives; as Mark commented he would always "be learning, no end." Perhaps, then, an outcome of such relationships and teaching approaches is the development of that elusive notion of lifelong learning. Certainly, it does indicate that where experiences and perceptions are positive, where interest is engaged, and the self is developed, an allegiance to learning is encouraged, but this requires a multifaceted set of contents and relationships, particularly in the nature of the teaching approach (see Woods 1995; Woods and Jeffrey 1996). In other words, this is not something which can be assumed to be created but rather is something which requires careful development and nurturing. That they were successful in this was shown by Sally Dean's comments:

> The kids had a lot more personality, and were a lot more outspoken than in other schools that I've been in. That's probably because there is only a few of them— so, they have the opportunity to speak out more—where, if there are 30 in the class, then the children are suppressed more. But, here, because they're more out-spoken, and also I think they feel more comfortable in their setting, they're pre-pared to let you know those things. I reckon they're encouraged, too. Like, with David and them...he trains them to just be themselves, and not just do this, do that. To stand up for themselves.

DISCUSSION

Neither David nor I, nor pupils or community, would seek to argue that Rana Primary is an idyllic setting. However, overall it is held to provide an environment which facilitates children learning, as well as engaging staff and parents in the processes and strategies, and indeed themselves learning.

This, then, provides the foundations for the ongoing reflec-tion-in-action and professional development of all members of the com-munity as they seek to become a creative school. Furthermore, it needs to be noted this becoming is a process and not a product; it is ongoing and developmental, a process of history, relationships, teaching, and leadership processes and styles, and not something that can be implanted or created without consideration of every aspect.

The overall outcome of a creative school, I suggest, is a sense of empowerment. The community feels that it is their school, that they have both a right and an obligation to participate in the school, and in the educative processes. Similarly, the pupils have the perception that in their school they can exert influence, are given responsibility, and are valued in terms of their opinions and person. This is further enhanced by an approach which focuses on teaching and learning with all members of the community underpinned by collaboration and negotiation. This created a particular environment wherein children learning was the goal and purpose.

But, of particular import is the approach to teaching and the marked influence this has upon children learning. Throughout the ethnography, primary influences were the way these teachers undertook their tasks, their approach to children learning and the relationships, focus on processes rather than content, and the creation of contexts where the development of the self is central. In short, underpinning the creative school is the creative teacher:

> These teachers are skilled at handling and turning to good use the tensions and dilemmas that pervade primary school life. They have a fund of knowledge—of subject-matter, pedagogy, and pupils—on which to draw, and a disposition to experiment in finding the optimum means to advance toward their aims. They possess the ability and flair to formulate and act upon hunches, to play with ideas, but within a disciplined framework. They have adaptability and flexibility to cope with ever-changing sets of circumstances (Woods 1995, p. 2).

Children learning in the Rana context is the outcome of a multifaceted interaction of context, history, relationships, and teaching processes. We need further insight into these complexities, only possible through spending time working with those involved and seeking their reality of experiences.

ACKNOWLEDGMENTS

Developed from the original paper (Cocklin and Davis 1996) I presented at the Ethnography and Education Conference, Oxford 1996, I acknowledge the input of Ken Davis as well as that by conference participants. Discussions with Peter Woods, Bob Jeffrey, Geoff Troman, and Mari Boyle at the Open University during the months I spent there influenced the content in a variety of ways, and I sincerely thank them while taking responsibility for the report. Last, but not least, this chapter would not have been possible without the efforts of all at Rana, my special thanks to them, and especially an appreciation for the ongoing contacts and support.

REFERENCES

Apple, M.W. 1986. *Teachers and Texts: A Political Economy of Class and Gender Relations in Education*. New York: Routledge & Kegan Paul.

Ball, S. 1994. *Education Reform: A Critical and Post-structural Approach*. Buckingham: Open University Press.

Bates, R. 1993. "Educational Reform: Its Role in the Economic Destruction of Society." *The Australian Administrator* 14(2&3): 1-12.

Cocklin, B. 1997. "Towards a Learning Community": The Case of Rana Primary School." *Education in Rural Australia* 7(2): 1-11.

Cocklin, B., and K. Davis. 1996. "'Creative Teachers' and 'Creative Schools': Towards a Learning Community." Paper presented at the Annual Ethnography and Education Conference, Oxford, September 9-10.

Cocklin, B., K. Coombe, and J. Retallick. 1996. "Learning Communities in Education: Directions for Professional Development." Paper Presented at the British Educational Research Association Conference, Lancaster, September 12-15.

Craft, A. 1996. "Nourishing Educator Creativity: An Holistic Approach to Continuing Professional Development." *British Journal of In-service Education* 22(3): 309-323.

Grundy, S. 1993. "Educational Leadership as Emancipatory Praxis." In *Gender Matters in Educational Administration and Policy*, edited by J. Blackmore and J. Kenway. London: The Falmer Press.

Hargreaves, A. 1994. *Changing Teachers, Changing Times*. Toronto: OISE Press.

Hargreaves, A. 1995. "Changing Teachers, Changing Times: Strategies for Leadership in an Age of Paradox." ACEA, Workshop: June-July.

Johnson, N. 1995. "Schools as Learning Communities: Curriculum Implications." Paper presented at the Australian Curriculum Studies Association Biennial Conference, University of Melbourne, 11-14.

Kleine-Kracht, P.A. 1993. "The Principal in a Learning Community." *Journal of School Leadership* 3(4): 391-399.

Marginson, S. 1993. *Education and Public Policy in Australia*. Melbourne: Cambridge University Press.

Pollard, A., P. Broadfoot, P. Croll, M. Osborn, and D. Abbott. 1994. *Changing English Primary Schools? The Impact of the Education Reform Act at Key Stage One*. London: Cassell.

Ritzer, G. 1993. *The McDonaldization of Society: An Investigation into the Changing Character of Contemporary Social Life*. Newbury Park: Pine Forge Press.

Schön, D. 1983. *The Reflective Practitioner*. New York: Basic Books.

Senge, P. 1990. *The Fifth Discipline: The Art and Practice of the Learning Organization*. New York: Doubleday.

Sugrue, C. 1997. *Complexities of Teaching: Child-centred Perspectives*. London: Falmer Press.

Smyth, J. 1995. "Teacher's Work and the Labor Process of Teaching: Central Problematics in Professional Development." In *Professional Development in Education: New Paradigms and Practices*, edited by T.R. Guskey and M. Huberman. New York: Teachers' College Press.

Woods, P. 1990. *Teacher Skills and Strategies*. Lewes: Falmer Press.

Woods, P. 1993. *Critical Events in Teaching and Learning*. London: Falmer Press.

Woods, P. 1995. *Creative Teachers in Primary Schools*. Buckingham: Open University Press.

Woods, P. 1998. "Critical Moments in the 'Creative Teaching' Research." In *Doing Research about Education*, edited by G. Walford. London: Falmer.

Woods, P., and B. Jeffrey. 1996. *Teachable Moments: The Art of Teaching in Primary Schools*. Buckingham: Open University Press.

Woods, P., B. Jeffrey, G. Troman, and M. Boyle. 1997. *Restructuring Schools, Reconstructing Teachers*. Buckingham: Open University Press.

NOTES ON CONTRIBUTORS

Shereen Benjamin completed the MA in Women's Studies and Educatio at the Institute of Education, University of London in the summer of 1997. She is currently teaching pupils who have been categorized as having "special educational needs" in a London comprehensive school.

Mari Boyle is a former primary teacher. She was until recently Research Fellow at the School of Education, the Open University, Milton Keynes, U.K., researching child-meaningful learning with particular reference to young bilingual children during the first two years of their school careers. She is currently preparing a book on this topic, and working toward a PhD. Her publications include: *Restructuring Schools, Restructuring Teachers* (Open University Press, 1997, with Peter Woods, Bob Jeffrey, and Geoff Troman).

Barry Cocklin is a Senior Lecturer, School of Education, at Charles Sturt University, Wagga Wagga, New South Wales. He taught in schools for 10 years before moving into the tertiary sector, and has spent time at Massey University (New Zealand), Newcastle University (Australia), and the past six years at Charles Sturt. With teaching involving courses in Sociology of Education, Educational Policy and Administration, and Qualitative Methodologies, his research and publications have covered areas including: adult students at secondary school; rural women principals and teachers; outcome-based education; teachers' workplace learning; critical theory and pedagogy; learning communities and "creative teachers"; and qualitative methodology and analysis. His particular interests lie in school-based research, and participant realities of their lived experiences.

Julia Flutter joined the research team for the "Making Your Way Through Secondary School" project in 1994 having recently completed her Masters degree with the University of Cambridge Department of Education. An early years educator for 10 years, and with a young family of her own, she is deeply concerned with the issues surrounding children's learning and development. Her personal interests lie in the influence of the social environment on children's attainment. Her research interests are broadly based, and have both psychological and sociological dimensions. She has taken part in projects which span pre-school education to year 11 and post-school transitions. She is currently acting as coordinator for "Effective Learning—Thinking About Learning, Talking About Learning," a school-based research initiative (directed by Jean Rudduck) with Homerton College and the Cambridgeshire Inspectorate (supported by Cambridgeshire LEA).

Eve Gregory is Reader in Educational Studies at Goldsmiths' College, University of London where she works with students on undergraduate, masters, and research degrees. Her own research interests are focused on cultural contexts and learning, the literacy practices of young children, bilingualism and early literacy, and family involvement in children's learning. She has directed ESRC and Leverhulme-funded research projects investigating children's out-of-school reading and transfer of cognitive strategies between home and school. Recent publications include *Making Sense of a New World: Learning to Read in a Second Language* (Paul Chapman, 1996) and *One Child, Many Worlds: Early Learning in Multicultural Communities* (Fulton/Teachers College Press, 1997, editor). Both her research and her teaching call upon her former experience as an early years teacher in multilingual classrooms.

Mary Jane Kehily has extensive teaching experience in many areas of education where her concerns have been with the ways in which education policy is translated into *lived experience* in the everyday context of the school. She has been actively involved in the teaching of personal and social education and has developed research interests in sexuality, schooling, and popular culture. After completing a graduate course at the Department of Cultural Studies, University of Birmingham, she worked as a researcher at the University of Birmingham and the Center for Educational Development, Appraisal and Research (CEDAR), University of Warwick. She is currently working on a research project which looks into children's relationships and is based at the Institute of Education, University of London.

Susi Long is an Assistant Professor in the Department of Instruction and Teacher Education at the University of South Carolina. The research reported in this volume was conducted during her doctoral study at the Ohio State University and received the National Council of Teachers of English 1997 Promising Researcher award. Her current research interests include the language and literacy developments of young children and "teacher as researcher," particularly, teacher as ethnographer.

Alexander Massey taught in state and private schools for 10 years, heading both music and drama departments, and has done LEA consultancy work and run workshops on supply teaching issues. He completed an MSc in Educational Research Methodology in 1995, and continued with DPhil research within the Department of Educational Studies, University of Oxford. Between 1995 and 1997 he was editor of the *Journal for Oxford Educational Research Students*, and he has published several papers on research methodology. He runs "Free Your Voice," a voice consultancy, for theaters, businesses, and therapy centers, and is a professional solo singer, performing opera, oratorio, cabaret, and folksong.

Jean Rudduck has been Director of Research at Homerton College, Cambridge since 1994. After teaching in a London secondary school, Jean Rudduck joined the Schools Council Research Team. She later moved to the University of East Anglia and was founder member of the Centre for Applied Research in Education (CARE). She was appointed Professor of Education at the University of Sheffield in 1984 and was Director of the Qualitative Studies in Education Research Group. Her early experience as a member of the Schools Council/Nuffield Foundation Humanities Curriculum Project led to a long-term interest in pupils' perspectives on teaching and learning. Recent books include: *Innovation and Change* (Open University Press, 1991), *Dimensions of Discipline* (HMSO, 1993, with David Gillborn and Jon Nixon), *Developing a Gender Policy in Secondary Schools* (Open University Press, 1994), *An Education that Empowers* (Triangle Press for BERA, 1995, editor), *School Improvement: What can Pupils Tell Us?* (David Fulton, 1996, with Roland Chaplain and Gwen Wallace).

Dinah Volk is an Associate Professor and Coordinator of the Early Childhood Program in the College of Education, Cleveland State University, Cleveland, Ohio. Before teaching at the university level, she taught young children for many years in day care centers and in public and parent-cooperative schools. Her research interests include the developing language and literacy of young bilingual children and their interactions with teachers, parents, and siblings. Her work with teachers on multicultural curriculum development is reflected in *Kaleidoscope: A Multicultural Approach for the Primary School Classroom*, a source book for teachers written with Y. De Gaetano and L.R. Williams.

Geoffrey Walford is Reader in Education Policy and a Fellow of Green College at the University of Oxford. He was previously Senior Lecturer in Sociology and Education Policy at Aston Business School, Aston University, Birmingham. He has academic degrees from Oxford, Kent, London, and the Open Universities, and is author of more than 100 academic articles and book chapters. His books include: *Life in Public Schools* (Methuen, 1986), *Restructuring Universities: Politics and power in the management of change* (Croom Helm, 1987), *Privatization and Privilege in Education* (Routledge, 1990), *City Technology College* (Open University Press, 1991, with Henry Miller), *Choice and Equity in Education* (Cassell, 1994), *Researching the Powerful in Education* (UCL Press, 1994, editor), *Educational Politics: Pressure Groups and Faith-based Schools* (Avebury, 1995), and *Affirming the Comprehensive Ideal* (Falmer, 1997, edited with Richard Pring). Within the Department of Educational Studies at the University of Oxford, he currently teaches on and has responsibility for the MSc in Educational Research Methodology course, and supervises research students. His current research foci are the relationships between central government policy and local processes of implementation, choice of schools, religiously based schools, and ethnographic research methodology.

Gwen Wallace is Emeritus Professor of Education at the University of Derby. She moved into higher education after 13 years of secondary school teaching, a degree from the Open University and an MSc and PhD from Aston University. Her early research focused on the development of middle schools and middle schooling. Her main interests lie in the relationship between school policies and teachers' practices, and between management structures and cultural changes. Her publications include four books on local management of schools (one with June Maw) and the coproduction (with Jean Rudduck and Roland Chaplain) of *School Improvement: What Can Pupils Tell Us?* (David Fulton, 1996). She also works with health professionals developing social research methods for evidence-based practice.

Ann Williams is a research fellow in the Department of Linguistic Science at the University of Reading. Having worked as a language teacher in a variety of educational contexts, her main area of interest is language and education. She has carried out ESRC funded research on the use of nonstandard dialects in school, the development of new dialects in new towns, the relationship between home and school literacy practices, and is currently investigating the role of adolescents in language change.

Peter Woods is Professor of Education in the Centre for Sociology and Social Research at the Open University. He has published widely in the areas of teacher-pupil interaction and school ethnography. His books include *Critical Events in Teaching and Learning* (Falmer, 1993), *Creative Teachers in Primary Schools* (Open University Press, 1995), *Teachable Moments: The Art of Teaching in Primary School* (Open University Press, 1996, with Bob Jeffrey), *Researching the Art of Teaching: Ethnography for Educational Use* (Routledge, 1996), and *Restructuring Schools; Reconstructing Teachers: Responding to Change in the Primary School* (Open University Press, 1997, with Bob Jeffrey, Geoff Troman, and Mari Boyle). For the past 10 years he has been researching creative teaching in primary schools. Current and recent projects include the effects of Ofsted inspections on primary teachers and their work; child-meaningful learning in a bilingual school; and the social construction of teacher stress and burnout.

Diversity in Higher Education

Edited by **Henry T. Frierson, Jr.**,
Educational Psychology Program,
School of Education, University of
North Carolina at Chapel Hill

**Volume 1, Mentoring and Diversity
in Higher Education**
1997, 216 pp. $78.50/£49.95
ISBN 0-7623-0086-8

CONTENTS: Preface. Introduction, *Henry T. Frierson, Jr.*
PART I. CONCEPTS OF MENTORING. An Operational Defi-
nition of Mentoring, *Charles C. Healy.* Mentor Roles in Grad-
uate Studies, *Morris Zelditch.* PART II. MENTORING
APPROACHES AND MODELS. An Examination of Effective
Mentoring Models in Academe, *Olga M. Welch.* Networking
Mentoring as a Preferred Model for Guiding Programs for Un-
derrepresented Students, *Marilyn Haring.* Models in Mentor-
ing through Faculty Development, *Marcia E. Canton and
David P. James.* Increasing Graduate Studies Interest and
Admissions among African-American Undergraduates: A
Role for Graduate Students, *Cheryl A. Boyce.* The Recruit-
ment and Retention of Talented African Americans in Sci-
ence: The Role of Mentoring, *Charles Woolston, Freeman A.
Hrabowski, III, and Kenneth I. Maton.* Mentoring as a Tool for
Increasing Minority Student Participation in Science, Mathe-
matics, Engineering, and Technology Undergraduate and
Graduate Programs, *William McHenry.* Refining and Expand-
ing the Role of Professional Associations to Increase the Pool
of Faculty Researchers of Color, *Stafford L. Hood and Jenni-
fer Boyce.* A Mentoring Approach Involving HBCU Faculty's
On-Site Involvement with Research University Faculty, *Will-
iam W. Malloy and Gloria L. Harbin.* PART III. THE CONSID-
ERATION OF COUNTERVAILING FACTORS RELATIVE TO
THE MENTORING EXPERIENCES OF SCHOLARS OF
COLOR. Negative Mentoring: An Examination of the Phenomenon as it Affects Minority Students, *Reginald Wilson.* An
Analysis of Five Pitfalls of Traditional Mentoring for People on
the Margins in Higher Education, *Theresa McCormick.*

JAI PRESS INC.
100 Prospect Street, P. O. Box 811
Stamford, Connecticut 06904-0811
Tel: (203) 323-9606 Fax: (203) 357-8446

Advances in Cognition and Educational Practice

Edited by **Jerry Carlson,** *School of Education University of California, Riverside*

Volume 5, Conceptual Issues in Research in Intelligence
1998, 330 pp. $78.50/£49.95
ISBN 0-7623-0423-5

Edited by **Welko Tomic,** *Faculty of Social Sciences, The Open University, The Netherlands* and
Johannes Kingma, *Department of Traumatology, University Hospital Groningen, The Netherlands*

CONTENTS: Preface, *Welko Tomic and Johannes Kingma.* Introduction: Issues in the Malleability of Intelligence, *Welko Tomic and Johannes Kingma.* The Schools: IQ Tests, Labels, and the Word "Intelligence," *James R. Flynn.* Intelligence as a Subsystem of Personality: From Spearman's G to Contemporary Models of Hot Processing, *John D. Mayer and Dennis C. Mitchell.* A Longitudinal Study of Factors Associated with Wechsler Verbal and Performance IQ Stores in Students from Low-Income, African American Families, *Frances A. Campbell and laura Nabors.* De Groot's Potentiality Theory of Intelligence: A Resume and a Validation Study, *Arie A.J. van Peet.* Relating Reading Achievement to Intelligence and Memory Capacity, *Ronald P. Carver.* Experimental Approaches to the Assessment and Development of Higher-Order Intellectual Processes, *Douglas H. Clements and Bonnie K. Nastasi.* The Detection of Interstimulus Relations: A Locus of Intelligence-related Differences, *Sal A. Soraci, Michael T. Carlin, and Richard A. Chechile.* Intelligence and Learning Potential: Theoretical and Research Issues, *Wilma C. M. Resing.* Inductive Reasoning and Fluid Intelligence: A Training Approach, *Karl Jozef Klauer.* Accelerating Intelligence Development through an Inductive Reasoning Training, *Welko Tomic and Johannes Kingma.* The Effects of Test Preparation, *Henk van der Molen, Jan te Nijenhuis, and Gert Keen.*

Also Available:
Volumes 2-4 (1994-1997) $78.50/£49.95 each
 Volume 1 (2 part set) $157.00/£99.90

JAI PRESS INC.
100 Prospect Street, P. O. Box 811
Stamford, Connecticut 06904-0811
Tel: (203) 323-9606 Fax: (203) 357-8446

Advances in Motivation and Achievement

Edited by **Martin L. Maehr** and **Paul R. Pintrich,**
School of Education, University of Michigan

The purpose of this series is to reflect current research and theory concerned with motivation and achievement in work, school, and play. Each volume focuses on a particular issue or theme. While the discussions are based on and fully reflect current developments in the field, a special goal of the series is to bring the best in social science to bear on socially significant problems.

Volume 10, 1997, 496 pp. $78.50/£49.95
ISBN 0-7623-0103-1

Also Available:
Volumes 1-9 (1984-1995) $78.50/£49.95 each

JAI PRESS INC.
100 Prospect Street, P. O. Box 811
Stamford, Connecticut 06904-0811
Tel: (203) 323-9606 Fax: (203) 357-8446

Advances in Confluent Education

Edited by **Joel H. Brown,** *Pacific Institute for Research and Evaluation, Berkeley*

Volume 1, Integrating Consciousness for Human Change
1996, 208 pp. $78.50/£49.95
ISBN 0-7623-0080-9

This volume draws from the first generation of Confluent Educators (George Brown, Laurence Iannaccone, and Stewart Shapiro) as well as second generation of researchers and practitioners. Intergrating Consciousness for Human Change is a research-based and process-oriented volume that explores the philosophical, psychological, and organizational/political aspects of awareness, responsibility, and change. It solidifies and deepens our understanding of an effective educational process at the individual and group levels within various social contexts.

CONTENTS: Foreword, *George I. Brown.* Introduction: Confluent Education in the Land of Oz, *Joel H. Brown.* Confluent Education: A Participator View of Knowledge, *Tone Kvernbekk.* Confluent Education: An Analysis from the Perspective of Merleau-Ponty's Philosophy, *Steve Hackbarth.* Confluent Education: A Coherent Vision of Teacher Education, *Lisa De-Meulle and Marianne D'Emidio-Caston.* The Confluent Approach to Organizational Change and Development, *James E. Barott and Jostein Kleiveland.* The Place of Group Dynamics In Confluent Education, *Stewart B. Shapiro and Peter J. Mortola.* Beyond Awareness: An Action Science Approach To Cross-Cultural Relations, A'Prolegomenon, *Debra Peters-Behrens.* Confluent Education and Evaluation Research, *Jordan Horowitz and Joel H. Brown.* School Diversity, the Economy, and Affect In The Curriculum, *Fernando E. Gapasin.* A Brief Retrospection, *Laurence Iannaccone.*

JAI PRESS INC.
100 Prospect Street, P. O. Box 811
Stamford, Connecticut 06904-0811
Tel: (203) 323-9606 Fax: (203) 357-8446

J
A
I

P
R
E
S
S

Advances in Special Education

Edited by **Anthony F. Rotatori,**
Department of Psychology,
Saint Xavier University

Volume 11, Issues, Practices,
and Concerns in Special Education
1998, 289 pp. $78.50/£49.95
ISBN 0-7623-0255-0

Edited by **Anthony F. Rotatori,** *Department of Psychology, Saint Xavier University,* **John O. Schwenn,** *Graduate Studies and Research, Emporia State University* and **Sandra Burkhardt,** *Department of Psychology, Saint Xavier University*

CONTENTS: National Educational Reform: General and Special Education, *Fred Litton and Joyce Fiddler.* Linguistically Appropriate Special Education, *Herbert Grossman.* Portfolio Assessment: An Individualized Approach for General and Special Educators, *Tammy Benson, Kathleen Atkins, and Fred Litton.* Classroom Disruption: Educational Theory as Applied to perception and Action in Regular and Special Education, *Barbara F. Zimmerman.* Community Counseling for Adults with Mental Disabilities: ADAPPT, *Sandra Burkhardt.* Curriculum and Teacher's Attitudes: The Impact of the Change Process in Special Education, *Sheila Marie Trzcinka.* The Effectiveness of Facilitative Communications on Specific Populations with Impaired Communicative Skills: Myth or Miracle, *Christine M. Kernwein.* HIV/AIDS Education and Prevention for Individuals with Exceptionalities, *Carrie J. Dacko.* Emotional First-Aids for Exceptional Learners, *Festus E. Obiakor, Gloria Campbell-Whatley, John O. Schwenn, and Elizabeth Dooley.* Fragile X Syndrome: Genetics, Characteristics, and Educational Implications, *Gail Harris-Schmidt and Dale Fast.* Cognitive-Behavioral Modification for Children and Young Adolescents with Special Problems, *Tim Wahlberg.* Assessment of Dementia and Depression in Adults with Mental Retardation, *Kirsten Mitchell.* Assessment and Treatment Implications for Alcohol and Substance Abuse Comorbid with Traumatic Brain Injury, *Randolph A. Stevens.* Sexual Abuse of Persons with Developmental Disabilities, *Kathleen Keating.*

Also Available:
Volumes 1-6, 8-10 (1980-1996) $78.50/£49.95 each
  Volume 7 (2 part set) $157.00/£99.90

JAI PRESS INC.
100 Prospect Street, P. O. Box 811
Stamford, Connecticut 06904-0811
Tel: (203) 323-9606 Fax: (203) 357-8446

International Perspectives on Education and Society

Edited by **Abraham Yogev**, *School of Education and Department of Sociology and Anthropology, Tel Aviv University*

Volume 4, Educational Reform in International Perspective
1994, 288 pp. $78.50/£49.95
ISBN 1-55938-739-4

Edited by **Abraham Yogev**, *School of Education, Tel Aviv University* and **Val D. Rust**, *School of Education, University of California, Los Angeles*

CONTENTS: Introduction: The Change Process and Educational Reform, *Val D. Rust*. PART I. CONCEPTUAL ISSUES. Problems of Educational Reforms in a Changing Society, *Torsten Husen*. Language and History: A Perspective on School Reform Movements, *Sol Cohen*. The Failure of Reform and the Macro-Politics of Education: Notes on a Theoretical Challenge, *Hans N. Weiler*. Conceptual Issues in Educational Reform: Ideology, the State, and the World Economic System, *Mark B. Ginsburg and Susan F. Cooper*. PART II. REFORM, IDEOLOGY AND THE STATE. Australian Education Inc.: The Corporate Reorganization of Public Education in Australia, *Susan L. Robertson*. Educational System Reform as Legitimation for Continuity: The Case of Brazil, *Francis Musa Boakari*. Educational Reform in Post-Revolutionary Iran: A Shift in Policy?, *Golnar Mehran*. The Spirit of Capitalism and School Reform in America, *Abraham Yogev*. PART III. EDUCATIONAL REFORM IN EASTERN EUROPE. Educational Reforms and the Discourse of Glasnost in Soviet Education, *Joseph Zajda*. The Polish Tradition and Western Patterns, *Krzystztof Kruszewski*. PART IV. SCHOOL REFORM AND DEVELOPMENT POLICIES. Two Perspectives on the Role of Education in Development: The World Bank versus the African View, *Ernestine K. Enomoto*. Education and Development Policies of India, *Vipula Chaturvedi and Mahesh Chaturvedi*.

Also Available:
Volumes 1-3 (1989-1993) $78.50/£49.95

JAI PRESS INC.
100 Prospect Street, P. O. Box 811
Stamford, Connecticut 06904-0811
Tel: (203) 323-9606 Fax: (203) 357-8446

J A I   P R E S S

Advances in Personal Construct Psychology

Edited by **Greg J. Neimeyer,** *Department of Psychology, University of Florida* and **Robert A. Neimeyer,** *Department of Psychology, University of Memphis*

Volume 4, 1997, 296 pp. $78.50/£49.95
ISBN 0-7623-0083-3

Also Available:
Volumes 1-3 (1990-1995) $78.50/£49.95

JAI PRESS INC.
100 Prospect Street, P.O. Box 811
Stamford, Connecticut 06904-0811
Tel: (203) 323-9606   Fax: (203) 357-8446